The Book of
WHITCHURCH

The Book of
WHITCHURCH

Parish & Community

GERRY WOODCOCK

HALSGROVE

First published in Great Britain in 2004.

Copyright © 2004 Gerry Woodcock.

All rights reserved. No part of this publication may be reproduced, stored in a retrieval system, or transmitted in any form or by any means without the prior permission of the copyright holder.

British Library Cataloguing-in-Publication Data.
A CIP record for this title is available from the British Library.

ISBN 1 84114 334 0

HALSGROVE

Halsgrove House
Lower Moor Way
Tiverton, Devon EX16 6SS
Tel: 01884 243242
Fax: 01884 243325
email: sales@halsgrove.com
website: www.halsgrove.com

Frontispiece photograph: *Haymaking at Higher Grenofen in the 1940s.*

Printed and bound by CPI Bath Press, Bath.

Whilst every care has been taken to ensure the accuracy of the information contained in this book, the publisher disclaims responsibility for any mistakes which may have been inadvertently included.

Contents

	Maps	6
	Acknowledgements	9
Chapter 1:	THE SETTING	11
Chapter 2:	WORKING	31
Chapter 3:	PLAYING	45
Chapter 4:	RESIDING	57
Chapter 5:	WORSHIPPING	71
Chapter 6:	CARING	83
Chapter 7:	SHARING	91
Chapter 8:	LEARNING	99
Chapter 9:	TRADING	109
Chapter 10:	TRAVELLING	115
Chapter 11:	GOVERNING	123
Chapter 12:	CONFRONTING	129
Chapter 13:	CELEBRATING	141
Chapter 14:	MURDERING	145
Chapter 15:	HEROES OR VILLAINS?	147
	Subscribers	156

THE BOOK OF WHITCHURCH

MAP ONE : WHITCHURCH PARISH - FEATURES

KEY

———————— = Present Parish Boundary

.... = Parish Boundary Before 1935

———————— = Roads

— — — — — — = Rivers or leats

Rivers
1. River Walkham
2. River Tavy
3. Taviton Brook
4. Tiddy Brook

Leat
5. Grimstone and Sortridge Leat

Bridges
6. Grenofen Bridge
7. Bedford Bridge
8. Merrivale Bridge

Features
9. Double Waters
10. Riland Reservoir
11. Windy Post
12. Honour Oak
13. The Pimple

Tors
14. Pew Tor
15. Staple Tors
16. Vixen Tor
17. Heckwood Tor
18. Feather Tor

Downs
19. Plaster Down
20. Shorts Down
21. West Down
22. Whitchurch Down

Settlements
23. Rixhill
24. Walreddon
25. Grenofen
26. The Village
27. Middlemoor
28. Caseytown
29. Taviton
30. Moorshop
31. Pennycomequick
32. Moortown
33. Merrivale

Roads
34. Whitchurch Road
35. Church Hill
36. Brook Lane
37. Anderton Lane
38. A386
39. B3357

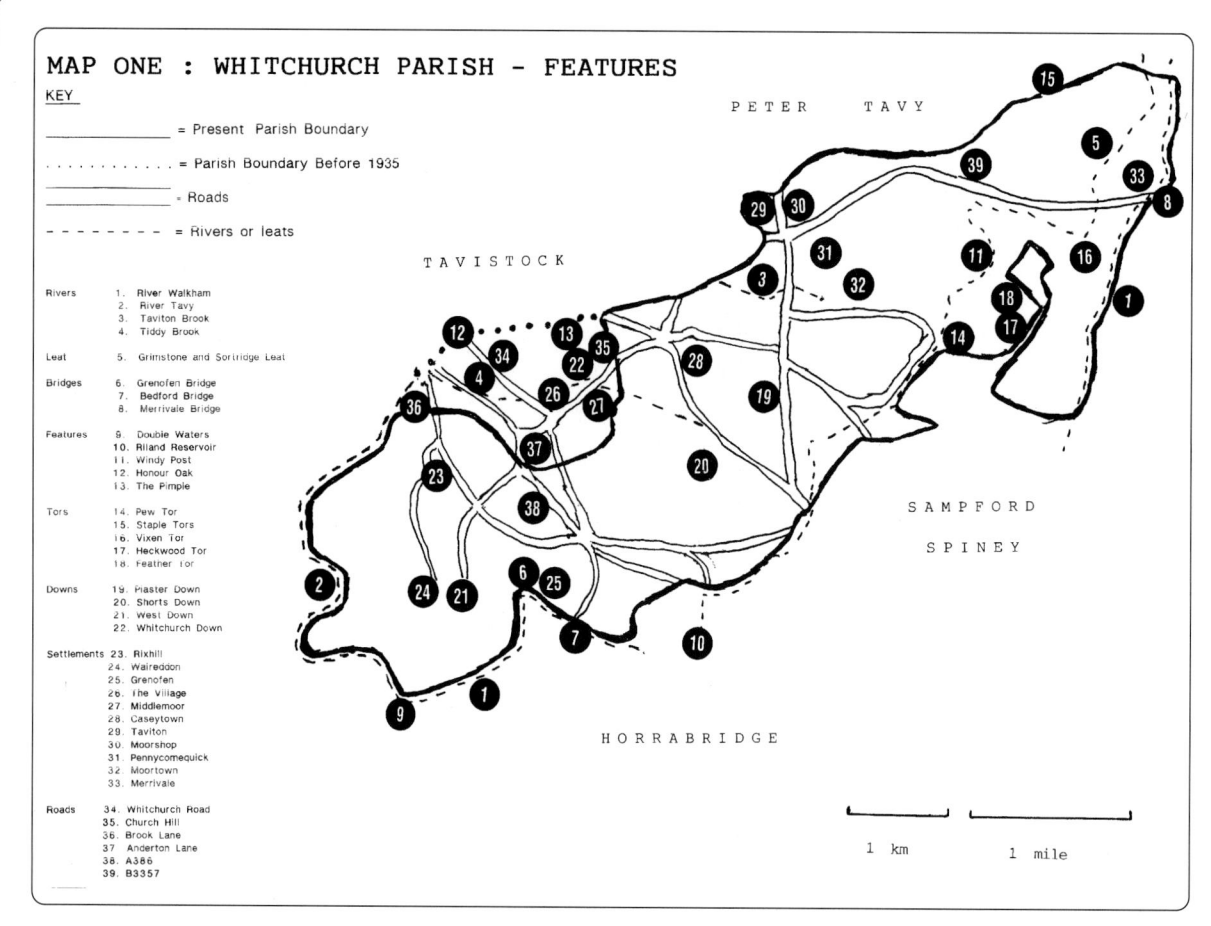

MAP TWO : WORKING AND PLAYING

KEY

———————— = Present Parish Boundary

.... = Parish Boundary Before 1935

Farms
40. Anderton
41. Higher Town
42. Wood Town
43. Higher Tor
44. Lower Tor
45. Higher Grenofen
46. Highlands
47. Ash
48. Ashlands
49. Ash Mill
50. Budghill
51. Taviton
52. Higher Quarry
53. Lower Quarry
54. Boyton
55. Fullamore
56. Lower Pennaton
57. Higher Pennaton
58. Stentaford
59. Birchy
60. Old Venn
61. Moortown
62. Oakley
63. Reddicliffe
64. Willsetton
65. Merrivale
66. Dennithorne
67. Prowtytown
68. Higher Longford
69. Lower Longford
70. Higher Collaton
71. Lower Collaton
72. Hecklake
73. Heckwood

Mines / Quarries
74. Merrivale Quarry
75. Pennycomequick Quarry
76. Wheal Surprise
77. Devon Burra Burra Mine
78. Great Sortridge Mine
79. East Sortridge Consols
80. Devon and Courtney Consols
81. Rixhill Mine
82. Anderton Mine
83. Gem Mine
84. Walkham and Poldice Mine
85. Virtuous Lady Mine

Sporting Venues
86. Old Racecourse:Finish
87. New Racecourse:Finish
88. The Ring
89. Whitchurch Cricket Ground
90. Old Cricket Ground
91. Old Football Ground
92. Tennis Club
93. Golf Course

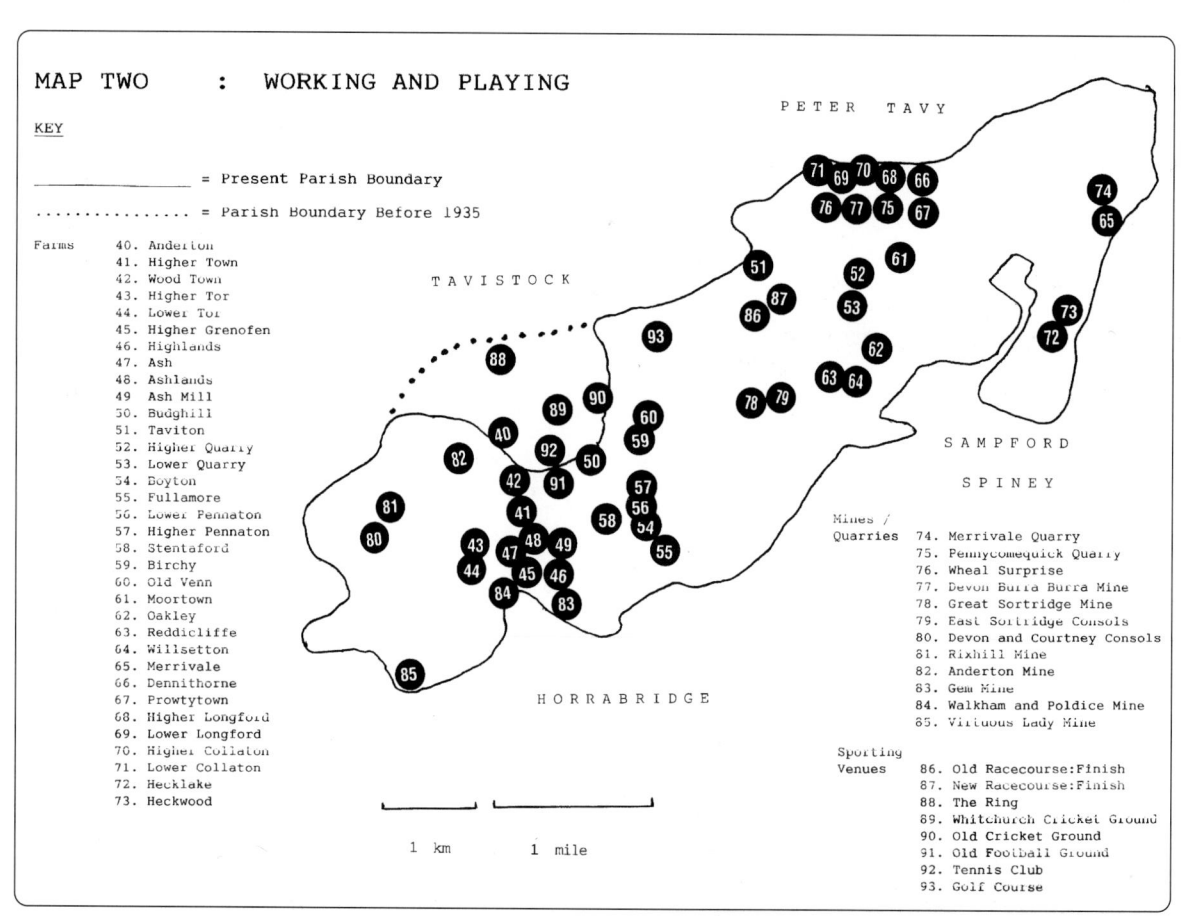

MAPS

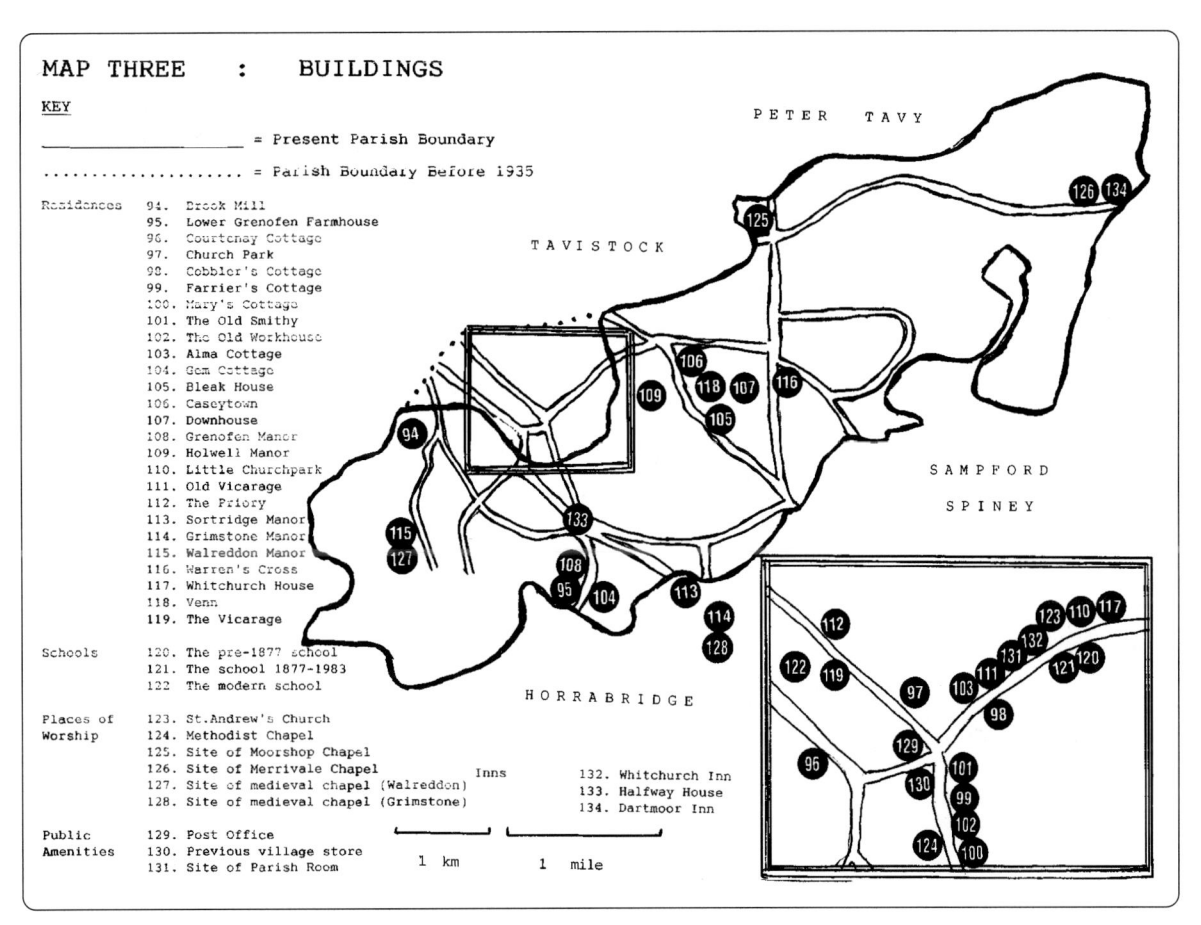

A section of John Speed's 1610 Map of Devonshire.

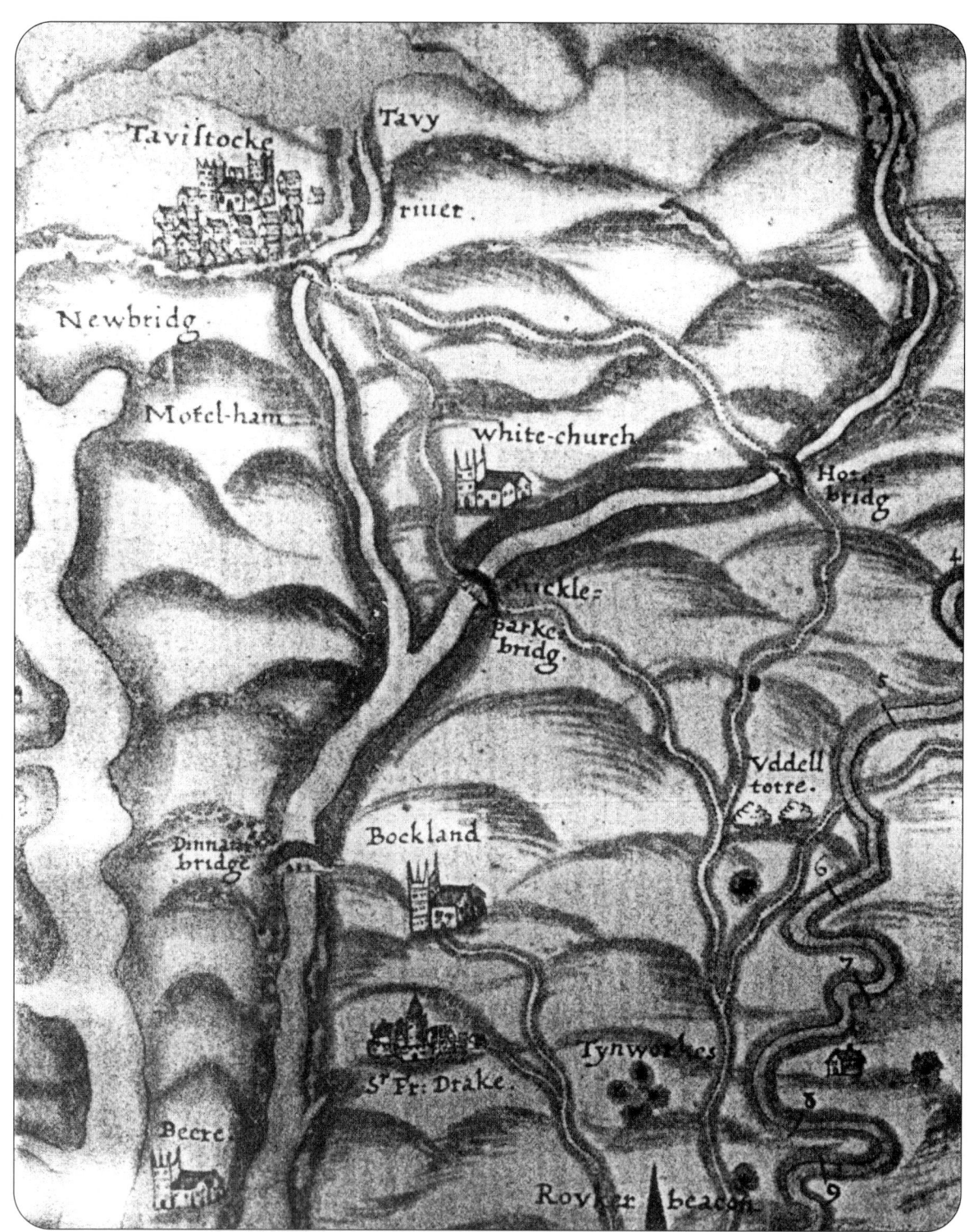

Three generations of the Plymouth-based Spry family contributed a wealth of local pictures and maps to the community in the sixteenth and seventeenth centuries. This is a section, featuring Whitchurch, of Robert Spry's map, drawn in 1584. It was sent to the Privy Council to illustrate the case for the construction of a waterway from the River Meavy to provide water for Plymouth, a project that was realised a few years later with the construction of Drake's Leat.

ACKNOWLEDGEMENTS

The people who understand a place best are the folk who live there, or have lived there at some point in the past. That is why my main sources for this study of Whitchurch are the residents, past and present. I am very grateful to the ones who kindly volunteered information, or patiently listened to my questions, or wrote helpful letters. To those who offered me the loan of pictures I also record my appreciation. This book appears because a large number of people have given generously of their time and attention.

I am indebted to the following who, in different ways, have provided me with the material on which the book is based:

Roy Acton, Clifford Alford, Joan Alford, Christine Allison, David Anthony, Malcolm Ashfold, John Baker, David and Susan Balment, Sabine Baring-Gould, Brian Barriball, Martin Beaver, William Beebe, Joy Beer, Dennis and Thelma Bishop, Stephanie Blanchard, R.J.E. Boggis, Frank Booker, Robert Bovett, Mike Brown, Lyn Browne, Merle Cary, Margaret Clark, George Cole, Don Connett, Ken Cook, Kit Cook, Margaret Cook, Jim Cooke, Winifred Cranch, William Crossing, David Dashper, Simon Dell, Wesley Dingle, Ian Doidge, Jane Doidge, William Doidge, Roy Downard, Bob and Linda Elliott, Joyce Elliott, Rosemary Estall, Kathleen Evans, Dorothy Findall, John Findall, Nicholas Findall, Vicky Fox, John Foxhall, Audrey Gay, Brian Giles, Grace Glen-Leary, David Gordon, Tom Greeves, Stephen Grey, Roger Grimley, Geoffrey Harland, Helen Harris, Peter Hearn, Eric Hemery, Graham Hingston-Jones, Pamela Jack, Brian Jones, John Jury, Ian Kilpatrick, Anthony Kingdom, Graham Kirkpatrick, Ian Mackintosh, Phil Maker, Roderick Martin, Trudy Massey, Chris Meadows, Joyce Metcalf, Alex Mettler, Margaretta Mudge, Rachel Newphry, Lena Nicol, Angela O'Shea-Warman, Mark Patrick, Margaret Perks, E.N. Masson Phillips, Peter and Sheila Plumb, Tom Quick, Paul Rendell, Pearce and Pat Richards, R. Richardson, Angela Rippon, John Robins, Alan Rowe, Courtenay Rowe, Derek Sach, Jenny Sanders, Richard Sellman, Harvey Sherriff, Richard Sleeman, Raymond Soper, Dick Spackman, Vic Stacey, Elisabeth Stanbrook, Mary Stanbrook, Peter Stanier, Frances Stephens, Amanda Sutherland, Shirley Thorington, Frank Toye, Gladys Tucker, John Vanstone, Jean Wans, Ken and Flo Watkins, Madeleine Waycott, West Devon Record Office (custodians of such source material as the Parish Vestry Records and the School Board Minute Books), John Weston, Andrew Williams, Mary Williams, Bryonie Wilton, Thelma Wood, R. Hansford Worth and Anne Wyatt.

I would like to record particular thanks to nine people. Ken Cook generously provided me with material that he had gathered for his excellent handbook on Whitchurch parish, published in 2002. Martin Beaver and David Gordon offered, from their respective exiles, a wealth of colourful and evocative detail about the village in mid-century. To Rod Martin, the secretary of the Local History Society, I owe the fact that many helpful sources and contacts were turned in my direction. Paul Rendell, a knowledgeable and committed writer on the local area, told me a good deal about the Walkham Valley. The other four are parishioners of long standing. Frank Toye and Richard Sleeman have kindly checked the typescript with the eyes of men who have lived through it all, or at least most of it. Flo and Ken Watkins have shown, meanwhile, not for the first time, a readiness to help that I have much appreciated. Their kindness is a reflection of one of the admirable features, then as now, of life in Whitchurch.

To all these kind people I owe a considerable debt. They are not, however, responsible for the book's shortcomings, which are entirely down to me.

All of these photographs are early-twentieth-century views of the village from the south.

Chapter 1

THE SETTING

Whitchurch is among the most common of place names. At the last count the AA list was in double figures, with examples in Scotland, Wales, the West Country, and the southern counties of England. It would appear that historically Britain was not short of settlements with white churches. In the West Country Devon, Somerset, Dorset and Hampshire each saw the emergence of a Whitchurch. There would seem to be an obvious explanation. When a stone building appeared as the focal point of a settlement it could well have been constructed of light-coloured local material. Its brightness would have been particularly striking if, as so often happened, the new church replaced a wooden building. This could have been the case with Devon's Whitchurch, situated as it is so close to the deposits of white elvan stone quarried in the district, and particularly on Roborough Down. It features in a number of local churches. If, however, this is the explanation for the name of our Whitchurch, then it follows that the village had a stone church at a remarkably early date: the Domesday Book refers quite clearly to 'Wicerce' in 1086. It is possible that there was a stone church of light-coloured appearance in the eleventh century, two centuries before the present structure, but no evidence of it has come to light, either documentary or archaeological.

There is a another, more likely explanation for the name of the parish. Saint White, or Wita, lies buried at Whitchurch Canonicorum in Dorset. She might be the same Celtic saint who appears as St Gwen or St Candida, these being the Welsh and Latin forms of 'White'. Alternatively, we may be dealing with Albanus, a companion of St Boniface of Crediton, who was martyred in 756 while on a mission to Germany. This man, appointed bishop of a German see, was, until recent times, commemorated in annual festivals in both Bavaria and Somerset, and is also remembered for his regular gift of a giant-sized cheese to a monastery in his diocese. If either the cheese-loving bishop or the saintly Celtic maiden is the true source of the place name of Devon's Whitchurch, then there is no need to wonder why, when the later medieval church was built, they were abandoned in favour of St Andrew. After the Norman Conquest both Celtic and English saints became unfashionable, and were in many places replaced by men with wider reputations. All that can be said with certainty on this subject is that the settlement of Whitchurch has known itself by that name for 1,000 years.

Whitchurch is a large parish. Its administrative boundaries may have been altered at various times, particularly on the occasion described in Chapter 11, but traditionally Whitchurch has always embraced five constituent parts. The first is the area closest to, and most alike, its big sister, the town of Tavistock. Centred on the Whitchurch Road, this district was thinly populated until the late 1800s. Ribbon development over the succeeding century swelled the population of suburban Whitchurch and resulted, by the end of the twentieth century, in the completion of an almost unbroken line of housing development between the historic centres of the two parishes.

The spine road was the old turnpike road out of Tavistock, running south-east through Whitchurch and Grenofen and on to Horrabridge and Plymouth. Having settled itself and put down roots, this sturdy oak then began sprouting offshoots, to the north Deer Park, Down Road, Westmoor, Whitham and Chollacott, and to the south Crelake and Mohun's Park. Stretching further, to be within touching distance of the old village of Whitchurch, came the late-twentieth-century additions of Anderton Court, Church Lea, Churchill Road, Friar's Walk, James Road, Newtake Road, Orchard Court, School Road, St Andrew's Road and Tiddy Brook Road.

The second element of the parish of Whitchurch is its core, the centre of the village. Here are the oldest buildings, all of them within a stone's throw of the crossroads, the point at which the Whitchurch Road meets, on the one side, Anderton Lane, and, on the other, Church Hill. The steep climb up the latter leads to the heart of the village, a cluster of four buildings that represent between them much of the historic communal life of the parish. Two of them, the church and the inn, are closely interconnected and have medieval origins. The other two, the village school and the Parish Room, both served the community for a substantial period before being superseded, one by an existing alternative and the other by a prospective replacement. The former building survives; the latter has been demolished.

Left: *Whitchurch Road in 1963.*

Below left: *The village, looking from the south in the 1950s.*

Below: *The village, looking from the south in the 1990s.*

Bottom: *Development on both sides of Whitchurch Road in the last quarter of the twentieth century.*

THE SETTING

The centre of the village: Church Hill.

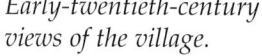

Early-twentieth-century views of the village.

THE SETTING

Two early-twentieth-century views of the village taken from different points on the road climbing out towards Grenofen.

The south-west of the parish, the area that includes Anderton, Walreddon, Buckator and Grenofen, features particularly the Rivers Tavy and Walkham. These two rivers form the boundary of Whitchurch for some distance, and their meeting-place at Double Waters marks the most southerly point of the parish. The two river valleys have provided not only a wealth of scenic beauty and natural history, but a number of examples of economic activity.

Occupying a substantial part of the parish of Whitchurch are the four Downs. West Down overlooks the valley of the Walkham between Grenofen *(above)* and Double Waters *(above right)*. Shorts Down and Plaster Down lie between the villages of Whitchurch and Sampford Spiney. But the most accessible, and the one that offers most in terms of interest and variety, is Whitchurch Down. The five roads which have over the years provided the access routes to the Down meet at Caseytown Cross, having come from Caseytown, Whitchurch village, Tavistock via Green Lane, Peter Tavy via Furzy Lane, and Horrabridge via Plaster Down. Farmers also, from time immemorial, drove their cattle and sheep onto the Down for grazing via Chollacott Lane. Whitchurch Down is a 459-acre site bounded by

Panorama from the Pimple, looking east.

THE SETTING

walled hedgebanks. Descriptions of it abound, some factual, some fanciful. Rachel Evans, in the middle of the nineteenth century, recalled 'travelling in an open carriage over the soft turf of Whitchurch Down on a summer's night.' She went on:

The wheels glided on without noise. There was perfect stillness around, while the moon beamed brightly on our path, and the delicious perfume of the heath flowers stole over our senses. On a marsh near us an ignis fatuus *waved its magic fire. The hills in the distance glowed with the conflagration of the turf cutters; whole acres were set burning to destroy the vegetation, and aid their labours in preparing peat which they cut for their winter fuel. There was a deep peace in the solitude around. Our carriage has since then rattled over the same soft turf, but on a far different occasion. The glare of day then revealed a busy multitude in gay attire, collected to enjoy the exciting sport of horse-racing.*

At about the same time the Queen of Tavistock folklorists, Mrs Bray, wrote:

Whitchurch Down is said to be very famous for the peril there incurred of being pixy-led. For there many an honest yeoman and stout farmer, especially if he should happen to take a cup too much, is very apt to lose his way. And whenever he does so he will declare, and offer to take his Bible oath upon it 'That as sure as ever he lived to tell it, whilst his head was running round like a mill wheel, he heard with his own ears they bits of pisgies, a laughing and a tacking their hands, all to see he led astray, and never able to find the right road, though he had travelled it scores of times'. And many good folk relate the same thing, and how the pigsies delight to lead the aged a-wandering about after dark.

Other visitors to the Down were gypsies, who made regular summer encampments there. The Furzy Lane Bridge was a popular spot. From there, old residents of the area will recall, the gypsies would strip the hedges of the young willow wood and make clothes-pegs for sale.

Whitchurch Down houses one particularly cherished feature. The extraordinary three-sided, hurdwick-stone-built edifice, known to everyone as 'the Pimple' (*right*), sits above Down Road and the Golf House. Built by the distinguished architect Sir Edwin Lutyens in 1914, it is a beautiful folly, but with a limited function – that of providing a cover for a service reservoir. The water was to supply 'Littlecourt', which Lutyens designed as the first residence in Down Road. It later served other properties. Responsibility for it, when it became redundant, was passed along a chain of public authorities, before in 2000 an anonymous buyer stepped in with a promise to maintain a much-loved landmark.

The land of the four Downs is common land. This applies also to Whitchurch Common, an area lying immediately to the south of the B3357 road, which attracts from the nearby car park on Pork Hill many walkers, ice-cream eaters, kite flyers, and people who enjoy a ravishing view. That these five areas within the parish are common land does not mean that ownership is common. It does mean that certain named local families enjoy rights there, principally of grazing. These relate to sheep, cattle and ponies, and involve specific detail regarding numbers and timings. There are also rules and conventions covering stone, peat, bracken and gorse. Such rights have their origins in the long-distant past, although they have been rationalised, codified and established in statute law at certain times. From the fourteenth century onwards the practice grew of having these rights incorporated into farm leases. The families concerned, some 80 at the last count, are the Whitchurch Commoners. An organisation to protect their rights and represent their interests was formed in the nineteenth century, although there had been instances

Panorama from the Pimple, looking south-east.

Main photograph: *Shorts Down.*
Left: *Furzy Lane Bridge.*

before that of the commoners taking joint action over specific matters. They continue to exercise significant influence in 2004, although, sadly, they are no longer alerted by the blowing of horns on the morning of a 'drift'. The term 'in venville' relates to the status of those who enjoy these common rights. It is applied both to the particular families concerned and to the parishes where the custom survives. Whitchurch is thus a 'venville parish'. The phrase is thought to derive from the Latin term 'fines villarum', meaning the rents payable by towns. 'Towns' in this context may be translated as 'farms'. The Whitchurch farmers concerned, in return for their rents, benefited from the common rights and had done so 'from the time whereof memory is not'. In some cases the payments were the responsibility of individual farmers. In others, a collective payment on behalf of the parish was made in return for the collective privileges which accrued. In 1505, for example, it is recorded that a rent of 12 pence was paid on behalf of the 'parochia de Whitechurche'.

In recent years the attentions of the commoners have focused on relations with the landowners, with the Dartmoor National Park Authority, with local authorities, and with users of the common lands, whether permanent residents, such as the Golf Club, or organisations seeking occasional use. They may also take action against fellow members who have been judged to have acted contrary to the spirit or the letter of the rules governing their rights. Non-members who use the commons risk their stock being impounded. Two examples of crusading activity in the twentieth century were the campaign to persuade the Water Authority to provide a drinking trough near the Pimple, and the battle with the Golf Club over a range of issues including the building of bunkers, Sunday play, and the activities of 'caddy-boys who are in the habit of driving cattle off the common.' The Whitchurch Commoners' Association meets annually as a body, and otherwise acts through its 16-member council, which meets four times a year. It is represented on the Dartmoor Commoners' Council, a wider body that represents the interests of all the commoners on Dartmoor.

A surviving entrance to Whitchurch Common. But how was it opened and closed?

THE SETTING

Whitchurch has one more element to go alongside its suburbia, the village, the river valleys, and the common lands. This is the high moorland. To move eastwards through the parish, along, for example, the B3357 road towards Princetown and the heart of Dartmoor, is to experience some spectacular scenery. Only a small part of Dartmoor is inside the boundaries of Whitchurch, but the stretch from Pork Hill to Merrivale affords opportunities to visit, or at least to see, the five tors that lie within the parish. They are:

Tor	Height Above Sea Level	OS Ref.
Feather Tor	1,120 feet	534742
Heckwood Tor	1,050 feet	537738
Pew Tor	1,050 feet	533736
Staple Tors	1,493 feet	542757
Vixen Tor	1,050 feet	543743

Pew Tor

Vixen Tor

Great Staple Tor

Vixen Tor

Staple Tors from an old postcard.

Feather Tor is close to one of the distinctive granite crosses that mark traditional routes across the moor. This particular path would appear to run from Whitchurch village to Heckwood Tor. The latter is just west of the Walkham, with some rock basins to its south. Pew Tor is interesting, both for its rock formations and for the evidence it affords of early quarrying. Staple Tors, which lie to the north of the other four tors and of Merrivale, consist of three separate rock formations. The shapes and forms that nature has produced in these piles of rocks are suggestive. They have given rise to every kind of reaction, from bewilderment through artistic admiration to strange cultic beliefs. The same is true of Vixen Tor, a highly visible and atmospheric feature overlooking the Walkham Valley. Its triple rock formation gives it an appearance most usually described as sphinx-like.

Within its boundaries, Whitchurch enfolds nine small settlements, or hamlets, in addition to the village. They are, from west to east:

Hamlet	Adult Population in 2002
Rixhill	13
Walreddon	12
Grenofen	174
Middlemoor	17
Caseytown	21
Taviton	16
Moorshop	47
Moortown	24
Merrivale	3

Rixhill seems to have had an earlier spelling as 'Rych Hill', and commemorates, in all probability, an early landowner. It sits between the Tavy and the Walkham, near the edge of West Down. Like its near-neighbour Anderton (the derivation of which is 'under the Down'), Rixhill was once the scene of mining activity, and sustained a significant population. All that has long gone.

Close by Rixhill is Walreddon, a small community that is centred on Walreddon Manor *(see Chapter 4)*. This is the site of one of the earliest settlements in the area. The great local historian W.G. Hoskins, in writing about the settlement of the Anglo-Saxons, describes the survival of 'Celtic clusters', and cites Walreddon as an example, the name meaning 'weala raeden' or 'community of Welsh'. In spite of its pre-Norman origins, it does not feature in the Domesday Survey, but first appears in an early-thirteenth-century document. A mansion had been built there by 1401, in which year Richard and Matilda Meavy obtained from the Bishop of Exeter a licence to hold services in the chapel there. The present building dates from the middle of the sixteenth century. The dwellings close by housed the servants who worked in the house and gardens and on the adjoining farm.

Like Walreddon, Grenofen was a settlement with an impressive manor-house at its heart (the story of the house is outlined in *Chapter 4*). Like Walreddon, the place was close to West Down and to the River Walkham. There was, however, a major difference. Walreddon remained shy and secluded, on a route to nowhere. Grenofen was close by the main thoroughfare between Tavistock and Plymouth. The place, the name of which means 'of the green marsh', became a major point on the turnpike road. Here was established a travellers' inn, around which the population grew. In the middle of the nineteenth century there

The view from Rixhill, looking north.

THE SETTING

Grenofen House, glimpsed through the trees from Grenofen Bridge, 1910.

Below left: *Cottages alongside the Halfway House at Grenofen, facing the site of the car park in 2003. Inhabited until the 1950s, they were demolished in the 1960s.*

was little except a toll-house, a few cottages, and a blacksmith's shop. In one of these cottages lived Sophia Oxenham, who, weather permitting, carried her portable harmonium to the Whitchurch Methodist Chapel each Sunday to play at the service. And here also lived her sister Mary who, with her husband John Bolt, was running a little grocery business by 1871.

Middlemoor presents an attractive and interesting picture, with a mixture of late-Victorian villas and cottages radically modernised a century later. The stream that runs through it, on its way to join the Tiddy Brook, provided the hamlet with water until the piped supply appeared in 1914. A particular feature is the sunken lane, some quarter of a mile long, that runs from Middlemoor to Shorts Down. This is undoubtedly one of the ancient 'hollow ways' so carefully described by W.G. Hoskins a generation ago. They were formed by the efforts of farmers of adjacent land who produced continuous banks close to the edge of their property, thus forming ditches which, occupying no man's land, became convenient rights of way, passing between farms or estates. Some hollow ways are medieval in origin. Others go back to Saxon, or even pre-Saxon times.

From Caseytown Cross, the five-road intersection, the most southerly route is a narrow lane leading across Plaster Down to Walkhampton and thence, originally, to Plympton Priory. This lane, until it opens up onto the Down at Bleak House, serves the hamlet of Caseytown. The name almost certainly derives from an early owner, a Case or a Cass or a Casey, and the origins are medieval. A petition to Wolsey, Chancellor of England, in 1518, mentions Caseytown by name, along with a number of other properties in the parish, such as Down House, Boyton, Oakley and Pennaton.

Taviton, near the northern boundary of the parish and accessible from the B3357 road soon after leaving Tavistock, is the site of an ancient settlement.

This photograph: *Middlemoor*
Below: *The Hollow Way between Middlemoor and Shorts Down.*

Above and below: *Holwell Cottages at Middlemoor, in 1965 and 1955 respectively.*

THE SETTING

If H.P.R. Finberg's interpretation is correct, then its half-virgate (some 15 acres) had come to a knight called Ermenald as a subtenancy by the time of the Domesday Survey. There was then enough arable land to keep a plough team busy as well as pasture for seven cows and 'in venville' rights to graze 40 sheep on the Down. The manor-house or barton stood near the point at which the narrow road to Nutley meets the B3357.

The Taviton Brook, a tributary of the Tavy, has been a major source of power over the centuries, and Taviton has had a number of mills. In the early-fifteenth century, for example, a tan-mill here was converted into a tucking-mill. By the end of that century the woollen industry had developed to the extent that there were 20 tucking-mills in the immediate area, of which three were at Taviton.

Moorshop centres on a crossroads, where the B3357, beyond Taviton, crosses an old, straight road running north–south from Peter Tavy to Horrabridge. Near this spot were, within living memory, a blacksmith's shop and a Methodist Chapel. The population, limited until recently to a handful of local farms, has been augmented by the popularity of the Longford Farm Caravan Site, the entrance to which is near the foot of Pork Hill.

The Old Smithy, Moorshop.

The suffix 'town' denotes, not a town in the modern sense, but a small, enclosed community or a farm. Moortown is thus the farm that commemorates in its name its fourteenth-century owner, William atte

Boundary wall of Moortown Farm.

Right: *The Rooke's family plot in Whitchurch churchyard.*

More. Lying in the east of the parish, between Whitchurch Common and Plaster Down, it consists of a small number of farms and cottages, distanced from main roads and from known tourist trails.

The last of Whitchurch's nine hamlets, and the most easterly one, is Merrivale. It is also the one with the smallest population. But this was not always so. Motorists who drive by as they cross the Walkham on the Tavistock–Princetown road may notice the inn and the quarry (both of which will feature in later chapters), but they may be unaware that here was once a community of about 100 people, with their own chapel, school, post office and inn; here every-body both lived and worked within hailing distance of each other. The name means 'pleasant open space', and the description fits. But living in such a remote spot through the rigours of a Dartmoor winter may not have been everyone's idea of an unbroken idyll.

Among the families who lived at Merrivale in its heyday was that of John and Ada Rooke. John had been born in 1873, the son of a stonemason. The family settled in Merrivale in the early years of the life of the quarry, when he was still a child. Young John got to know Ada Clarke, who lived a few doors away along Walkham Terrace. Ada had been born in Aldershot and was the daughter of an Army pensioner called William Clarke. She was the same age as John, and they grew up together. They were both 22 when, in October 1895, they were married at Tavistock's Registry Office. They continued to live at Merrivale, where John had followed his father into the quarry. George, their first-born, arrived in November 1897. Three other children followed – Dorothy, William and Percy. As John and Ada grew older they began to assume, within the community, an unofficial position of some authority. This was enhanced by Ada's role as midwife, albeit unqualified, to the community. Her slightly haughty style earned her the nickname 'Lady John'. She and John were to lose two of their sons in quick succession. George, at 19, was killed in the First World War. Percy, at 20, died as a result of a road accident in West Street, Tavistock.

Above and left: *Merrivale in 1910.*

Merrivale – the inn and roadside buildings in the 1920s.

THE SETTING

In addition to the two rivers, the Tavy and the Walkham, that mark its south-western boundary, Whitchurch has three significant waterways, as well as a number of minor streams and leats. The Tiddy Brook enjoys, between Plaster Down and Brook, a short but busy life. Tumbling impatiently down via Bishopsmead to join Mother Tavy, this bubbly little upstart on more than one occasion caused serious flooding before being strait-jacketed by storm pipes and the like. Taviton Brook has suffered no such fate. But then it has behaved rather better. Flowing along the northern reaches of the parish in a westerly direction, under bridges at Pennycomequick and Furzy Lane, it serves Taviton before joining the Tavy near the foot of Green Lane. A reliable old workhorse, it has over the centuries supplied other leats, supported both farms and mines, and provided power for the various activities at the old settlement at Taviton. And then there is the Sortridge and Grimstone Leat, following a seven-mile course, nearly all of which is within the boundaries of the parish. Taking its water from the River Walkham near the foot of Great Mis Tor, it flows in a south-westerly direction by Merrivale, across Whitchurch Common and Plaster Down, to service the two farms from which it derives its name. At Grimstone a storage reservoir helped to maintain the flow to water-wheels at the local mines. A mile or so to the south the leat returns its contents to the Walkham at Horrabridge. Its journey contains many interesting features, including evidence of man's exploitation of such resources as tin, granite and peat.

The leat crosses ancient tracks and aqueducts, flows under clapper bridges, and also provides many examples of bull's-eye stones. These were devices by which water could be diverted into branch channels. They could, alternatively, be closed by bungs. Along the course of the leat a number of farms, homes, mines and quarries benefited from the operation of these stones.

Above left and above: *Two examples, on the Sortridge and Grimstone Leat, of bull's-eye stones.*

Left: *The Sortridge and Grimstone Leat crosses Whitchurch Common.*

Eric Hemery, the doyen of modern Dartmoor writers, describes a walk along the Sortridge and Grimstone Leat thus:

A highly scenic walk, in which the wild and rugged country at the source is progressively exchanged for the gentle undulations and soft pastel colours and woodlands of the Lower Walkham Valley and the wide waters of the Tavy and Tamar estuaries backed by the Cornish moors.

The practice of 'beating the bounds' developed from the sixteenth century. Parishes were at that time first given limited civil duties and tax-raising powers, and it became important for each parish to know exactly how far its authority extended. Early perambulations were undertaken for the prime purpose of asserting doubtful boundaries. In the nineteenth century the meetings of the Whitchurch Parish Vestry regularly appointed 'certain gentlemen' to undertake the task. The need for these exercises may have receded, but the tradition has survived, with recent beatings having taken place in 1992 and 2000.

Whitchurch's immediate neighbours through the ages have been Tavistock to the west (see *The Book of Tavistock*), Peter Tavy to the north (see *The Book of Peter Tavy with Cudlipptown*), Sampford Spiney to the east, and Walkhampton and Buckland Monachorum to the south (see *The Book of Buckland Monachorum with Yelverton*). To these was added, in the twentieth century, Horrabridge, which came late to parish status. Among early examples of boundary markers was the famed 'Honour Oak', so named because French prisoner-of-war officers on parole in Tavistock during the Napoleonic Wars were put on their honour not to stray beyond this point. This marked the boundary with Tavistock. In the same way the bridge over the Walkham at Horrabridge was the meeting-point of three parishes – Whitchurch, Sampford Spiney and Buckland Monachorum. Alterations to the boundaries have taken place over the years, sometimes amid controversy. (These will be discussed in Chapter 11.)

Beating the bounds in 2000, at the boundary stone at Merrivale.

Right: *The old oak that marked the parish boundary on Whitchurch Road also bears this plate.*
Main: *When this picture was taken the bridge at Horrabridge was still the meeting-point of three parishes.*

HONOUR OAK TREE
MARKED BOUNDARY OF FRENCH PRISONERS ON PAROLE IN TAVISTOCK FROM PRINCETOWN DURING THE NAPOLEONIC WAR (1803 - 14). ALSO WHERE MONEY WAS DEPOSITED IN EXCHANGE FOR FOOD DURING A CHOLERA OUTBREAK IN 1832.

Left: Lion Steve Grummitt helps Tavistock Mayor Judith Williams to bury a time capsule at the site of the new boundary stone on Whitchurch Down.

THE SETTING

Animal and plant life abounds in Whitchurch. Foxes are common, as are otters, badgers, rabbits and squirrels. The moorland streams carry minnows and in the lowland areas there are plentiful sticklebacks and common eels. Upland areas display heather, gorse, thorn bushes and some coniferous trees planted as wind-breaks, while the valleys show a variety of lush grassland, deciduous trees and wild flowers. In the moorland areas can be seen lapwings, skylarks and curlews, while the valleys are home to such garden birds as blackbirds, thrushes and tits. Lizards and adders abound, and there is a large population of bats, particularly attracted by the inviting habitats provided by disused mines.

The climate of Whitchurch may be described as 'moist'. Annual rainfall is between 50 and 60 inches, with more than 70 inches being recorded in some years on the higher moorland. Temperatures are high compared with other regions of the country, the difference between Whitchurch and a village in eastern England working out at an average of five degrees on any one day. Neither thunder nor frosts are common phenomena. There have, however, been occasions when harsh conditions took a grip of the area and brought movement to a halt. Heavy snowfalls occurred, for instance, in 1881, 1891, 1927, 1929, 1946, 1962 and 1978. If you were young, these were occasions for exciting breaks with routine and for days off school. Grown-ups tended to stress the inconvenience and the potential threats to life and limb. For everyone concerned there was the opportunity to gather enough anecdotes to dine out on the stories for years to come.

Two eye-witness accounts, one from 1891 and one from 1962, are given below.

On the evening of Monday 9 March 1891, Frederick Weekes, a music teacher, boarded a train at Tavistock to take him home to Plymouth. The train had crossed the River Walkham when it came to a halt. Mr Weekes recounted what happened next:

The driver got off his engine, lamp in hand. 'You're here for the night', he cried. He went back to consult with the guard of the train and took ten minutes to reach the engine again. He had to try twenty times at least before he could stand against the wind and the fine drifting snow. He unhooked the engine, telling us he must drive to Horrabridge. In about three quarters of an hour he returned, having had to get off his engine and remove trees about six times. He told us to get out and he would take us to Horrabridge on the engine. I was one of the first to jump out and was immediately up to my waist in snow which I ploughed through and working against wind and blinding snow I reached the engine. Fourteen of us were wedged up on the engine. Crossing the Magpie Viaduct was awful. It really seemed as if we should be lifted up bodily and thrown over and then when we came to a deep cutting the snow rushed up as through a funnel. The fine snow coming up from beneath, the steam coming down on us from above, the howling wind and noise of the engine – we held our

Right: *Someone living in Walreddon Manor in 1891 left a window slightly open overnight. This was the scene in the room the next morning.*

In 1891 the Princetown train got stuck a short distance outside the Whitchurch parish boundary.

breath and wondered what would come next. At last we reached Horrabridge Station.

During the winter of 1962–3 Peter and Sheila Plumb were living at Merrivale, where they ran the Dartmoor Inn. Peter recalls leaving home in the car with their two daughters, who had hair appointments in Tavistock, but, finding the road blocked at Pork Hill, they abandoned the car and walked home. The following day Peter and a neighbour dug the vehicle out of a deep drift and managed to get into Tavistock, where food supplies were taken on board. Conditions were by now, however, deteriorating, and he had to stay overnight. Meanwhile, a van delivering bread to Dartmoor Prison became stuck at Merrivale. Sheila remembers:

The two men in the van abandoned it and walked back down the hill to the inn. The weather had by now worsened dramatically and they had to stay. They proved very helpful. We had by then been using water from the leat for two or three days as all the water pipes were frozen. The men carried buckets of water, checked the roof-space for snow, and fought their way up the garden to feed the hens. It was some weeks before the water-supply was restored. A little later, when the road at Merrivale had been reopened to allow for one-way traffic, a van carrying meat to the prison became stuck on Merrivale Hill, and the contents of the van had to be unloaded and stored in the inn. Help later arrived in the shape of a prison officer, four prisoners, and a tractor and trailer, but the supplies did not reach Princetown until the next day. Because of further snowfalls the five men had to stay overnight in the bar of the Dartmoor Inn!

Two centuries before the Mother's Pride van got stuck in the snow at Merrivale, Revd John Swete described the scene that met him as he passed 'Merrivile' on one of his tours of the region. He wrote:

On Merrivile Down we had a view of a singular Torr called Vixen, and, beyond, the Downs of Sampford Spiney and Walkampton. From this, by an unpleasant descent, we came to Merrivile Bridge and hamlet. The River Walkham here tumbles over as rocky a channel as can be imagined, forming through the whole course a succession of waterfalls.

At about the same time Revd S. Shaw was passing through on his 'Tour of the West of England'. He wrote:

This being market day, we met a number of the people flocking to Tavistock with grain, a few sheep, and an abundance of michaelmas geese. The common vehicles of the country are panniers and horses, nor did we meet a single carriage the whole day.

Pennington Lane in 1963. The snows came on 29 December 1962. The road was cleared a few days before Easter in 1963.

Another late-eighteenth-century visitor was William Marshall, the author of *The Rural Economy of the West of England*. He described the local villages as 'few and small, with farm houses and many cottages, being happily scattered over the arrears of the townships.' And of the people, Marshall was surely thinking of Whitchurch when he pronounced that 'many of the women are of elegant figure.' Of the local middle class he was more cryptic. They were, he considered, not unlike their counterparts in other regions, 'except what arises from an over-rated estimate of themselves.' Unfortunately, more recent commentators have not been so forthcoming about the parish or its neighbours. In the authoritative *Shell Guide to Devon*, for example, the entry on Whitchurch is limited to three sentences. The first describes it as 'a parish of disused mines, of moorlands, and a golf course, two miles from Tavistock.' The second gives a brief account of Walreddon Manor. The third reads: 'Holwell is another old house in the parish.' And that is it.

That Whitchurch is a settlement of some antiquity is confirmed by its appearance in the Domesday Book. But the story of man's relationship with the land, and the capacity of the former to exploit the possibilities of the latter, goes back much earlier than the Norman Conquest. We may assume, without evidence, an early population of hunter-gatherers, and, later, neolithic settlements of stock-keeping farmers.

But it is the Bronze Age, the second millennium BC, that affords us our first genuine glimpses of the lives of our Whitchurch ancestors. Dartmoor is covered with reminders of the people of that period, including hut circles, menhirs, avenues of standing stones, burial chambers, boundary walls, and whole villages. One of the most spectacular sites, at Merrivale, lies just beyond the Whitchurch boundary. But there are also remnants within the parish, particularly on Whitchurch Common.

Prehistoric man made his mark on the landscape, and this can be seen locally in both the development of field systems and boundaries or reaves, and in the early exploitation of tin and copper deposits. That so little seems to have survived in Whitchurch in terms of either his bones or his tools may be attributed to the high levels of acidity in the soil.

THE SETTING

Places like Whitchurch were not affected by the Roman occupation to any appreciable extent. A number of stones with Latin inscriptions, commemorating important local officials, have surfaced in the area, and a quantity of Roman coins were found in the parish in 1818. But the evidence from the Roman and Celtic periods is very scant. The Celts provided some place names, like those of the Rivers Tavy and Tiddy. We are also told that after the Anglo-Saxon invasions, a Celtic cultural laager (the settlement of the Welsh) survived at Walreddon.

William the Conqueror's Domesday Survey of 1086 was an operation concerned with taxation. Tax liability was assessed on the basis of land, the key unit of the latter being the hide. Definitions of a hide tended to be rather imprecise, but it is generally considered to encompass about 120 acres. The Devon acre was about one-fifth larger than the statute acre. Whitchurch – 'Wicerce' – was assessed on the basis of one hide. The entry reads:

Roald holds Whitchurch himself. Saewin held in before 1066. It paid tax for 1 hide. Land for 12 ploughs. In lordship 3 ploughs; 8 slaves. 20 villagers and 15 smallholders with 5 ploughs. Meadow, 20 acres, pasture 1 league long and 4 furlongs wide. Formerly 30s; value now 70s.

The Domesday picture is of a small community. Five centuries on, the size of the population was probably very little changed. In 1600 the vicar of the parish, William Skirrett, noted that he had 53 'howseholders, poore and rytche'. This is not too far away from the figure of 75, which was the number of householders eligible in 1613 for the payment of Church Rates. (Something like a quarter of the latter figure were assessed for this payment on the basis of their ownership of property rather than their residence.) The Protestations Returns in 1641 contain 135 names, which seems rather high, even allowing for the fact that many whose name appeared were not householders. All the names were written, perhaps significantly, in the same hand. The surnames that appear in the list are as follows:

Addams, Addamor, Arundell, Ayshe, Bickford, Bloye, Bonde, Brishe, Brocadon, Brounsdon, Burgin, Burne, Carer, Castleford, Chubb, Cole, Crewe, Cudlipp, Dodge, Dracke, Edmond, Gawde, Gaye, Glanvill, Goodinge, Halls, Hamlin, Heane, Hocadaye, Hooper, House, Howard, Humphrey, Jackman, Jope, Kemble, Kindsman, Kinge, Knighton, Lange, Lavers, Macye, Maddiford, Madge, Mariot, Marwood, Matacot, Maynard, Nickell, Oxenham, Paidge, Palmer, Peterfield, Philp, Radford, Reddall, Rider, Rowe, Skirrett, Sowton, Spiller, Sprye, Stackwill, Stacye, Talbat, Taler, Taverner, Tom, Treneman, Voysey, Walter, Wicket, Wills, Withe.

The first national census taken in 1801 recorded the population of the parish of Whitchurch as 478. Figures for subsequent censuses were:

1801	478	1871	1,098
1811	595	1881	1,067
1821	692	1891	1,144
1831	791	1901	1,536
1841	918	1911	1,484
1851	1,156	1921	1,477
1861	1,340	1931	1,411

The pattern over these 130 years is clear. There was a steady increase in the early years of the nineteenth century, and an accelerating rate of growth in the middle years of the century. This was due, not so much to changes in the agricultural sector as to the rapid development of mining interests in and around the parish. The 1860s, that saw the beginning of the end of these activities, witnessed a sharp decline in the population, which was not reversed until some significant housing development took place on the Whitchurch Road around the turn of the century. The upturn was not sustained. The *Tavistock Gazette* wrote 'with disappointment' that the 1911 census had shown a decline, albeit a small one, and this 'notwithstanding the establishment of a railway halt'.

The nineteenth century censuses give us clear indications of the distribution of population within the parish. The 1851 survey may serve as an example. It came at a point at which the population had doubled

Kistvaen (burial site) on Barn Hill, Whitchurch Common.

```
Ipfe.Ru.ten. WICERCE.Sauuin teneb T.R.E.7 geldb
p.I.hida.Tra.e.xII.car.In dnio st.III.car.7 VIII.serui.
7 xx.uilli 7 xv.bord.cu.v.car.Ibi.xx.ac pti.Paftura.I.
leu lg.7 IIII.q3 lat.Silua.II.leu lg.7 IIII.q3 lat.
Olim.xxx.folid.Modo ual lxx.folid.
```

The Domesday entry, in its original form.

over a period of 40 years and was set fair to expand still further over the next decade or so. It will be noted that Horrabridge was not at that time a separate parish and that the land of that village was shared between three parishes, of which Whitchurch was one.

The Population of the Parish in 1851	
Horrabridge Village	310
Farms	306
Farm cottages	109
Other cottages	117
Middlemoor	67
Merrivale	38
Rixhill	39
Village Centre	61
Whitchurch Road	63
Grenofen House	17
Holwell House	15
Vicarage	14
TOTAL	1,156

In 1935, as will be described in Chapter 11, a part of the parish was transferred to Tavistock. This was followed, in 1950, by the creation of a new parish, Horrabridge, which was formed by bringing together parts of Whitchurch, Sampford Spiney and Buckland Monachorum. The result of these changes was a considerable reduction in the area of the parish. Moreover, the lost acres contained the homes of more than half the population. The last four counts of the century produced the following figures: 1961: 463; 1971: 445; 1981: 484; 1991: 511.

Jane Doidge, herself a well-known Whitchurch parishioner, has studied the parish registers, and has produced some interesting conclusions about marriage patterns. She discovered, for example, that the vast majority of parishioners who got married between 1813 and 1950 chose partners from nearby. The figures are shown at the bottom of the page.

The first half of the twentieth century saw an increase over the previous century in the number of marriages involving a Whitchurch resident and someone from more than 15 miles away (15 per cent of the total as against 7 per cent). The increase is, however, a surprisingly modest one. In spite of social changes and transport developments, the great majority of young men and women in the parish continued to find their partners within walking distance. It need only be added that the term 'within walking distance' has a rather different meaning for late-twentieth- and early-twenty-first-century folk than it had for their Victorian forbears.

If the spread of public transport in the first half of the twentieth century was not as important a factor in bringing about social change as was once thought, then what of the increase in the availability of private transport in the second half of the century? The increase in the number of cars has been extraordinary. In 1991 only 6 per cent of Whitchurch households were carless. Half of them had one car, while 36 per cent owned two cars and 8 per cent owned three or more. The 1991 census also revealed that 83 per cent of households were owner-occupied. Privately rented accommodation accounted for 12 per cent of the market, the remaining 5 per cent being local authority housing. One other interesting demographic development emerges from the figures. In 1981 there were 177 inhabitants below the age of 25 and 117 above the age of 55. Ten years later the figures for these two categories were 157 and 144. Whether, in contemplating the future of Whitchurch, the trend so clearly illustrated by these figures should be a cause for comfort, or alarm, or neither, must be a matter of opinion.

Some children, and others, drawn to the novelty of the camera in the village during 1908.

| Period | Distance from Whitchurch of Residence of Chosen Partner | | | |
	Within 5 miles	5–10 miles	10–15 miles	Elsewhere
1813–82	552	40	46	52
1883–1950	490	40	60	110

Chapter 2

WORKING

Over the last 200 years or so there have been between 30 and 50 working farms in the parish of Whitchurch. At the beginning of the twenty-first century these included, in the western part of the parish, three in the Anderton area (Anderton, Higher Town, and Wood Town), two at Rixhill (Higher Tor and Lower Tor), and five at Grenofen (Higher Grenofen, Highlands, Ash, Ashlands and Ash Mill). Covering much of the central part of the parish are Budghill, Taviton, and, centred on Plaster Down, Higher Quarry, Lower Quarry, Boyton, Fullamore, Lower Pennaton, Higher Pennaton, Stentaford, Birchy and Old Venn. Further east, in Moortown, Moorshop, Merrivale and the border lands with Sampford Spiney, are Moortown, Oakley, Reddicliffe, Willsetton, Merrivale, Dennithorne, Prowtytown, Higher Longford, Lower Longford, Higher Collaton, Lower Collaton, Hecklake and Heckwood. The origins of some of these names lie in the mists of antiquity. Some obviously derive from physical features in the immediate area: Ash, Oak, Tor, Fen, Thorn, Wood, Vale, Hill, Cliff, Lake, Moor, etc. Others reflect human activity: Quarry, Ford, and so on. A number can certainly be identified with the names of individuals or families. Tristram Risdon, the seventeenth-century antiquary, told us that:

Moretown hath long been in the tenure of Moringe, a family which anciently wrote themselves De La More, and they bear for their armories six martlets sable in a silver field.

The Prouta family gave their name to Prowtytown, and Dunna was, we may assume, an early owner of Dennithorne, where he presumably had a thorn bush. Fourteenth-century records give us the names of John de Aysshe, William atte Torre, William atte Fenne, and Ralph atte Wode.

Of other well-known, albeit slightly more recent, farming dynasties in the parish, the one that holds the record for continuity is probably that of the Willcocks. The family ran Anderton Farm for the best part of three centuries. Already established there by 1730, they were shown in the 1870s as owning 332 acres with a gross estimated rental of £356. The Skinners of Budghill have their place in local folklore because Emily Jane, the widow who ran the farm through much of the first half of the twentieth century, was fiercely possessive of her three adult children and strongly resistant to any potential suitors. The son, Frank, owned a pre-war Austin 7, which was reputed to make only one journey a week, when Frank drove it to Tavistock Market. Emily also launched a ten-year vendetta against her neighbours, the Beavers, after discovering two of their guests shooting rabbits on her land. The Doidges are an old Plaster Down dynasty, long associated with Pennington (or Pennaton as it has sometimes been recorded), and also with Fullamore, which William Doidge bought in 1954.

William Soper was 47 when, in 1870, he left the village of Stokenham, five miles east of Kingsbridge, and the farm where he had lived for some years. He was to go west, but this was not the Californian trail, and the distances were not measured in hundreds of miles. His destination was Whitchurch, and the journey was only some 40 miles. Nevertheless, it involved a major upheaval. His wagon, loaded up

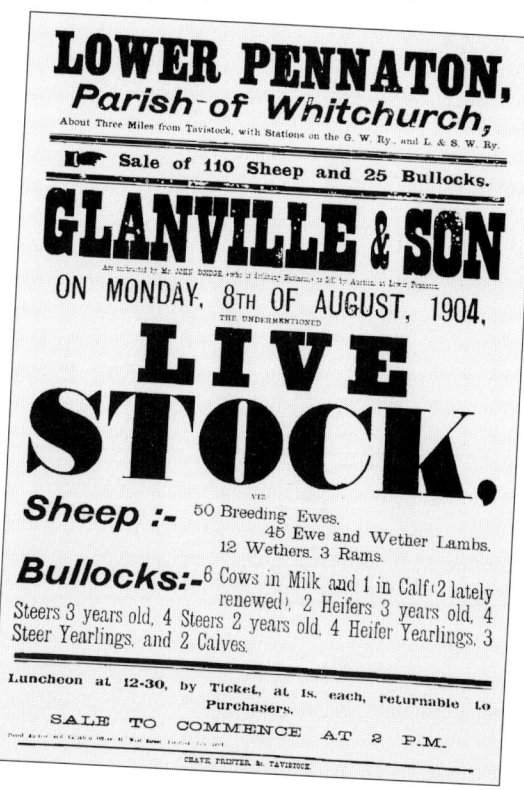

John Doidge sells his stock in 1904.

Main: *William Doidge cutting corn in the 1930s. He bought his first tractor for £274 in 1941.*
Below: *John Samuel Doidge thatches a hayrick in 1919.*

the night before so that an early start could be made, carried all his furniture and household effects. Alongside him was his wife Catherine, half his age, but already the mother of four children. William's first wife had died after producing six young Sopers. Catherine was now proving to be equally fertile. The journey, which was to bring the family to its new home at Ash Farm, began at six o'clock in the morning. The two horses, fit and fresh, made good progress in the morning, but in the afternoon, as they reached Cadover Bridge, the 'fore-hoss', the colt 'in chains', had to be rested, and there was a break for refreshment. Then it was on to Yelverton and, with everyone now thoroughly weary, came the climb up Grenofen Hill. The shaft horse was now showing signs of fatigue. From Grenofen, however, it was all downhill, and Ash Farm was reached at nine o'clock. William and Catherine were, during their life at Ash, to add five more children to the four that they had brought with them from the South Hams. William, of course, had also fathered six in his first marriage. He was to farm the 140 acres of Ash Farm until his death in 1894 at the age of 71. His young wife predeceased him by one year. They are both buried in Whitchurch churchyard.

William Soper

Catherine Soper

Four generations of the Soper family, 1958. Left to right: Harry (then 54), William (85), Jonathan (not yet 1), Raymond (26).

WORKING

For almost 100 years Lower Longford Farm at Moorshop has been home and workplace to four generations of the Dingle family. It began in 1911 when William Dingle, a Stoke Climsland butcher, bought the 94-acre farm. A practical and versatile man, he took readily to farm life, passing the business on ultimately to his son William Gerald. Thereafter, it was inherited in the next generation by Gerald Wesley, who continued to work the farm along with his son John Wesley beyond the close of the twentieth century. Gerald Wesley is, as his name suggests, a man of faith and of commitment to the Methodist cause. A local preacher, he delights in being close to nature, loves Dartmoor, and is proud of his local roots.

Above: *Sheep shearing in 1951. Gerald Wesley Dingle holds the clipper. His father William attends to the three-foot diameter wheel resting on triangular feet, fitted with a connecting chain. A cog drives the shaft for the clipper.*

John Henry Hearn of Bratton Clovelly was an impulsive man. As a youngster he had travelled up to London on the new railway and secured himself a job as a trainee tailor. One day, while working in the shop, he was reprimanded for breaching company rules by speaking to another member of the staff while on duty. John Henry thereupon decided that life was better in Devon, and he immediately and impulsively returned home to Bratton Clovelly. It was the late 1860s. A few years later a 138-acre farm at Whitchurch called Oakley came onto the market, when the Glanvilles, who had been there for some time, decided to move to the neighbouring farm, Willsetton. Borrowing the £3,000 that was required for the purchase from his brother James, who had wisely married the daughter of a Plymouth land agent, young Hearn now headed south, pausing only on the way to collect a wife, Charlotte Palmer, at Germansweek. By the mid-1870s John Henry and Charlotte were happily settled at Oakley (leigh or ley refers to land on the edge of the common which has been cleared and taken into cultivation).

They had three children, John, Thomas and Bessie. The two boys attended the small private school run by John Gaud at 4 Fern Hill Villas, in the parish. They and their sister all worked on the family farm for some years. They grew one acre of mangels, one-and-a-half acres of turnips, 14,000 flat-pole cabbages, a dozen rows of potatoes, one acre of barley, three to four acres of oats, and one acre of wheat, the straw being used for the thatching of hayricks and the grain for chicken corn. The animal population is not known.

In 1919 John Henry retired, and Thomas inherited the concern, John and Bessie having moved away. He ran the farm for 32 years, employing four workers, three of them living-in. Livestock during this period was listed as seven cows, ten heifers, four workhorses, 50 ewes grazing on the moor, plus 100 mares and followers. The latter ran out on the moor until 1928, when they were sold following the imposition of a levy on horses impounded after straying on to the main roads. In 1951 John, representing the third generation of Hearns at Oakley, inherited a farm without electricity, in which everything was still done by hand and horse. He modernised the business and improved the buildings, working the farm with his wife Minnie and a little casual help. In the 1980s he passed it on to his only son, Peter, under whose management sheep numbers increased to nearly 500. At the time of writing he and his wife Margaret have four children.

A stone wall at Oakley Farm, typical of many such boundaries of medieval origin.

Bill Toye

In the middle years of the twentieth century there was no better-known character in Whitchurch than Bill Toye. He farmed at Whiteacres, close to the village. David Gordon, one of a number of village boys who came under the spell of Mr Toye's mechanical ingenuity, recalled the origins of Bill's, and Whitchurch's, first tractor at the beginning of the Second World War:

My stepfather had a 12hp Ford, which he stored in 1939 and then gave to Bill as his tractor. This inventive man cut away the rear upper sides and roof to make a light pick-up, geared down the engine, fitted a tow-bar for a trailer for harvesting, and fashioned a wooden adaptor on the drive-shaft so that he could mow the hay. As it had to run on the cheap fuel, not petrol, it was warmed up on a small amount of precious petrol before being turned over to TVO. To the delight of we lads, there were invariably bangs and groans from the complaining engine before it burst into life with clouds of choking black smoke. Bill also had a shed, which was his secret world, a place for rest, for talk, for advice, but most of all for making things. Here were workbenches, hand tools, and a treasure trove of bits and pieces of wood and metal from which new parts were designed to make machines run again. There was no electricity, but hurricane lamps, a forge, a treadle-lathe, and a grindstone.

Above: *Bill Toye in his farmyard.*

Right: *Machinery on the Toye farm – the hay rake.*

Below: *Bill's tractor.*

Bottom right: *The hay mower on the Toye farm.*

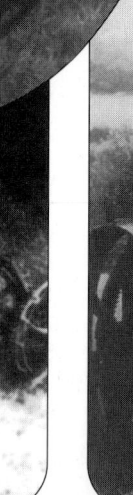

Above: *Noel Beaver* (right) *outside his home, Whitchurch House, in 1947, standing alongside the last Squire of Grenofen, Henry Chichester.*

Below: *Noel's stepson, David Gordon, who took over the running of the business when his stepfather died in 1949.*

David Gordon's stepfather was Noel Beaver. His arrival in the village in 1938 created, at first, a little apprehension. Here, moving into the former vicarage, was a stranger, a professional naval officer, a 'toff', with money. The extent to which he and his family became part of village life was to form an interesting chapter in the story of Whitchurch over the next half century. Noel was an innovative farmer, but his ideas were occasionally greeted with coolness. An extreme example was his introduction, during the war, of a powered wire across the kale field, moveable each day, which ensured systematic grazing. It took an inspection by two policemen to dispel the rumours that this fence was part of an elaborate apparatus enclosing a spy nest. The innovations continued, and neighbours were gradually won over by such breakthroughs as silage making and using hay poles to make hay in bad weather.

When Noel Beaver died in 1949 his stepson David Gordon, already an enthusiastic young farmer, took over the running of the business and continued the pattern of innovation, particularly in the area of pioneering grassland methods. Of stockmanship he had already learned a good deal. As a lad he had been responsible for seven Hereford bulls, whose behaviour, he noted, was peaceable enough when they were together in fields or buildings, but decidedly aggressive when surrounded by an audience of, presumably, admiring cows on the moor.

As a breed, Whitchurch farmers have tended, over the years, to be fiercely independent. They have also often felt themselves to be the victims of uncaring governments, ignorant townsmen, or unhelpful weather. The foot-and-mouth epidemic of 2001 hit the local area particularly hard. There is also a long history of farm accidents, underlining how hazardous the work can be. The Hamlyn family, who farmed Dennithorne, lost two sons in this way. Luscombe, in the 1920s, fell under a loaded cart in Moor Lane, and the cartwheel ran over his chest. Some years later George died when using an unguarded belt-driven circular saw. Hazards of a different kind have arisen periodically from poaching and rustling, particularly of sheep. The latter is, however, less prevalent than it was in the middle of the nineteenth century, when Rachel Evans wrote of Whitchurch Down that 'sheep stealing is common amongst the labourers of the small farmers and 'night work' is carried on almost with impunity.'

The geographical variations within the parish, the rugged moorlands, the common lands of the Downs, the feeding pastures of the lower valleys, provide the keys to the farming activities that are carried on. Cattle, such as Galloway and Aberdeen Angus, are grazed on the moor and brought back to home farms for supplementary feeding during the winter. Sheep provide for the mutton and dairy trades. Arable farming is inevitably limited by the nature of both the soil and the climate. The overall picture is of a

Left: *A common feature of Whitchurch farms – black-faced sheep.*

number of family farms and smallholdings, most of them between 50 and 100 acres. The biggest transformation to have taken place was that which replaced subsistence agriculture, the activity of providing for the immediate needs of the family, by farming as an economic activity. This radical development led to major changes in the appearance of the countryside and the nature of the operation. The strip system, which we now know operated in parts of the parish, gave way to partial enclosure. The increased demand for food led to more land being taken into use and to the formation of clusters, or hamlets, while sheep farming expanded to meet the demands of the local woollen industry.

Developments in the twentieth century have included two major initiatives to meet the problems of rising costs. On the one hand there has been wholesale mechanisation of what was up to the nineteenth century a labour-intensive industry. On the other hand a number of smaller farmers have increasingly seen their future in terms of diversification, and this has included stretching out to meet the holiday trade by offering facilities for accommodation in various forms.

Agriculture has always been the dominant economic activity in the parish of Whitchurch. For a long period quarrying played a secondary, albeit significant, role. Much of the activity of Dartmoor's granite industry lies beyond the boundaries of the parish, but some has been conducted within Whitchurch, in such areas as Whitchurch Common, Heckwood, Pew Tor, Merrivale and Staple Tors. The most accessible stone was that which lay in abundance as loose clitter around the high tors. Such moorstones were carted down to Tavistock in the nineteenth century and taken from there by canal to Morwellham for onward transportation to distant parts. In 1847, 3,032 tons were recorded as following this route. The coming of the railway to Tavistock in 1859 and the subsequent closing of the Tavistock Canal did nothing to ease the immediate problem of ready transport into the town.

In the nineteenth century the method of splitting the granite was by 'feather and tare'. Two 'feathers' (curved iron guides) were inserted into each of a series of holes which had been made along a line of the stone's natural grain. Between each pair of feathers was inserted an iron rod called a 'tare', which was then struck by a sledgehammer. Tares were hit in turn. Increasingly, the demand for moorstone came from towns and cities that required paving blocks for their streets and pavements. The rectangular blocks thus provided were known as 'setts', the masons who fashioned them, the 'settmakers', worked in situ at low benches formed by two upright stones supporting a slab across the top. Here the craftsman stood, facing uphill with his feet protected in the opening below the bench. Surviving evidence on Great Staple Tor indicates that the settmakers often worked in rows of three or four.

Their workplaces were known as 'bankers'. In the 1860s, in support of the settmakers, were three smiths' shops, at Pew Tor, Merrivale and Barn Hill.

Inset: *Evidence of 'feather and tare' on Great Staple Tor.*
Main: *Settmakers' bankers on Great Staple Tor.*

WORKING

Three glimpses of Merrivale Quarry.

The increased demand for building material towards the end of the nineteenth century led to the opening of Whitchurch's best-known, and Dartmoor's longest-lived, quarry. The person responsible for the opening, in 1875, of the Tor Quarry, or Merrivale Quarry, was William Duke, a man who, although he had been born in Jersey, knew both the business and the area, having worked at Foggintor. When he died in 1898 he passed the concern on to his son, Cornelius, who continued to operate it under the name 'C. Duke & Co'. The quarry became more profitable after the turn of the century, as demand grew from all over the country for material for major buildings and public works, and by the time the First World War broke out in 1914 the labour force had tripled beyond the 50 who were employed in 1890. The problem of transport to one of the railheads at Princetown or Tavistock remained unsolved, in spite of grand plans to provide a one-mile link that would have connected the quarry with a point on the branch line that joined Princetown and Yelverton. Meanwhile, the damage done to the roads of Whitchurch and Tavistock by the heavily laden wagons on their way to the latter caused the courts to insist that C. Duke & Co. should pay compensation for 'the extraordinary wear and tear'. Successive owners of the business were the Dartmoor Granite Company in 1930, Anselm Odling Ltd in 1947, and the Merrivale Granite Company in 1976. One of its employees, George Cole, who started work there between the wars, was later to recall:

I got a job making granite paving stones and kerbs. These had to be flat, square, and surface dressed. I was given a 7lb short hammer, some chisels and edge-trimming tools, and after brief instructions left to get on with it. The first week or two were hell. To begin with, I frequently missed the head of the chisel and my knuckles got a terrible pounding. Also the side of your hand and the little finger became impregnated with tiny splinters of granite. We were paid by the foot for the dressed stones and were lucky to earn 30 shillings a week.

The Merrivale Quarry closed in 1997. In its last few years it had provided the material for projects as close as the new bridge over the Walkham a few yards away and as distant as the memorial, in the South Atlantic, to the casualties of the Falklands conflict. Its closure brought to an end a period that had seen the rise and fall of not only a working quarry, but a living community.

The Anderton Mine

Left: *The water-wheel and tram from adit level.*

Below: *The engine-house.*

Bottom right: *Diagram of the workings in 1847.*

Bottom left: *Main shaft.*

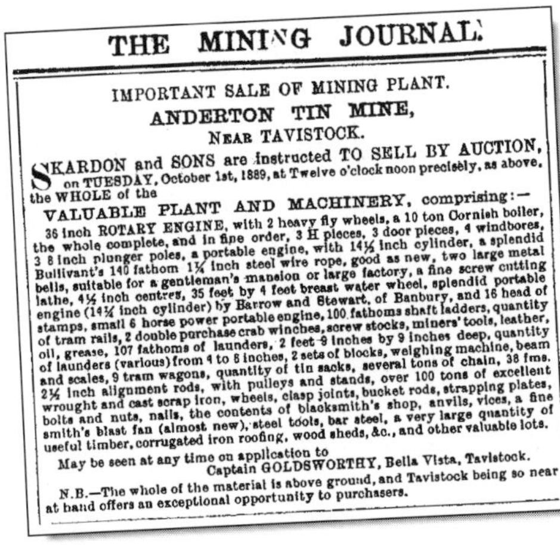

Left: *A sale notice from 1889.*

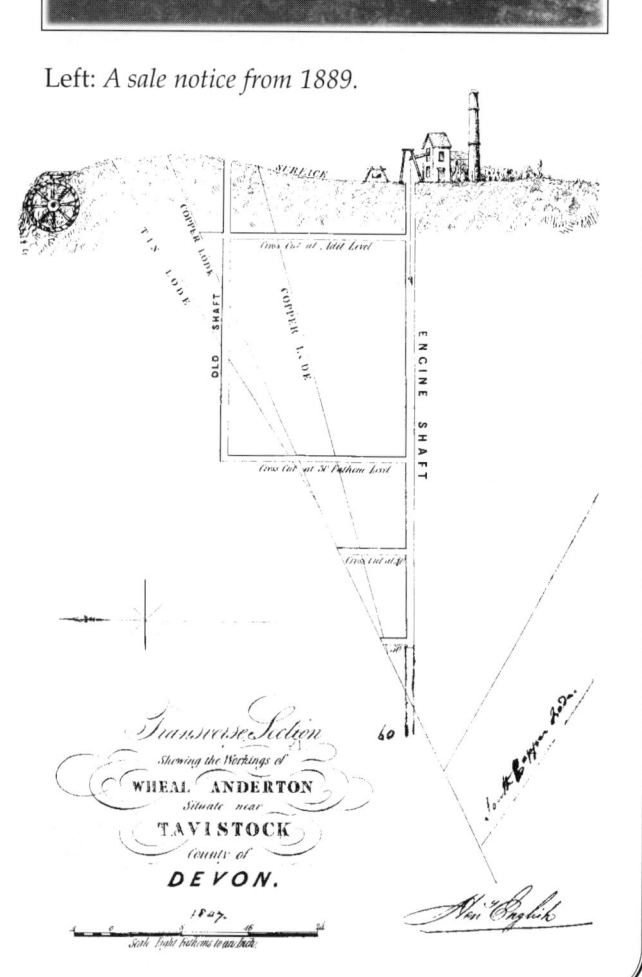

Left: *Apple crusher, dressed but abandoned, at Merrivale. Why?*

A considerable number of other quarries – more modest in scale, less productive and more obscure – dotted the parochial landscape. Their remains, sometimes substantial, sometimes mere scratchings of the surface, may today be traced, discovered, or fallen into. On Whitchurch Down, for example, there are remains on the golf course, near The Ring, to the south of Torlands, and at Pennycomequick. The latter, a substantial operation, appears to have provided material for such local buildings in the early-twentieth century as the Golf House and the house known as Warren's Cross.

Merrivale, as well as featuring a prominent quarry, was also the site of a nineteenth-century mine, alternatively named Merrivale Bridge Mine or Wheal Fortune. It was one of more than 20 in the parish that, at some point near the middle of the century, produced modest amounts of copper, tin, lead and arsenic. This was a period of wild speculation in which the spectacular success of some ventures led to crazy over-confidence as to what might lie beneath each hillside or in each valley. The story of the Whitchurch mines is one of a succession of enterprises which, with a few exceptions, were short-lived and not very productive. It was an unusual year that saw more than half a dozen mines all operating at the same time. At Moorshop were Wheal Surprise and the Devon Burra Burra Mine. At Lower Longford Farm the existence of large mounds of spoil and the occasional experience of subsidence provide evidence of these workings, although the only figures of production, which relate to the latter, suggest a total of 190 tons of copper ore for the ten years from 1863.

A cluster of three mines on Plaster Down – Great West Sortridge, Great Sortridge and East Sortridge Consols – are said to have been active from 1856, but no production figures are recorded, and they may be described as small, prospecting works. Evidence of the latter two has been obliterated or obscured, but the site of the Great West Mine was clearly marked by the survival, on the western edge of Plaster Down, of a tall stack. There was then a clutch of five mines to the west of the village. Near the slopes of the Tavy Valley were the Devon and Courtney Consols Mines, the former producing 1,510 tons of copper ore and 3 tons of lead ore between 1852 and 1861, and the latter realising 280 tons of copper ore between 1869 and 1878. The other three, grouped on either side of the main Tavistock to Horrabridge road, and between the Tavy and the Tiddy Brook, were the Rixhill Mine and the Old and New Anderton Mines. The first of these produced 153 tons of black tin between 1852 and 1855. The Old Anderton Mine realised 174 tons of black tin between 1852 and 1862. The New Anderton Mine, in production from 1882 to 1889, recorded 202 tons of the same product. All three worked the same tin lode, in a more or less east–west alignment, and the last two were, for a time, known as Tavistock United.

An example of the vicissitudes of mining activity in this area is provided by the story of Sortridge Consols, earlier known as Wheal Robert. Opened and closed three times during the nineteenth century, it survived until 1903, in spite of losing two of its men, one being the mine captain, in a drowning accident in 1883. This mine was connected to the more stable and productive Franco Mine, and was sited close to the Walkham. The other mines in the parish were in the Walkham Valley. Following the river's flow, from east to west, there were the George and Huckworthy Bridge Mine, the Furzehill Mine, and Walkhampton Consols. These were all fairly modest undertakings, but the next one, Wheal Franco, was of a different order. Opened in 1823, it was, by 1840, operating in the valley on both sides of Bedford (Magpie) Bridge with a workforce exceeding 130. By 1862 the mine had produced more than 10,000 tons of copper ore, which had been sold for £51,500. Thereafter, decline set in, exacerbated by a drainage problem which even adits and six water-wheels could not overcome. The mine was abandoned in 1875. A short distance along the valley is the site once occupied by West Sortridge Consols, originally Gem Mine. The house above it, Gem Cottage, served as the Count House to this mine. Here the supervising bailiff weighed the ore and took dues amounting to one shilling for every ton he weighed. The Walkham and Poldice Mine, nearby, was another enterprise that had alternative names, this time Old Poldice, Devon Poldice, and Walkham United. Opened in 1865 on a site where there is evidence of earlier tin workings, dating probably from the seventeenth century, it was closed in 1890. Lower Grenofen Farm may well have been the house of the mine captain.

The last of the mines strung along the valley of the Walkham before its meeting with the Tavy was the Virtuous Lady. Tradition has it that this mine, which was certainly being worked in the sixteenth century, was named after Queen Elizabeth I. Its operation, thereafter, was sporadic, with its most prosperous period coming in the middle years of the nineteenth century, when copper and tin ore were transported via Orestocks to Morwellham for shipment to South Wales for smelting. Although the mine has now been closed for more than a century, the site contains a wealth of detail including the mine captain's house.

The local mining industry never developed to the point at which it became a permanent employer

The remains of Gem Mine in about 1880, with the railway viaduct providing a backcloth.

The Walkham and Poldice Mine in 1887.

~ WORKING ~

Above: *The old wooden viaduct, near Double Waters, built to carry water to the 'Virtuous Lady' and to other neighbouring mines. The icicles, shown in this 1890 picture, indicate leaks.*

Right: *One of many such stones in local churchyards.*

Below: *Virtuous Lady Mine, pictured on a 1907 postcard.*

of labour, although a number of Whitchurch men did work in more stable mining enterprises in neighbouring parishes. The members of the mining community did suffer from a range of factors in their working conditions that tended to make their lives shorter than those of the average workers. There were the dangers associated with flooding, explosions and rockfalls, and the diseases to which their work made them prey. Long days of labour were lengthened even further by long walks to and from home. And job insecurity remained an ever-present fact of life. Such rewards as there were came in one of two forms. The miner might be a tutworker, in which case he received a wage but was required to provide his own tools and equipment out of his earnings. The alternative arrangement, the tribute system, was one in which the worker received a percentage of the value of ores produced, less the cost of tools and equipment. It should finally be noted that in mining, as in every industry, the workforce included people, in this case many women and children, who were not engaged in the direct act of production. Alongside the miners were large numbers of surface workers, processing the various stages to which the ores were submitted after extraction.

The 1851 census indicated that 33 per cent of the working population of Whitchurch were at that time engaged in agriculture and 20 per cent in mining and quarrying. If to these totals are added the 19 per cent who were domestic servants, it will be seen that more than two-thirds of workers fell into one of those three occupation groups. This left small numbers covering a variety of trades, such as tailors, cordwainers, painters, carpenters, millers, dressmakers and masons, as well as a handful of professional people and a few still employed in the once-extensive wool industry. One constant feature of the employment pattern has been the existence of a number of jobs servicing agriculture, or related to it. These included blacksmiths – who also served the local mines and quarries.

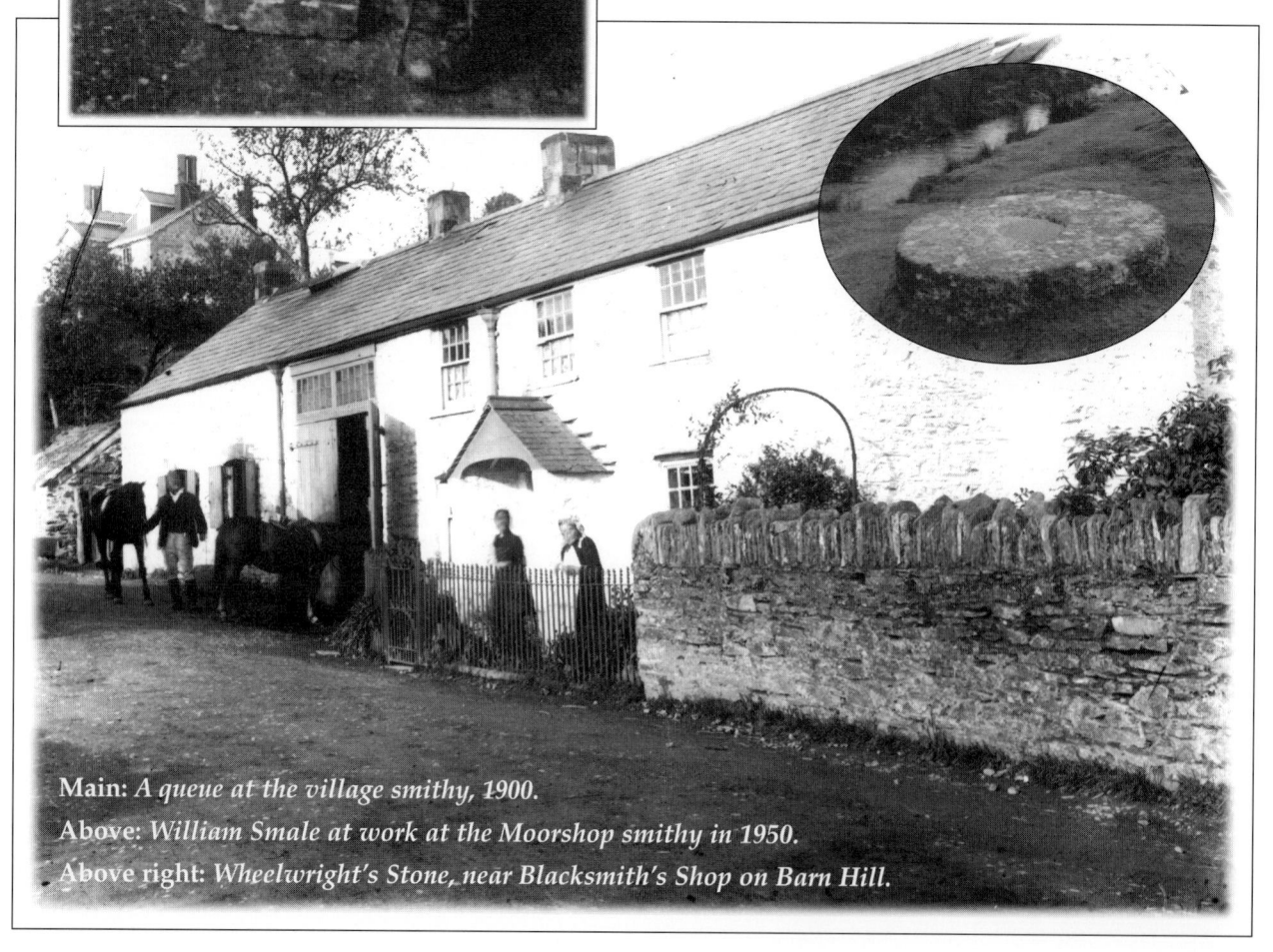

Main: *A queue at the village smithy, 1900.*
Above: *William Smale at work at the Moorshop smithy in 1950.*
Above right: *Wheelwright's Stone, near Blacksmith's Shop on Barn Hill.*

Equine occupations have always been a feature of village life, whether it be trainers, grooms or breeders. Into this category came Sidney Horrell, the famed breeder of Dartmoor ponies. Born at Buctor, he later lived at Higher Tor, Walreddon, and began showing ponies in 1920. His 'Virtuous Lady' was his first prizewinner, and her daughter, 'Midget', became a champion mare. 'Peter Tavy the Second' was a stallion who won competitions at the Devon and Cornwall County Shows, as well as at the Royal Show at Stoneleigh.

A range of other industries have been conducted in the parish from time to time. During the nineteenth century there was some elvan quarrying near Grenofen Bridge, and, further along the Walkham Valley, near Magpie Bridge, stood both a brickworks and a mill, the latter producing, at different times, sausages and violin strings! Later, between the wars, a hand laundry was operated for some years, just off the main Tavistock to Plymouth road. The proprietor was E.O. Carter, the foreman was Harry Yard, and those on the pay-roll numbered 24. Beyond the usual services, it offered free public access to a garden between building and road which featured a pond, adorned by a fountain, and was home to goldfish and terrapins.

The first half of the twentieth century saw the closing chapter in the long history of village-based tradesmen and craftsmen serving the local community. Richard Westlake conducted his business as the village cobbler on Church Hill until into the 1960s. A courteous man, he remained constantly unperturbed by the mountain of shoes awaiting repair that occasionally faced him. His emporium is well remembered by older Whitchurch folk for its strong smells of leather and polish. Kathleen Evans recalls that:

Even to a child it seemed a small building. There was just enough room for a high counter, behind which was a platform on which Mr Westlake sat, with his lasts, tools, and sewing machine, alongside two shelves for incoming and finished repairs. Rubber stick-on soles or 'tacks' on toes and heels of working boots were always done by father when the footwear was brand new, but leather soles and 'best shoes' went to the cobbler, who did a very good job.

Most trades became closely identified with particular families. The Sleeman brothers were the jobbing builders, joiners and coffin makers. From their store-shed each morning Stan and Percy would load their materials onto the flat-bedded side-car of their motor bike. Last to go on was the wooden extension ladder. This operation complete, they would ride though the village with style and panache. If only they had known that their practice of wearing their caps back-to-front would become *de rigueur* among the young half a century on! Another well-known dynasty were the Toyes. Bill Toye, he of the improvised tractor and the shed with its secrets, had a sister Flossy who regularly, over the years – hatless and in all weathers – made her twice-daily visits to the homes of villagers, cheerfully delivering milk from churns carried by a horse and trap, and always ready to deliver a letter or a message for a house-bound customer. The Toyes had mining in their blood. Bill's father had, according to his son, died of 'gold dust in his lungs'. Frank was another member of the clan, becoming a respected stonemason and a pioneer of local cricket.

Living on Chapel Hill, near their cousins the Toyes, were the Mundays. Bill Munday was a universally liked figure, both as an organiser of village events, including children's parties, and as an understanding employer in his sausage-making business. His son Don became known as an entertainer and acrobat. Lil McCall, Bill's sister, worked for several years at Whitchurch House. Her genial son Bob, disabled following a childhood fall from the wall of the village school, became a skilled stockman and later an expert lorry driver. These families, and others who will appear later, were among the stalwarts of the village community in the twentieth century. The people who were at the hub of parish activities were rather different from their counterparts in previous centuries. Revd Beebe, vicar of Whitchurch in the early 1900s, lamented the disappearance of the traditional dynasties who had, for a long time, guided the fortunes of the parish. 'Moringes, Skirrets, Glanvilles, Drakes, Courtneys, and Arundells', he wrote, 'all have gone.' He put it down to the combined effects of the bottle and the gaming-table. There is, of course, no chance of similar misfortunes striking the present generation of village worthies.

Sidney Horrell and Peter Tavy the Second.

A Whitchurch shooting party, equipped with all necessities including the megaphone. On the far right stands Reginald Chapman, two places away from his father George. They were members of a well-known local family.

The hunt at its traditional Boxing Day meet at the Whitchurch Inn. This particular year was 1962, and the occasion took place three days before the coming of the big snow.

Chapter 3

PLAYING

The earliest sports to be conducted in the parish of Whitchurch would undoubtedly have been the traditional triad of hunting, shooting and fishing. Hunting has been carried on for centuries for three reasons, to produce food, to provide sport, and to conduct culls of those animals thought to be posing a threat to other species by their behaviour or by their numbers. Dartmoor's attractiveness as a hunting field to lords, if not kings, and certainly to abbots, was very evident in the Middle Ages. Principal quarries were deer, hares and foxes. The eighteenth century saw fox-hunting become an organised sport for gentlemen, with strict rules of behaviour and etiquette, and by the end of that century there was at least one pack of hounds very active in the immediate area. One of the foremost patrons of the sport was Richard Sleeman, the vicar of Whitchurch in the middle years of the nineteenth century, who kept his own pack at the vicarage. He had developed a taste for the hunt as a young man when he had served a term as curate to the famous 'hunting parson' Jack Russell.

The Lamerton Foxhounds, formed by a Mr Morgan in 1840, included Whitchurch Down in its territory. A number of changes of ownership and mastership in succeeding years led finally to the emergence of Spooner's Harriers, a pack named after Clarence Spooner. Plymouth-based cavalry officers were among the strongest supporters of the hunt, arriving by train along with their steeds. Harriers eventually became foxhounds, and the hunt was renamed the 'Spooner's and West Dartmoor Hunt'.

Shooting parties were frequently organised, usually from the base of one of the large houses in the parish. Poaching, always a large-scale industry, offered the prospect of a different kind of shooting experience, and was certainly helped by the coming of the motor car. Meanwhile, the Whitchurch Rifle Club was formed in 1904 under the presidency of Colonel William Jesse of Ashbrooke. It originally met in the school before moving to the Parish Room in 1906, where it held its inaugural meeting on 3 February, with Colonel Jesse and Captain Halford Thompson firing the first shots. Thereafter it met every Tuesday evening between 7 o'clock and 9 o'clock, charging an annual subscription of one shilling and attracting some 40 members. It continued to operate until 1962, and had only three secretaries during its life, two of whom were Richard Sleemans, father and son.

The existence within the parish of long stretches of the Tavy and the Walkham has provided opportunities for the third of the traditional country sports, fishing. Revd Beebe wished to add to the list wrestling and cock-fighting, and, given the universal popularity of the latter and the extraordinary level of interest in the South West in the former, there is no reason to doubt that Whitchurch saw its fair share of these activities.

The sport for which Whitchurch became renowned, and which attracted considerable numbers of spectators, was horse-racing. The best description of the scene is given by the Tavistock authoress Rachel Evans. Writing in 1846, she described what she saw on Whitchurch Down:

The hum of voices rose merrily on our ear, mingled with loud shouts of laughter and the neighing of the impatient steeds. Vociferous cries of 'names, weights, and colours of the riders' intruded on our attention. Ballad singers bawled their loudest ditties to the listening rustics. Our old friend Punch and Judy fought and chattered as loudly as ever, while a band of musicians played our national airs amidst the continually increasing din and uproar. Vehicles of all descriptions lined the sides of the course. Booths and gay streamers denoted the vicinity of good cheer, while a handsome stand protected the charms of a number of ladies from the too powerful rays of a noonday sun. In the same elevated position were placed the umpires of the day, bending forward to see the necessary preparations for the coming race. At a given signal the jockeys vault into their saddles and, with conscious pride, pace their horses along the cleared course. A bell rings, and for a moment the utmost quiet prevails. 'Are you ready?' 'Yes'; 'Off'; sound through the air, and away speed the contending coursers, outstripping the wind itself in their gigantic efforts. They ascend a hill and for a second are lost to the gaze of the anxious spectators. A moment more, and they again appear, rounding the eminence, and coming up the course with the fury of the wild horse of the desert. On they come, while the roar of the multitude rises higher. On they come with flashing eyeballs, dilated nostrils, and strained limbs, scarcely touching the earth beneath them. The crack of the whip is never needed, for the demon of emulation is spurring them on. The wild ambition of man has been imparted to the noble animals. One more breathless moment and the goal is attained. Two of the horses have come neck-to-neck. The race is to begin again! And where is the third noble animal, so beautiful and sleek and stately as he appeared when he first set out? Oh, he is distanced, or he has bolted, or his strength is done up, or (as I once witnessed) his limb is dislocated. Yes, we saw the miserable creature led off the course with his head pendant, his mouth foaming, his sides panting, and his whole frame trembling with the excruciating pain he endured, while a heartless multitude looked calmly on, or turned their heads to behold another victim of their sport.

The spectacle of which Miss Evans so evidently disapproved became an annual event on the Down in the middle of the eighteenth century. In 1753 the fourth Duke of Bedford donated 'a silver pint mug and a silver tumbler to be run for by horses and some other prizes to be sported for on Whitchurch Down.' The 'other prizes' were probably awarded to the winners of wrestling competitions, which often, in that period, shared an occasion with a race meeting. Over the years the popularity of this annual midsummer meeting increased. The prize money was enhanced each year, the quality of the fields improved, and the number of visitors increased to the point where all the rooms in all the local inns were booked well ahead of the event. In 1811 a Plymouth newspaper was reporting a high level of interest in the city on the eve of the annual meeting, to the extent that: 'horses, coaches, chaises, gigs, and even the mourning coaches throughout Plymouth, Stonehouse, and Dock are all in requisition.'

The meeting had, since the 1770s, become a two-day event, and had become very much a social occasion, with a ball 'attended by nearly all the rank, beauty, and fashion, of the neighbourhood.' It also became a commercially well-organised event, with bookmakers licensed and traders wishing to erect a booth or tent being charged a rental of half a guinea (52p). Local newspapers got used to calling it 'the annual diversion'. The extent to which the enterprise was dependent on the sponsorship of the Duke was illustrated in the 1830s, when the sixth Duke asked his staff to advise him on whether he should continue his support. John Benson, the Duke's Tavistock steward, opined that 'I do not mean to say that the races are of no benefit to local trade, but that I think no great injury could arise from their discontinuance.' The writing was on the wall. The death of the Duke in 1839 provided the opportunity, and in the 1840s the seventh Duke reduced the ducal subsidies in stages. Rachel Evans was overjoyed:

It is not likely that the turfy slopes of Whitchurch Down will ever more resound to the shouts of the victorious jockey or be the site of the tavern or gambling house. But the playful colts fling their manes in the air and bound over the shaven course at liberty. May they long be preserved from the fate of 'the high-mettled rider' made food by the hounds!

Miss Evans was too sanguine. The races continued, with the vacuum created by the Duke's withdrawal being largely filled by the gentlemen of the Plymouth Garrison. *The Devonshire Chronicle* of 15 May 1849 contained a description of how the betting was conducted:

A large group congregated together, with books and pencils all in readiness, waiting some favourable opportunity to set the machinery in motion. Some one at last, rather more impatient than the others, would begin by saying 'Come Sir, I'll lay you 2 to 1, etc'. Another would follow, another, and another, until nothing but one continual din of '8 to 4; 10 to 5; 12 to 1 etc' could be heard, the answers generally being negatived, by the pencil and book, mechanism rapidly working, to set down the odds. Occasionally, however, a sound would issue from out the group of 'No Sir! My book is made up', which accounts, no doubt, for the rumour that some considerable amount of cash changed hands on this occasion.

In 1850 the Race Committee asked the Duke of Bedford whether he would renew his sponsorship. The Duke offered £10, with conditions, one of which was that the event should not feature any 'demoralisation or drunkenness'. The committee declined the offer. The occasion that year was marred by an accident. On their way home from the Down to Tavistock at the end of the day's sport a chandler called Merrifield and a farrier called Minhinnick challenged each other to a race. On reaching Vigo Bridge, Merrifield's horse swerved as it tried to take the sharp bend, and plunged into the river. Horse and rider were both killed.

From the following year, 1851, we get the fullest description of the sideshows at the event. *The Plymouth and Devonport Journal* described:

Booths, shows, stalls, shooting galleries, ale and porter enclosures, gingerbread stands, sandwich shops, all built of canvas, moveable when all the trade is over. There were thimble-riggers, peg-and-garter spectators, royal whirligigs. The special constables were busy, ordering everybody to go everywhere. A clown danced, laughed, and cried, and did anything to please the folk outside the Temple of Philosophy.

In 1857 there were, in attendance, two brass bands, one having been hired while the other simply turned up. While it was felt that the stewards did their job as well as they could, there was some grumbling about delays. The first race, scheduled for noon, got off at 3 o'clock. The 1860s saw a falling-off in the level of public interest, and the 1868 meeting was the last of a series.

Over the next decade the local racing public had to be content with the kind of event that took place on the Down on the morning of Monday 2 September 1878. Several hundred people gathered following a rumour that John Babbage and Richard Prout had challenged each other to a horse-race. The course was described as 'over a mile of the ground which was wont to be used when the races were an institution.' Prout won by a neck. The suggestion that this indicated the survival of a healthy appetite for the sport led to a revival of the annual meeting, now to be held at Heathfield, between 1880 and 1886, and to an abortive attempt to bring it home to the Down in 1887. The only racing on the Down thereafter was in the form of hunt point-to-point meetings for a few years on either side of the First World War.

The traditional Whitchurch racecourse, the 'old course', had its starting point near the crossroads at Moorshop, and proceeded eastwards through Lower Longford, Quarry, and Moortown, before returning via Oakley Cottage, Wilsetton, and Warren's Cross. A good view of the finish, near Pixie Cross, could be had from the nearby grandstand. The 'new course', used in the twentieth century, started near Furzy Bridge and proceeded westwards via Taviton and Torland. There was then a straight level run due east to the finishing point, near which a stand on the rising ground would have afforded an excellent view of the whole race.

One morning in 1920 young Master Abel was walking across this area on his way to school from his home at Pennycomequick. There had been racing on the previous day. And there, beneath his feet, was a half-crown. More than 70 years later Mr Abel, in his Whitchurch home, recalled the incident vividly and relived the experience of being a boy in 1920 for whom a half-crown in the pocket meant sudden access to a different world.

The traditional parish boundary between Whitchurch and Tavistock crossed Whitchurch Down, and crossed also that part of it where the Tavistock Cricket Club had its home from the moment of its formation in 1849. 'The Ring' is a spectacular ground and a beguiling setting, but, in spite of being historically partly in Whitchurch and happily calling one of its ends the 'Whitchurch End', this is the home of the Tavistock Club. It is sufficient here to point to the number of Whitchurch men who have made outstanding contributions to the life of that club. There was, first of all, its first captain. Richard Sleeman was born in 1813, the son of the vicar of Whitchurch. He was himself destined for the Church, and his first job, as noted above, was as curate to Jack Russell, the hunting parson. In 1848 he succeeded his father as the vicar of Whitchurch. In the following year, at the age of 36, he was one of the pioneers who established the Tavistock Cricket Club in its home on the Down, only a few minutes' walk from his vicarage. His playing career took him through to the age of 55, but he retired from the captaincy 11 years earlier, in 1857. Thereafter, as well as playing, he took over responsibility for the care of the ground, and thus became The Ring's first

Right: *Parish boundary stone at The Ring, incorporated into the circle of boundary stones around the ground.*

The Ring in 1900.

curator. He died in 1870 at the age of 57, only two years after hanging up his cricket boots. Over the years he had spent a lot of time at The Ring, reflecting his deep love of the game. There was, though, another factor at work. Summer days on Whitchurch Down must have afforded some respite from the noise, not only from the pack of hounds that he maintained at the vicarage, but also from the 15 children that he reared within its walls. As a cricketer he could, perhaps, be described as no more than a steady middle-order batsman. Of his qualities as a captain we have no idea. His position in the annals of the club remained secure – he was the first captain. The next generation of cricketers at The Ring in the 1870s and '80s also featured a vicar of Whitchurch. This was Revd Samuel W. Featherstone, affectionately known as Sammy, who succeeded his father as vicar of the parish in 1883. His long playing career was one of the most consistently successful in the club's history. Although predominantly a bowler, he made a lot of runs, topping the club averages, for example, in 1880 with an average of 34. He was described in 1885 as 'one of the best bowlers in the west of England, a fast run getter, and a good all-round player.' In 1888 he played for Devon. In one game for Tavistock he took six wickets, all clean bowled, with consecutive balls. Sammy was a young, dashing, popular cricketer, with a lot of natural talent, who led by example and by radiating an infectious enthusiasm for the game. The nearness of his home to the ground made it possible for him to offer regular hospitality. One wonders how the other residents of the vicarage, family and staff, reacted when, as frequently happened in the middle of a wet afternoon, with play abandoned, two dozen cricketers and two umpires arrived to occupy the place and to while away the soggy hours with talk, laughter and refreshment. Featherstone also had a sense of humour. Not many could have carried off what he achieved when, attending a temperance meeting, he persuaded his earnest audience that his own experience as 'a partial abstainer' had made life more difficult for him than it would have been if he had been a teetotaller.

Edward Chilcott was the club captain for 11 seasons in the last years of the nineteenth century. His playing career had begun at Cambridge, where he was a Rugby Blue. His father had established a law firm at Tavistock, and Edward entered it, taking over its leadership when his father retired in the 1890s. The family home, Chollacott Lane House, was

Edward Chilcott

in Whitchurch parish and was a stone's throw from both the cricket ground and the golf course. Edward, who was a natural ball player, spent a good deal of time at both venues, captaining, at different times, both clubs. As a cricketer he was blessed with a good eye and great agility. Described in 1885 as 'a fast run-getter and a sensational hitter', he made nine from one hit on one occasion during that season. He also set very high standards in the field and could be very critical of players, even senior ones, who he thought were guilty of slackness.

David Gordon, Ceylon-born and Whitchurch-reared, played for three seasons at The Ring in the middle of the twentieth century, sharing the summers with undergraduate studies at Oxford and days on the farm with Bill Toye. His was a natural cricketing talent. It was recognised by the county selectors when he played for Tavistock against a Devon XI in a match in August 1949 to celebrate the centenary of the club. His match analysis of 11 for 104 resulted in his selection to face Dorset, and it seemed clear that the county officials were eyeing him as a future county captain.

Stuart Munday belongs to a dynasty deeply rooted in Whitchurch. Having joined the club in 1965, he was to play in five succeeding decades, and to hold, at one time or another, most of the club offices. A strong personality, he has been at the centre of a number of controversies within the club. There was never any doubt in anyone's mind, whether you agreed with him or not, that he maintained, throughout his career, a strong loyalty to the club and to its interests as he saw them.

These, then, were examples of Whitchurch men who played for Tavistock and whose cricketing theatre was The Ring. In the early years of the twentieth century two other significant cricket figures settled in

The 'Chilcott seat', halfway up Down Road and a short step from The Ring.

David Gordon appears fourth from the left as the Tavistock side takes the field in the centenary match in August 1949.

Whitchurch parish. They were near-neighbours at Middlemoor. One was a retired soldier, Colonel Alexander Ward-Young, who, in his early career, had played a good deal of cricket to a high level. When he died in 1934 he was, at his own insistence, buried at Horrabridge in his cricket blazer. The other was Rowland Powell-Williams, who had played county cricket for Warwickshire. Both men gave encouragement to local cricket, and both were involved in the running of a Whitchurch Cricket Club, which is known to have been operating up to 1907. In that year it was reported to have 'expired', only to be revived in the following year, from which time it continued until the First World War. During this period the Colonel was president and Powell-Williams a committee member. The vicar, Revd Beebe, was treasurer, and William Batten of Oakley Villas was the secretary, while Elizabeth Lovell was the kindly farmer who provided a field twice a week. A typical season would see between 12 and 20 fixtures, half of them at home, against the likes of Bere Alston, Brentor, Calstock, Mary Tavy, Yelverton and Tavistock Grammar School. The costs of running the club produced deficits of the order of 75 pence in 1909 and £5 in 1912, but the committee managed to deal with debts by raising money at popular musical concerts in the village. One such, in 1912, featured 'some talented lady and gentlemen artistes from Plymouth', and a bravura performance from Victor Earl, the possessor of 'a sweet tenor voice'. Victor's final offering, 'My Sweetheart When a Boy', must have had a different reception than it would have from a modern audience.

The Whitchurch Cricket Club suspended activities in 1914, and the long gap that followed covered both world wars. There was a revival after the Second World War, and the club went into action again under the captaincy of Charlie Sparrow, playing on the Down, in the area opposite Middlemoor, which was later to be a football field. The foundations were thus laid in the late 1940s for the full-scale revival which came in 1949, and which was down to the generosity of young David Gordon, back at Whitchurch House after army service and eager both to throw himself into the farm and to offer some tangible support to local cricket. He made available a field adjoining the drive to the house, the only condition being the willingness of club members to help if required at harvest time. The Wayfarers were born.

The story of the Whitchurch Wayfarers in the half-century or so since its reincarnation has been one of considerable success based on principles of self-help and high levels of commitment. The ground is in excellent order, and in 2001 Kate Allenby, Olympic modern pentathlon medallist, some of whose schooling was at Whitchurch, opened a new pavilion. The picture in the early years of the twenty-first century is of a club running two sides in the Senior Devon League, four colts' teams at the various age levels, and a ladies' team. It is a well-run, happy outfit with a large membership and strong local support.

It is said that a football club operated in a field close by the Halfway House for a time between the

The Wayfarers

Left: *The Whitchurch Club in the 1950s. Left to right, back row: Bob McCall, David Toye, Ron Bowman, John Adams, Maurice Woods, Roy Curtis, Bob Elliott; front: Bill Brown, Ken Watkins, Ray Martin, Courtney Rowe, Frank Toye; lurking: Mrs Woods and ?.*

Below: *A group of club members prepare the foundations for the new pavilion in 1974, to be constructed mainly from reclaimed Nissen huts. Left to right, standing: David Endacott, John Cornall, Andrew Watkins, Vic Stacey, Bob Elliott; bending: Den Crocker, Bob McCall.*

Above: *Match against Tavistock Seconds on the Wayfarers' ground in 1973. Visiting batsman Jack Taylor faces the home attack in the hands of Vic Stacey. John Pocknell is at the non-striker's end. John Doidge keeps wicket. Brian Barriball, at mid-on, prepares to pounce. Bob Elliott is in the gully. The umpire is Francis Sprague. The result was a home win.*

The Wayfarers in the 1960s. Left to right, standing: Martin Elford, Stuart Munday, Russell Bartlett, Ken Mackay, Les Tucker, Dennis Towl; sitting: Francis Sprague, David Endacott, Bob McCall, Bill Crocker, Barry Chappell, Ian Mackay, Derek Glanville, John Doidge.

wars, calling itself the Grenofen Grapplers. If this is so, this may have been the first soccer club in the parish. Of the Whitchurch Villa Football Club we can be more certain. It owed its origins to a meeting held in the Parish Room on 18 November 1920, at which it was decided to form a football club 'under Association rules'. Quick off the mark, their first fixture was in the following month, when they played a local derby against Horrabridge, and won 3–1. The club played on a field known as 'The Level', at the top of the hill on the road going out of the village towards Grenofen. Here, with a shed providing basic changing accommodation, the club had its home between the two wars. After the Second World War permission was obtained from the Whitchurch Commoners to play on the level area of the Down on the opposite side of the road from Middlemoor, where, it appears, there had once been a hockey pitch. This ground was shared for a time with a club known as Wescon United, founded and managed by a William Blowe. The name of the club derived from a cooperative venture involving young members of the Wesleyan and Congregational Churches. The Whitchurch Football Club was disbanded in 1996, when it was unable, because of planning constraints, to provide the kind of changing facilities on which the league authorities insisted. Since then the pitch has been used by junior teams.

The Whitchurch Tennis Club was formed in 1921, its first president being Frank Radcliffe of Holwell. The club had initially just one grass court, in the grounds of Anderton Cottage. In 1926 the bowling-green alongside became the second court.

Improvements to the facilities were made by the traditional pattern of fund-raising efforts, including concerts, jumble sales, whist drives, etc., and in 1956 it became possible to construct a hard court. The club president was now General Frederick Barron of Greystones, and other prominent supporters of the cause included Ernest Mercy of Bellever, a bank

Right: *Players and officials of Wescon United on the Whitchurch football pitch in 1964.*

Below: *Whitchurch Villa in the 1940s.*
Left to right, back row: *T. Worden, J. Endacott, mascot 'Nipper', S. Goode, L. Rice, S. Doidge, H. Palmer, W. Munday, D. Toye, J. Martin, R. McCall;* middle row: *R. Minhinnick, H. Doidge, G. Norman;*
front row: *J. Frise, S. Frise, C. Toye, C. Berryman, J. Willcock.*

The Tennis Club

Left: *A few hardy souls gather at the old courts on 24 March 1983 to mark the end of an era.*

Below: *Playing the first match on the hard court. Left to right: Harry Mudge, Jimmy Angell, Roy Curtis, Ken Watkins.*

Below: *A 1948 moment. Joan Doidge plays a forehand as a train on the GWR line passes behind her.*

Below left: *The celebration tea in April 1956. Left to right, background: Ken Watkins, Mr and Mrs Pearce, Mr and Mrs Barron, Mr and Mrs Mercy, Mr and Mrs Perkin, Mrs Mudge; foreground: Mrs and Mr Gerry, Roy Curtis, Robert and Gill Warren.*

Below right: *All that remains of the old Tennis Club premises is this gate, produced for the club by one of its members, Den Bishop, and sited at the entrance from Anderton Lane.*

manager, George G. Pearse, of Wingate, a lawyer, and Allan Gerry, the vicar. The club captain, who was to maintain a close and affectionate interest in the fortunes of the club for the rest of the century and into the next, along with his wife Flo, was Ken Watkins. After the opening day, in April 1956, 100 supporters and guests gathered in the Parish Room for a celebration tea.

A second hard court followed in 1967, but, as far as Anderton was concerned, the writing was on the wall. In 1983 the decisive move was made to amalgamate with the Tavistock Tennis Club, and to move to the latter's premises in the town. For a time 'Whitchurch' came before 'Tavistock' in the name of the club. Sadly, if inevitably, this was bound to change.

The Golf Club, with its course in the majestic setting of Whitchurch Down, was founded in 1890. In November of that year a dozen people, meeting at the Bedford Hotel in Tavistock, decided to approach the lords of the manor of the two parishes that shared responsibility for the Down. Within a month, approval had been obtained, the club had been formally launched, and a slate of rules had been drawn up. Rule 3 declared that half guineas should be payable as entrance fees, as annual subscriptions, and as 'green money'. Military and naval officers were to be exempt from the entrance levy. Under the helpful patronage of the Duke of Bedford a nine-hole course was laid out and was in use by February 1891, attracting into membership, within the first year, 23 gentlemen and ten ladies. Competitions were speedily organised and in June 1891, in a wooded area on the Whitchurch side of the Pimple, the first clubhouse opened its doors. The replacement of the latter in 1895 by another building on the same site was quickly followed by an extension of the course to 5,300 yards and 18 holes. A professional was hired and paid 12s. (60p) a week, plus any profits he could make on the sale of balls. The head greenkeeper received a wage of 13s. (65p). To attract patrons from Plymouth arrangements were made with the railway companies to offer discounted tickets. The GWR station was particularly handy for the course, the distance in between being the manageable, albeit steep, Down Road. Having arrived at the clubhouse you could buy a cup of tea or a tot of whisky for threepence, and bread and butter or cake for twopence.

In 1905 the club had built a two-storeyed house of wood and iron to accommodate its growing membership, which had by now reached 200, one-third of whom were ladies. This in turn gave way, in 1915, to a clubhouse on the site of the present one. Between the wars there were a significant number of serving officers in membership, as well as an increasing number of juniors. Between 1934 and 1960 there was also an artisans' section, whose members paid less and enjoyed fewer facilities, although they were allowed to drink at the bar during Sunday lunchtimes.

Main and left: The third clubhouse, 1905, and the fourth clubhouse, 1915.

During the later twentieth and early twenty-first centuries, the activities of the club continued to expand. There have been a number of major revisions to the course and the clubhouse was purchased in 1957, while membership has grown to something like 800. The modern era, in which the club celebrated its centenary to general acclaim, has been a relatively peaceful one. But it was not always so. In the early part of the twentieth century there were confrontations over major issues of principle. One such was Sunday play, effectively resisted by the Commoners until 1924. When the latter finally capitulated, the Whitchurch Parochial Church Council could not contain its indignation:

> ... it is with deep regret together with shame and bewilderment that we have to record the fact that on March 31 the Whitchurch Commoners by 11 votes to 10 upset the tradition of 35 years and granted permission to the Golf Club to play golf on the Down on Sundays from 12.30 to 6p.m.

An even longer and more bruising battle was the one fought over the bunkers that the club wanted to construct. Four years of hand-to-hand combat were only brought to an end by a legal judgement and by compensation payments, and the 'battle of the bunkers' left its wounds. The Golf Club has, over the years, brought significant benefits to the parish. A considerable number of Whitchurch people have been involved in its organisation, and a number have been employed either on the course or in the house. These have included, over the years, a number of village lads who worked as caddies. According to the club by-laws of 1895, caddies were to earn fourpence a round, but could also be paid between a penny and threepence for balls retrieved. Only 'respectable boys of good behaviour' were employed. The other obvious benefit to the parish came in the form of additional numbers of visitors and tourists, lured by the attractiveness of a beautiful course, affording at the same time both fine sport and wonderful scenery.

Above: Puss in Boots, *1997. Left to right, standing:* Sue Riozzi, Karen Pawley, Barbara Butterfield, Trudy Massey, Sian Demery, Lyn Stevens, Lydia Philpotts; *kneeling:* Mac McEwen, Ben Pearce, Barbara Sherrell.

Left: *The first pantomime in 1974. Den Bishop is pictured among the children, who include Susan Jury, Julie Smith, Michelle Bradley and Natalie Wilton.*

Below: *Mike Maker, Don Munday, Steve Eslick, Russell Bartlett and Den Bishop.*

PLAYING

Left: In 1984 the Youth Theatre Group tackled Jesus Christ, Superstar. *Here a crowd of children appeal to Christ for healing. Jesus was played by Andrew Williams, who was to find himself, 20 years on, back in Whitchurch as curate of St Andrew's.*

Below: Aladdin *in 1992. Pictured are: Sally John, Trudy Eales, Mandy Jackman and Glyn John.*

Below: Players in Pantoland, 1994. *The whole company are pictured. Carol Eager sits at the centre of the second row from the front, flanked by Trudy Eales on her right and Judith Johns on her left.*

Whitchurch is proud to have a theatrical tradition, associated for a number of years with the Parish Room. One element of this was provided by the Youth Club, which was particularly active in the 1970s and which established a pattern of entertainments and parties for the parish's senior citizens.

February 1974 saw the beginning of the 'Whitchurch Pantomime' tradition. The first production was *Blubeard*. *The Tavistock Times* wrote that:

> ... considering the disadvantages of the Whitchurch Hall stage, the cast achieved a smoothness which could perhaps teach some of the professional shows a thing or two.

Den Bishop as Ann 'kept up a continuous patter which had the crowds laughing throughout the show.' Harry Kennen as Count Ten 'showed amazing agility', and 'held the audience with delight when he sailed into a Maurice Chevalier number.' Dr Edith Strong gave 'an outstanding piece of showmanship' as Madame La Snoop. The young dancers had been trained by Carole Eager at her School of Dancing, and Miss Eager and Edith Gray were the co-producers. The demand for tickets was such that an extra performance was arranged.

Once under way, and with press notices like that, there was no stopping them. The series of pantomimes ran:

1974 Blubeard	1989 Goldilocks
1975 The Pied Piper	1990 Dick Whittington
1976 Humpty Dumpty	1991 Humpty Dumpty
1977 Dick Whittington	1992 Aladdin
1978 Tommy Tucker	1993 Red Riding Hood
1979 Cinderella	1994 Players in Pantoland
1980 Mother Hubbard	1995 Robinson Crusoe
1981 The Queen of Hearts	1996 Beauty and the Beast
1982 Aladdin	1997 Puss in Boots
1983 Robinson Crusoe	1998 Sleeping Beauty
1984 Jack and the Beanstalk	1999 Cinderella
1985 Sleeping Beauty	2001 Snow White
1986 Babes in the Wood	2003 The Old Woman Who
1987 Cinderella	Lived in a Shoe
1988 Mother Goose	

In addition, the company put on, for a number of years, an annual summer show:

1975 The Roaring Twenties	1984 The Good Old Days
1980 The Good Old Days	1978 Old Time Music Hall
1976 A Show for Summer	1985 Let the People Sing
1981 Thank You for the Music	1979 That's Entertainment
1977 Holiday Fayre	1986 The Wizard of Oz

The backbone of this operation was a group called the Whitchurch Players and Dancers. Its founder was Carole Eager, the manager of the stage-dance school that bears her name. She wrote all the shows and produced all of them up to 1997, when the mantle fell to her erstwhile pupil Trudy Massey (née Eales), who also took on the responsibility of running the dance school. Others who have served the group faithfully

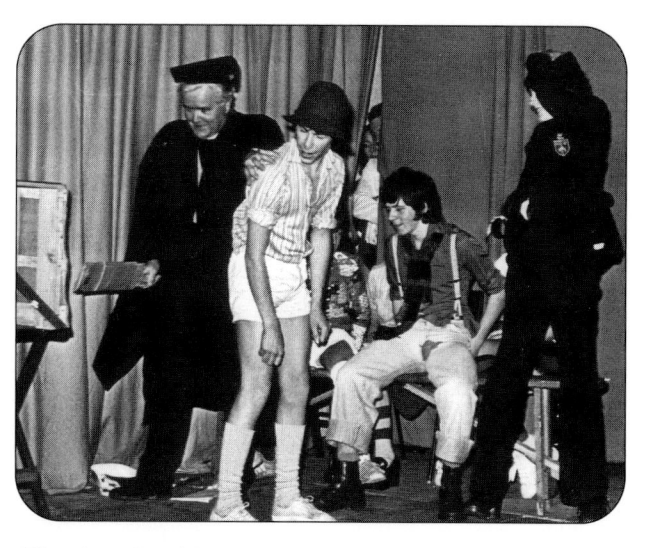

The vicar, Revd Harry Kennen, wields the cane, Nicholas Maker takes the punishment, David Rowe ruminates, and Paul Blowey looks alarmed.

The Youth Theatre's Oliver *in 1982, featuring, left to right: Ben Portman, Christopher Bowles, Andrew Williams, Edward Rippon, Katherine Duncan, Clare Turner, Marianne Kilpatrick, Sally Anniss.*

over the years have included Derek Cruze, Sue Sellis, and Geoff and Margaret Bradford. In 2003 the officers were: Mac McEwen, president; Sue Riozzi, chairperson; Nicky Dore, secretary; Julie Harris, treasurer. The Parish Room remained the home of the event until 1999. Its demolition left the group with no alternative but to seek shelter in the Wharf at Tavistock. In spite of the move, the identity with Whitchurch remains, as the continuing title of the group reaffirms. The 1970s, which saw the origins of these traditions of theatre and entertainment in the Parish Room, saw also the formation of a youth theatre group, which offered a succession of annual shows from 1979. Spearheaded by such young theatrical and musical talents as Andrew Williams and James Lunt, these proved to be performances of high quality and were much appreciated by villagers of all ages, as well as by visitors. The main run of productions ended in the mid-1880s when a number of the leading figures moved away to university, but younger members who had been involved remained to continue the distinctive spirit and vigour of youth theatre.

Chapter 4

RESIDING

Whitchurch boasts a fine range of sturdy old farmhouses. Anderton, Dennithorne, Heckwood, Lower Collaton, Moortown, Prowtytown, Stentaford, Venn and Wilsetton all have origins in the seventeenth century, or in some cases earlier. They have, of course, been subject to alteration over the years, some in a more radical form than others. Venn, for example, is a Tudor building with seventeenth-century additions and nineteenth-century alterations, which was abandoned for a time in the twentieth century and used as an animal shelter, before being reincarnated as a modern dwelling in 2001. Many of the houses share such common features as the through-passage or the familiar three-room plan. Brook Mill Farmhouse, a Tavyside building in the Walreddon area, is the site of a medieval mill. In 1969, when Hugh Brian Cooke, the previous owner of the Waterways Garage, bought the property, it had been lived in by Alfred Cory Mortimore for some years. In the later stages 'Morty', who was 82 in 1969, had been living in one room in a home that had become derelict, damp and run-down. Major renovations were undertaken in the Cooke era to this magnificent, but decayed old building.

Woodtown is in the same part of the parish as Brook Mill. The original name of this seventeenth-century house was Attwoode. In the twentieth century, when it shed much of its substantial lands in a series of sales, there were a number of changes of ownership until it was bought in 1966 by Mrs Ruth Graham, breeder of cattle and dogs. Its owner at the time of writing, Frances Stephens, has, with her husband Mike, done a great deal of renovation, and in so doing has revealed some of the house's oldest, and most interesting, features.

Close by Woodtown, at Rixhill, is Lower Tor Farmhouse. Its origins lie in the sixteenth century, with a stable and a lean-to being added in the eighteenth century. Here for some years in the middle of the twentieth century lived Frank Hodge, who, after emigrating to America and enlisting in the US Cavalry, returned to England after the war and bought the farm. His reputation for taming difficult horses was unrivalled. Among other skills, his charges would learn how to get him home after a long evening in the Market Inn.

Higher Grenofen Farmhouse displays all the features of a rebuilt longhouse, dating from the

Above: *The house at Brook Mill Farm in 1969.*

Left: *In 1969, on the first floor of the Brook Mill Farmhouse, one of the millstones survived, with the vertical driving mechanism in situ.*

Above: *Woodtown in 1996.*

Left: *A medieval door at Woodtown.*

Clockwise from top: *Lower Grenofen Farmhouse; Boyton Farmhouse; Fullamore Farmhouse; Higher Pennington Farmhouse.*

RESIDING

Main: *Higher Grenofen Farmhouse, 1930s.*

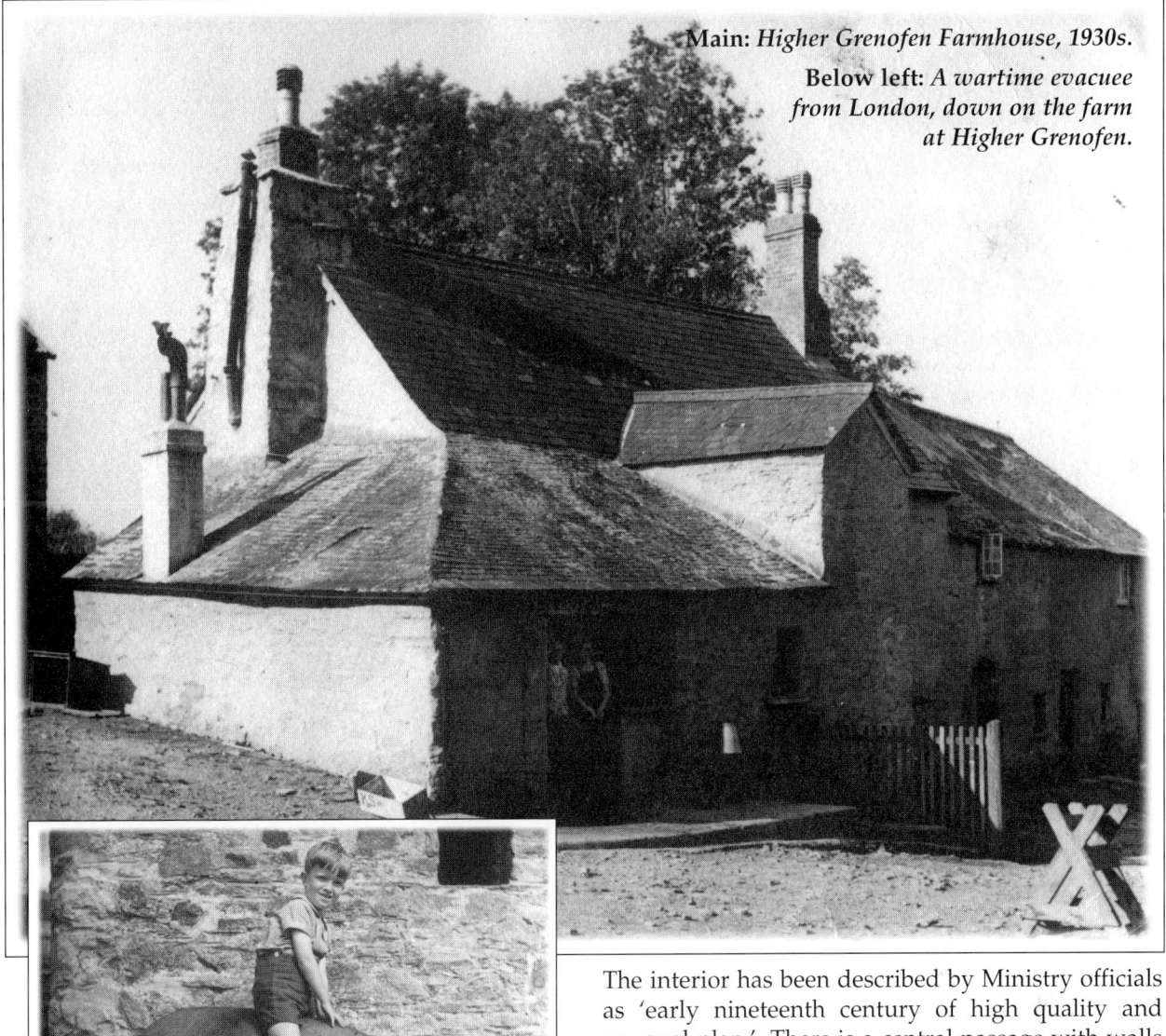

Below left: *A wartime evacuee from London, down on the farm at Higher Grenofen.*

early-seventeenth century. The shippen was two-storeyed, the presumption being that the upper floor housed the farm servants. The position of the house, close to the main Tavistock–Plymouth road, encouraged the early development of what have become common farmhouse practices in efforts to diversify. Bed-and-breakfast accommodation was already being offered in 1934.

Lower Grenofen Farmhouse, by the Walkham, may well have been built as a home for the captain of the nearby Walkham and Poldice Mine.

Boyton is one of the farmhouses that lie broadly in the Plaster Down area of the parish. The property is first mentioned, as 'Bawton', in a document of 1518. The interior has been described by Ministry officials as 'early nineteenth century of high quality and unusual plan.' There is a central passage with walls curved to both right and left of the entrance, forming a semi-circular inner porch. To the rear the walls are also curved, forming a circular area with a vaulted ceiling.

Close to Boyton is Fullamore. The house has mid-seventeenth-century origins, the rear wing being, in all probability, of the original date. Used for a time as a cider store, its access door has its frame cut back to allow the passage of barrels. Alterations in the eighteenth century saw the separation of the passage and the shippen from the house. Higher Pennington is in the same area.

Higher Quarry Farmhouse, described as 'an interesting and a well-built house', forms part of the hamlet of Moortown, towards the eastern part of the parish. Fine views are obtained from the rear of the house, facing south-west, which was the original entrance. Outside the house there are a number of features of interest including 'a profusion of gateposts', an assembly of old granite troughs and millstones, and two ancient stone barns. The house itself dates from the middle years of the seventeenth century.

Clockwise from above: *Lower Quarry; Alma Cottage; Cobbler's Cottage; Mary's Cottage (named after Mary Sleeman) in the 1960s; Church Park Cottages.*

RESIDING

Lower Quarry is in the same vicinity and of the same age as Higher Quarry. Ownership over the last two centuries has been dominated by two families. In the nineteenth century there was John Shazell, who was bequeathed the property by Richard Edgcumbe. John passed it on to his son, also John but with a second name of Edgcumbe in recognition of the benefactor. The two John Shazells were in occupation from 1839 to 1888. From 1902 to 1948 the property belonged to Jonathan Peek, or to members of his family.

Oakley Farmhouse, situated between Plaster Down and Moortown, has Elizabethan origins. Wooden panelling, originally in the hall and reset in the nineteenth-century passage, carries an inscription with the initials 'WH' and 'IP' and the date 29 May 1655. Major reconstruction to the house was carried out in the 1880s and again in the 1920s.

If Whitchurch is a parish of farmhouses, it is also a parish of cottages, many of them traditionally inhabited by farm workers, miners, or quarrymen. The term 'cottage' covers, of course, a wide range of dwellings from modest abodes to substantial residences. There is Courtenay Cottage, for example, in the Rixhill area, with its long association with the Cranch family. There are the cottages known as Church Park, built by the Duke of Bedford in 1852 as a small part of the great design by the Bedford establishment to ease the housing problem in the area. These four cottages cost, to build, a total of £368. There are also the traditional village cottages, whose names act as continuing reminders of their past, such as Cobbler's Cottage or Farrier's Cottage. A number of these cottages, in the village or in satellites such as Middlemoor, have been adapted, some of them radically, to meet modern needs.

Mrs Kathleen Evans, living in Exeter in 2003, has provided a fine description of a childhood spent in one of the Holwell Cottages at Middlemoor. Here she lived, as Kathleen Giles, for the first 16 years of her life, from 1931 to 1947. She writes:

Our cottage had four rooms. Next door had only two and a lean-to kitchen at the back. Downstairs floors were flagstoned, walls were cob and very thick, and the roof was slated, and was generously coated with a layer of cement whenever it sprang a leak. There was no sanitation or proper drainage. The water supply, one outdoor tap next door and one cold tap in our kitchen, came from a spring in the field behind. If the cows from Holwell House got into the enclosure and knocked the cover off the cistern, the water contained tadpoles, pine needles, and various body parts of frogs, mice, birds etc. Lighting was by oil-lamp or candles, and heating by coal or Valor Oil Stove. The small cottage was occupied by the under-gardener at Holwell House. My father was the chauffeur. He did general machinery maintenance, lawn-mowing, and relief milking if the cowman was ill. The cowman lived in Shorts Cottage and the head gardener in the Lodge. Most of the bigger houses in Middlemoor were occupied by retired army and navy officers, and the cottages by workers on the land or on the local estate. Wives did domestic work for families in the larger houses or took in washing or dressmaking.

Above: *An Endacott family picture from 1917. John and Rose are surrounded by their children. Left to right, back row: George (undergraduate), John junr (soldier), Marion; front: Charles, Ada.*

Left: *Edward Ham, long-serving gardener for the Chilcotts.*

In the latter half of the nineteenth century the mile between the centres of Tavistock and Whitchurch was settled by the professional and commercial middle classes. Some of these were people who had done well in the professional and business worlds and who were seeking a less stressful living environment, or a setting in which to display the fruits of their success, or simply a bit of land on which to keep a couple of ponies for the children or grandchildren.

There were also those who were taking early steps on the social-climbing ladder, and for whom the acquisition of a Whitchurch Road residence marked a significant stage in the rise of their family fortunes. Two examples may suffice. In 1904 the Chilcotts, Tavistock's foremost legal dynasty, built Chollacott Lane House. A generation later the Endacotts moved into Number 1 Oakley Villas, on the opposite side of the road. Both families made significant contributions to the life of the parish.

Housing developments in the latter part of the twentieth century have given further emphasis to the population imbalance in the parish between a populous west and a sparsely populated east. The two areas that have received the most attention from developers have been Grenofen, and Whitchurch Road between the village and Chollacott.

Of the grandest and most substantial dwellings in the parish, full as they are of character and of history, ten have been selected to provide a cross-section of homes that fall into this category.

Caseytown

The hamlet of Caseytown, the small settlement that straddles the narrow lane from Whitchurch Down leading to Bleak House and on to Walkhampton, takes its name from the house. The house, in turn, derives its name from an early owner, a Cass, Case, or Casey. Medieval in origin, the old property was replaced in 1867 by a new residence built for the Cudlipp family. There is, however, clear evidence of the substantial use of masonry taken from earlier buildings, an early date stone in a rear wall giving,

Friar's Walk.

Church Lea.

Below: *The new school is the centrepiece in a 1990s view looking eastwards across Whitchurch Road, showing some of the older development, clinging to the main road, and some of the modern estates.*

Above: Downhouse in the 1920s.

Right: Dr Hughes outside the front door of Downhouse, with family members.

for example, a seventeenth-century date. A brass plate on a stable door bearing the inscription 'White Rose 1810' is a reminder of the closeness of the house to the popular racecourse on Whitchurch Down.

Downhouse

Formed on the basis of a group of cottages, Downhouse, on the northern edge of Plaster Down, dates from around 1800, but was much altered and 'gentrified' in the middle of the nineteenth century. Originally the house was approached by a drive from Venn Bungalow. The track that exists across the moor at the time of writing dates from the middle of the twentieth century. In the last half of the nineteenth century the house was occupied successively by Edwin Pearce and William Phillips, the latter a mine captain from Gulworthy who sired at least 14 children. In about 1900 it passed to Robert Harry Hughes, MA MB Cantab, a Plymouth doctor, who added the porch. His family sold the house, in 1940, to Commander Geoffrey Dixon, a grandson of Captain Phillips. Lt Commander John Fison appeared briefly in the 1950s, but fell on hard times. Charlie and Dolly White then moved in, refugees from a hectic business life in Gosport, where they had run a laundry. They farmed with gusto, until the cruel winter of 1963 destroyed their enthusiasm for 'the good life'. At this point, says the owner in 2003, Geoffrey Harland, a man with a naval background, 'I came along and took it off their hands.' The house has a benevolent, well-behaved ghost.

Grenofen Manor

In 1833 Mrs Bray wrote of Grenofen Manor as 'a house surrounded by delightful grounds, lawns and trees, with below the Walkham winding in the most beautiful manner through the valley.' A century and a half later the Ministry of the Environment described it, more prosaically, as:

> ... a large two-storey house, eighteenth century in character, of rubble with a slate roof. Rebuilt in 1750, there are no remains of the original Manor House incorporated in the present building.

The first owners of the original house of whom we have information, at the beginning of the eighteenth century, appear to have been a family with Redruth origins called the Pollards. They sold it to the Knightons, who carried out the substantial mid-century alterations. This dynasty survived the disinheriting, in the 1760s, of the oldest son, who, it was said, had 'by irregular conduct and imprudent marriage incurred the displeasure of his father.' The young man's unpardonable sin had been to marry the daughter of a Tavistock doctor. In 1830 the property was sold at public auction, the agents advertising it as:

> ... calculated in every respect for the residence of a large genteel family, as it is replete with every accommodation suitable thereto, and commands the most picturesque and romantic prospects, sheltered by spreading lofty pine and other luxuriant trees.

The buyer was Revd Jonathan Philips Carpenter of Mount Tavy, who added a large ballroom and a drawing-room. His oldest daughter Harriet married William Henry Chichester of Arlington Court. By this route the property came into the hands of the family who were to live there for the remaining 100 years that the manor was to remain a private home. The nineteenth century saw the further expansion of both the house and the gardens, while the development of the collections of glass, china and pictures turned it into a typical residence of a Victorian gentleman. A mangenese mine was opened on the estate and the GWR drove its Tavistock–Plymouth railway line through the property. Of the latter, it was claimed that the Chichesters enjoyed special privileges from the company, possibly through share ownership, which included the right to have trains stop on demand just a few yards from the house. The impression was strengthened by Henry Chichester's

Bottom: Miss Chichester dominates this group scene at Grenofen House in 1894. The back row includes: Miss Brooks, Mrs Coppin, Mrs Creber, and three unknowns; middle, left to right: Mrs Symons, Mrs Witheridge, Master Chichester, Master Gaud; front, left to right: Miss Hirtzel, Miss Melluish, Mrs Featherstone, Miss Poppin.

Squire Chichester and his dog enjoy the solitude of the lane alongside his house.

Grenofen House in the 1930s.

devotion to the hobby of train-spotting. It was Henry's father, William Henry Chichester, gentleman, landlord and sportsman, who took up residence at Grenofen in 1853, and who was listed in 1873 as owning 1,230 acres of land. He died in 1911 and was succeeded by his son Henry, who reigned as squire until his own death in 1955. Henry was a public figure, a local councillor, poor law guardian, and magistrate. He died a bachelor, in spite of having a reputation for being something of a ladies' man. His sister Gertrude inherited the property. The addition of 'Clark' to the family name came about as a result of Gertrude's marriage. The estate passed, in turn, to her son, Captain H.P. Chichester-Clark. He sold it, in 1956, to Cyril Smythe, who turned the house to commercial purposes, including the manufacture of plastic products. In 1979, with the building requiring major renovation, the property was divided up and sold, becoming for a time a country club, before its conversion, in 1987, into a number of residential apartments.

Holwell Manor

Holwell, the 'place of the holy well', near Middlemoor, was the site of a medieval mansion which, for more than three centuries, was the seat of the Glanville family, one of the most illustrious dynasties in the area. They were established there from the latter part of the fourteenth century, and it remained in the possession of the family even after Judge Glanville had decamped in the late-sixteenth century to his newly-built mansion at Kilworthy. Holwell was sold in 1790 to John Moore Knighton, a member of the family who had recently virtually rebuilt Grenofen Manor, and were now to give Holwell the same treatment.

Thereafter, it was, for a short time, the residence of John Taylor, that remarkable mining engineer whose drive and foresight found their fullest local expression in the construction of the Tavistock Canal. He moved away in 1812 and the house was subsequently sold to John Scobell. The 1851 census found a household consisting of John Deacon and his wife, with their two sons and three daughters. They had been living there for 17 years and were looked after by a staff of eight living-in servants, one lady's maid, one housekeeper, a footman and a governess, one cook, two housemaids, and one groom. The last 40 years of the century saw the occupancy of William Pryce Michell, a retired Tavistock doctor who, having moved into Holwell, began a second career as philanthropist and supporter of every good Whitchurch cause. He encouraged charitable enterprises and was a particularly generous benefactor of two of the village's key institutions, the church and the school. He was followed, in the early years of the new century, by George Martin and Richard Hancock, by Frank Radcliffe between the wars, and by Colonel Michael Allen and Captain Edward Madgwick thereafter.

Right: William Pryce Michell outside his front door at Holwell House.

Holwell House

Little Churchpark

In 1939 Sir Ernest Whiteside Huddleston retired at the age of 65, after a long and distinguished career, first in the army and then in the colonial service. He had been married to Elsie Barlow-Smith, but she had died in 1931, leaving him with a son and a daughter, both in their twenties. Following a re-marriage, to Lorna Box, and his subsequent retirement, the family moved in 1939 to Whitchurch, where Sir Ernest had a house built close to the village church. It was to be called Little Churchpark. Emma Muriel Box, the new Lady Huddleston's sister, also joined the household. The two sisters became very well known in dog circles, their speciality being golden retrievers. During the rest of Sir Ernest's life, and after his death in 1959, a frequent visitor to stay with his father and stepmother was Father Trevor Huddleston of the Anglican Community of the Resurrection at Mirfield. He became a national figure following the publication in 1956 of his book *Nought for Your Comfort*, a searing attack on the apartheid regime in South Africa, based on his own experiences of life in that country. In the same year that the book appeared he preached in Whitchurch church, the first of a number of occasions when he found an opportunity to combine a family visit with some professional work. A charismatic, albeit very humble and modest, figure, he was to continue for many years his work in South

The Old Vicarage, then known as Whitchurch Farm, in the 1890s, with three of the Lovell children. Left to right: Harold, Bessie, Florence.

The old farmhouse dairy, now the kitchen of The Old Vicarage.

Below and inset: The Priory in 1900 and The Priory's medieval porch tower.

Above: *Little Churchpark.*

Left: *Sir Ernest Huddleston.*

Right: *Miss Box with some of her prizewinners.*

Africa alongside his concern for the poor of London (where he may have been the only bishop to live in a council-house) and his devotion to the Mirfield community.

The Old Vicarage

The house halfway up Church Hill has been known as 'The Old Vicarage' for a few years. It has, however, never been the vicarage. The nearest one can come to an explanation for its modern designation is that at one point a curate lodged there for a time. The history of the building is that of a village-centre farmhouse, formerly known as Home Farm, and before that as Whitchurch Farm. William Beer farmed here from the 1870s to the end of the century. Then began the Lovell era. The family were substantial landowners in the area between Church Hill and Chollacott, and played a prominent role in village affairs over a period of half a century. Joseph Lovell, who brought his young family here, probably in 1900, died in 1905 at the age of 40, his widow Elizabeth being left to run the farm and raise Ethel, Bertha, Bessie, Florence and Harold. Eventually, Harold came of age and took over the business. On his death in 1946 the house was sold for £5,000. The property comprised two reception rooms, kitchen, dairy, three bedrooms, two attics, electricity, water, gas, telephone, a converted tithe barn, stables, shippens, a garage and 35 acres of land. Postwar residents have included Francis and Mabel Adams, Lily Campbell, Rosemary Phillott, and Percy and Margaret Perks. The new name appears to have been adopted in 1955.

The Priory

If 'The Old Vicarage' is a misnomer, so is 'The Priory'. The *Tavistock Gazette* noted the moment when the new name was adopted. 'Tiddybrook Castle', it reported in March 1884, 'has been almost entirely rebuilt by Mr J. Dennis. It is now to be known as The Priory, and presents a romantic aspect.' The old name, Tiddybrook, is the name of the narrow stream that flows past the house from the Down above it. The building is essentially a substantial farmhouse on the road between Whitchurch and Tavistock. Its most interesting feature is a square entrance tower dating from the fourteenth century. This was obviously part of the original structure. The rest is mainly the work of the nineteenth century, and of a Tavistock builder called John Dennis. The *Gazette's* use of the word 'castle' reflects the size and appearance of the building, but there is no reason to think from its castellated adornments that it ever had any military function. It was almost certainly a large farmhouse.

The new resident, who moved in when Mr Dennis had completed his task, had other ideas about the origins of his new home. He took up the idea that the building had a religious origin. According to this theory, which had the support of a number of writers, the Bishop of Exeter had, in the early-fourteenth century, ordered that Tavistock Abbey should establish in Whitchurch a chantry, where four priests could be accommodated. If this place had, indeed, been the one chosen for that foundation, then surely it would not do to continue to call the restored house 'Tiddybrook'. Something more in keeping with the solemnity of its history and the dignity of its presence was required. How about 'The Priory'? And The Priory it has remained ever since, through a subsequent history in which the building has been at different times a school and a domestic dwelling.

The Argall family occupied the house up until the First World War, after which it passed quickly from Henry Vincent Soltau to Commander Charles Bentinck Burke and Major E. Stanley Rogers. In 1930 came James Samuel Bookless, a much-travelled industrialist with a past encouraging paper manufacture in India and a present as a member of Devon County Council. In 1957 his family sold out to the proprietors of Tavyside School, an independent

Sortridge in 1965.

Walreddon in 1922.

institution that had been operating for some years on Mount Tavy Road. The building housed this school for some years (see Chapter 8) before reverting, before the end of the century, to a residential function. (Chapter 5 contains more discussion of the origins of the name of the house and of the 'chantry' story.)

Sortridge Manor

Close by the old road from Whitchurch to Horrabridge, and midway between the two villages, lies Sortridge. Built in 1558 by John Skerrett, a Tavistock man ambitious enough to become both churchwarden and father-in-law of Judge Glanville, it remained in his family for some years, during which period close family links united the illustrious occupants of Sortridge, Holwell and Kilworthy. In the middle of the seventeenth century Sortridge came by marriage to John Pengelly of Anthony in Cornwall.

From him it passed down a line of Pengellys until the early years of the twentieth century. Two tablets in the church tell us something about this dynasty, including the lady who was 'grave without preciseness, facetious without levity'. The Pengellys provided two eighteenth-century vicars of the parish, and the house was, for a time, the vicarage. In 1904 the estate, consisting of some 400 acres, was sold to a Plymouth stockbroker and subsequently broken up, the bulk of it, the house with 140 acres, being bought by Mrs Selina Watford, whose daughter Norma took up residence in 1909 after marrying Colonel Charles Marwood Tucker. Colonel Tucker lived there until his death at the age of 90 in 1955, taking seriously the responsibilities that came his way as squire, benefactor, employer, county councillor, magistrate and deputy lieutenant of the county. He was also a strong campaigner on Dartmoor issues, including the creation of a national park. Between 1955 and 1961 the manor passed to two further owners before being bought by Wing Commander Smythe, and subsequently by Commander George Stubley. Michael Heseltine lived here for a time during the period when he was the prospective, and then the actual, Member of Parliament for the Tavistock Constituency. He recalls, in his autobiography:

> ... renting in September 1965 accommodation in the wing of a house called Sortridge. It was an austere stone house, owned by a Wing Commander Smythe, and was much in need of repair, but it housed us while we looked for something else.

The building was, in all probability, originally rectangular in design, but a series of alterations, some of them necessitated by the effects of three fires, have resulted in the form visible at the time of writing, which is of one long west wing extending north–south, with two parallel wings turning eastwards. The front and porch doorway may be part of the original construction.

Walreddon Manor

In the peninsula bounded by the Tavy and the Walkham, which forms the western part of Whitchurch parish, Walreddon Manor is an outstanding feature. The house was built in a place that, according to its name, had been a Celtic settlement. The survival in a ground-floor room of the arms of Edward VI (1547–53) in moulded plaster is clear evidence of the period of origin. A sturdy house made of granite and local hurdwick stone, it has two parallel wings. The front, facing south-west, was entirely remodelled towards the end of the seventeenth century, but the remains of the original building, with its mullioned windows, may still be seen at the back. Flanking the house is a fine medieval barn.

A lane from the road gives access to 'Lady Howard's Walk', so named after the lady who was born in the house in 1596 and whose ghost haunts the surroundings. Lady Mary Howard was a member of the Fitz family who lived at Fitzford a mile away in Tavistock parish, and who used Walreddon as a dower-house.

When Lady Mary died in 1671 she left Walreddon to her cousin, Sir William Courtenay. It remained in the ownership of that family, who became Earls of Devon, until 1953. Over these three centuries the land hereabouts formed a part of the Courtenay estate, the main nucleus of which was at Powderham, the family's home on the other side of the county. The 182 acres that the family owned at Walreddon in 1900 was augmented to 699 acres by purchases that were made in the Duke of Bedford's sale in 1911. By 1939 this had been reduced to 689 acres through the sale of ten one-acre building plots. In 1953 the whole lot was sold. Over the same three centuries the family made occasional use of the manor-house themselves, but more often it housed a tenant, who needed both to be rich and to enjoy seclusion. Edward Eyre fell into that category. (He and Lady Mary will both make repeat appearances in Chapter 15.) Among recent residents, the couple who made most impact on the life of the local community were Archie and Pamela Jack, who lived here in the 1960s and '70s. Major Jack settled into a new chapter of a life that had already included winning the Sword of Honour at Woolwich, becoming a fencing blue, competing in the 1936 Olympics in Berlin, gaining a fluent command of Hindustani, conducting wartime operations in the Balkans, working as an SOE saboteur, being awarded the Military Cross, and winning prizes for ocean racing and big-game hunting. More recent owners have included Hugh Hudson, the oscar-winning film director, and Zak Goldsmith, the noted environmentalist.

Whitchurch House

When Henry Pengelly, vicar of Whitchurch, died at his ancestral home at Sortridge in 1823 it proved to be the end of a long period in which that house had served as the parish vicarage. Mr Pengelly's successor, Peter Sleeman, had a suitable new home built for himself conveniently close to the church. It was to be lived in by himself and by his seven successors over the next 100 years. Peter's son Richard, who followed him into the living, raised a large family within its walls.

The 1851 census recorded a household of 14 people – Richard and Annette Sleeman with their three sons and nine living-in servants, one footman, two grooms, one child's maid, one nursery maid, one housemaid, one laundress, one kitchenmaid, and one cook. The enterprise was to grow over succeeding years as the vicar and his wife produced a further 12 children and expanded their staff proportionately. It was said that a beech tree was planted along the vicarage drive to celebrate the arrival of each new Sleeman.

The last of the vicars to live here was Revd William Beebe. When he died in 1938 the Church Commissioners decided to sell the building. It was bought by a retired naval officer, Commander Noel Herbrand Beaver. In the following year he moved in with his wife Marjorie, son Martin and stepson David. Commander Beaver had enjoyed a long naval career, including service in the First World War, but now, at the age of 47, all that was behind him. Or so he thought. Within a year of the family's arrival in Whitchurch the Second World War broke out and he was recalled to the service. (Something of the story of Whitchurch House during that war, with Marjorie Beaver at the centre, is given in Chapter 15.)

Noel Beaver died in 1949. His stepson David Gordon took over responsibility for the farm, while his widow Marjorie continued to run the house in such a way as to make it the centre for a wide range of local activities. She died in 1987 and the house was sold six years later.

Above: *Marjorie Beaver with her two sons, David and Martin.*
This photograph: *Whitchurch House, formerly the vicarage, in 1900.*

Chapter 5

WORSHIPPING

The name of the parish, Whitchurch, is the best possible indication of how central a position the church has occupied in the life of the local community. It seems probable that a forerunner of the present building, dating from the Saxon period, occupied the site. The fourteenth century saw the construction of its replacement, a place of worship dedicated, not to St White, but to St Andrew. There were, during that period at least two private chapels in the parish, at Grimstone and Walreddon. The new church was to see, in the first few years of its life, the stormiest period of its history. The advowson, the right to appoint to the living, rested with the lord of the manor. In the early years of the century the powerful Abbot of nearby Tavistock Abbey, Robert Champeaux, on discovering how substantial the revenues were from the small parish, managed to acquire that right from one Walter Labbe. He went on to formulate a scheme under which income from the Parish Church would go to the Abbey, where, Champeaux promised, it would be used to establish and maintain, in Whitchurch, a chantry, staffed by an arch-priest and three assistants, who would replace the existing priest. These four men would jointly share a semi-monastic life as well as conduct the services of the church and care for the souls of the parishioners. They were also to maintain a programme of intercession on behalf of a list of notables, who, living or dead, were to be similarly prayed for until the end of time. The first name on this select list was that of the Abbot, followed in second and third places by the King and Queen, and in fourth place by the Bishop of Exeter. Both the Bishop and the King, unsurprisingly, gave their approval to this plan, which was to take effect on the death of the existing, and first, rector of Whitchurch, James Fraunceis. By the time of this latter event, March 1331, Tavistock had a new abbot, named Bonus, and Exeter had a new bishop called Grandisson. The son of Walter Labbe, the man who had lost the advowson a few years earlier, now repudiated his father's concession, demanded his traditional right on the basis of inheritance, and appointed, to fill the vacant living, Master David Aliam. Abbot Bonus thereupon made a different appointment, and the two sides prepared for trench warfare. Bishop Grandisson sided with Labbe, insisting that Aliam be instituted, and to ensure that this happened he enlisted the support of the powerful Abbot of Buckland, who decided to make a personal visit to Whitchurch. When he arrived he found the church doors barricaded. Outside was an armed guard under the command of four Tavistock monks. The Abbot of Buckland was forced to withdraw, having excommunicated all the obstructors. Bishop Grandisson now appealed to the Government, and, with this final throw of the dice, won his battle against the troublesome Bonus. In a flurry of excommunications and sackings, the Abbot of Tavistock retired to Avignon, from whence he had originally come.

Master Aliam thus became the second rector of Whitchurch. The revenues from the parish continued, however, to find their way to Tavistock Abbey where the Abbot continued to hold the advowson until it passed to the Crown at the time of the Dissolution of the Monasteries. And what of the Champeaux-Stapeldon plan for the establishment of a chantry? It was simply dropped. It was never implemented, and nothing more was heard of it. Then, towards the end of the nineteenth century, the story was revived. It was now claimed that the scheme had not only been devised in the fourteenth century, but had been put into effect and had operated for a time. It was further asserted, without any evidence, that the Tiddybrook Farmhouse had housed the chantry. In recognition of this, Tiddybrook House, the name of which sounded too frivolous for a building that had, at one time, had such a serious function, was redesignated 'The Priory'. The original plan for a chantry had, of course, made no mention of Tiddybrook. Anyone reading the proposal would assume that the intention was that the chantry, if it were to materialise, would form part of the church building that had, at that time, undertaken the original stages of its construction. If the chantry had become a reality it would undoubtedly have formed part of the new St Andrew's Church rather than Tiddybrook Farm. But a myth had been created. And all because the new owner of the grandly restored Tiddybrook House felt that the existing name was not posh enough.

The interior of the church comprises nave, north aisle, south transept, chancel and the later south transept aisle. The chancel was dated by Nikolaus

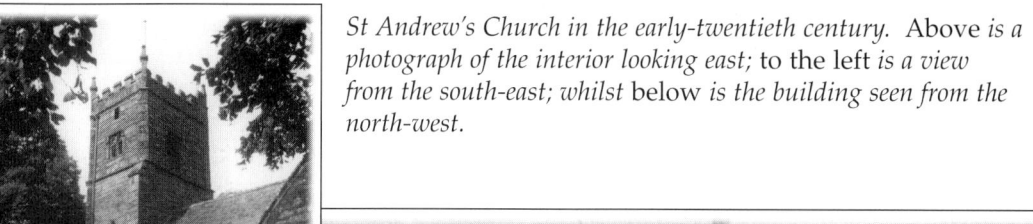

St Andrew's Church in the early-twentieth century. Above is a photograph of the interior looking east; to the left is a view from the south-east; whilst below is the building seen from the north-west.

Pevsner at c.1300, on account of 'the intersecting tracery of the east window, the one remaining north window and the characteristic recess for an Easter Sepulchre inside.' Only the south door is older. Most of the rest is in the Perpendicular style, principally fifteenth century in origin. This applies also to the font, which is octagonal and features on its panels alternate shields with the crosses of St Andrew and St George. Unfortunately, none of the medieval glass survived the seventeenth century. The old roofs are wagon-shaped, with good bosses on the beams, some in the nave carved with faces.

Other interesting details include, in the north aisle, a portion of rood-screen, transferred here from Moretonhampstead in 1857, and consisting of three bays and doors. There is a squint in the south transept, piscinae in the chancel and in the transept, a sundial outside the porch and the stoup inside it. There are also fine family memorials to the Mooringes of Moortown and the Pengellys of Sortridge. The former features members of the family kneeling, some holding skulls. The inscription reads:

Neere hereby lie the bodys of those whose names are underneath. Here lyeth the body of Paschaw the wife of John Allyn gent, sometime the wife of Richard Mooringe gent, who was buried ye 5 day of May 162[?]. Also the body of Garteryed the daughter of Anthony Mooringe who was buried the xi day of November 1617. Also the body of John son of Anthony Mooringe who was buried the ix day of Feb 1620. Also the body of Alce the wife of Anthony Mooringe gentlmen who was buried the viii of January 1639. Also the body of Anthony son of Anthony Mooringe who was buried the xxiiii day of January 1627. Also the body of Mary the daughter of Anthony Mooringe who was buried the v day of June 163[?].

The Pengelly memorial includes a vivid relief of the Rising of the Dead, as well as some choice mini eulogies. Among the latter are:

Mrs Margaret Pengelly, a virgin of great modesty and piety, died Jan 1715 aged 22.

Francis Pengelly esq Barrister at Law, in which capacitie as in all other parts of his conduct, he appeared to be a man of great ability, industry, and integrity. He left this world Jan 1 1722. His monument of his great worth, and her just sense of it, was erected by his widow.

Mrs Mary Pengelly, wife of John Francis Pengelly esq of Sortridge. Her learning was elegant and comprehensive, grave without preciseness, facetious without levity. She died Dec 4 1778.

The church contains a number of other memorials to such families as the Courtenays, Drakes, Jupes, Scobells, Sleemans, Sowters and Sprys. In the vaults beneath lie the remains of a number of members of the Courtenay family.

In the 1870s a thorough programme of renovation of the church was carried out, at a total cost of some £1,500. Choir stalls and a new vestry were added, the old 'horse box' pews disappeared, and the south porch was rebuilt. Another notable addition was the Michell Chapel, constructed in 1904 as a result of a bequest of William Pryce Michell of Holwell. It was built of local stone, with a roof of cradled oak and a floor of Oregon pine. Named originally after the donor, this chapel was refurbished in 1975 and dedicated to St Margaret of Scotland.

Seating arrangements throughout the church remained, for some time, an interestingly accurate reflection of the parish's various social strata.

Right: *William Henry Chichester of Grenofen, churchwarden 1856–1906.*

Below: *Church benefactor, William Pryce Michell of Holwell, provider of the Michell Chapel.*

Clockwise from top:
George Johnston, 1870–78;
Samuel Featherstone senr, 1878–83;
Samuel Featherstone junr, 1883–98;
William Chambers senr, 1898–1900;
William Chambers junr, 1900–07;
William Beebe, 1907–38.

WORSHIPPING

Richard Sleeman, 1848–70.

The comparison was with a theatre, in which the most favoured places were reserved for those who paid the highest prices for their season tickets. Tenants had their own area, as did servants. The theatre analogy was followed in 1901, when the vicar announced that 'all seats in the church are free as soon as the five-minute bell ceases ringing.' The abolition of seat renting was to follow a few years later.

The Victorian period, for all its sense of stability and continuity, did produce some controversies, although not on the scale that led to the riots of the fourteenth century. Typical of the upsets in an otherwise tranquil period was the threat, in 1879, from the sexton, John Laver, to resign unless he was given an increase on his half-a-crown (12$\frac{1}{2}$p.) a week salary. He agreed to continue to dig graves, for which he was paid 'by those requiring his services'. The other duties, such as that of pew opener, he refused to do. The Vestry took a tough line and refused to give way to Mr Laver's demands. He was allowed to resign and Joseph Spry of Walreddon was appointed in his place.

There was, during this period, a wider field of dispute about the direction in which the Church of England should be going, and these national issues were reflected at parish level. By the end of the century the influence of the Oxford Movement had touched, in one way or another, most parishes in the country, producing, in some cases, controversy between High and Low Church parties. Much depended on the incumbent, although in Whitchurch there developed a strong tradition of parochial opinion being expressed, particularly through the churchwardens. The general position taken up by the latter was to warn their vicar of the dangers of going too far in the direction of more elaborate ritual. Two examples, small in themselves perhaps, will indicate the theme. In 1904 it was agreed with vicar Chambers that 'people in the south part of the church should turn with the choir to the east at the Creed.' Two years later, there was strong objection to Mr Chambers receiving, as a gift from a lady parishioner, a pair of candlesticks. The vicar argued that they could be put on the alter and 'utilised for lighting only in a legal manner', but the churchwardens countered that 'many members of the congregation would be averse to the introduction of candles on the communion table.' The gift was declined.

The first vicar of Whitchurch whom we can identify was James Fraunceis, who was appointed in 1321 and died ten years later, and the fortieth was Simon May, appointed in 1992. The list, with the years of appointments, is as follows:

Vicars of Whitchurch	1524 William Drake	1785 Henry Pengelly
	1547 John Huxtable	1823 Peter Sleeman
1321 James Fraunceis	1554 Roger Irelande	1848 Richard Sleeman
1331 David Aliam	1587 William Skirrett	1870 George Johnston
1354 Philip Chori	1611 John Ellistone	1878 Samuel Featherstone senr
1356 Walter Wyot	1622 John Polewheele	1883 Samuel Featherstone junr
1362 William Smyth	1653 Degory Polewheele	1898 William Chambers senr
1390 Henry Smyth	1697 Christopher Furneaux	1900 William Chambers junr
1398 John Raddych	1727 Henry Pengelly	1907 William Beebe
1432 William Macy	1738 Philip Hicks	1938 Guy Warmington
? John George	1740 Thomas Salmon	1953 Allan Gerry
1503 John Wynne	1758 John Weston	1970 Harry Kennen
1503 Robert Barber	1767 John Gandy	1978 Ivo Morshead
1517 William Davy	1769 William Bedford	1992 Simon May

We know little about the personalities or careers of the early pastors. Since the eighteenth century three vicarages can be identified. Up to 1823 the vicar lived at Sortridge House, and between 1823 and 1938 at Whitchurch House. Since the latter date the vicarage has been 204 Whitchurch Road. Messrs Fraunceis and Aliam appear to have had their careers overshadowed by the local politics of the age, involving two abbots, a bishop, a lord of the manor, and some 'bovver boys' from Tavistock. Aliam also enjoyed the distinction, or luck, of being one of only two local pastors (the other was the vicar of Bradstone) to survive the Black Death. If the Smyths were fathers and sons, then this was to happen on at least three future occasions, with the Sleemans, the Featherstones, and the Chamberses, and possibly also with the Pengellys and the Polewheeles. William Drake, who was vicar at the time that another Drake was born at nearby Crowndale, might well have been a relative of Francis. A century on, Degory Polewheele was one of those who joined in the virulent campaign against the rancorous Puritan minister who then held the Tavistock pulpit, Thomas Larkham. When in 1659 the Council of State planned to undermine Larkham's position by organising a series of hostile lectures in his own church, Polewheele was one of those, representing the more moderate Anglican position, who was chosen to deliver one of the talks. Christopher Furneaux, who succeeded him as vicar of Whitchurch, moved here from a living at Torrington. His imposing tomb is by the entrance to the south porch. Among the items of church plate is a flagon inscribed 'The gift of C Furneaux to the Church of Whitchurch 1706.' For a time he combined the job with that of headmaster of Tavistock Grammar School. Philip Hicks did the same thing. The appearances of the names of Skirrett and Pengelly are reminders of the long association of the church with Sortridge. John Weston, a Kingsbridge man, had been vicar of St Leonards, and his sudden death took him back there. Richard Sleeman is the first of the vicars of whom we have photographs.

Each of these modern pastors has made a unique contribution to the life of the church and of the parish, from Richard Sleeman, sportsman extraordinaire, to Simon May, with pioneering work in the field of family worship. The most influential and longest-serving of them was the man once described as a 'kindly philosopher', William Newton Percy Beebe. The son of a former vicar of Yeovil, he won several rowing cups at Oxford and represented the university at chess. Ordained in 1883, he came to Whitchurch via a living at Brighton. He had also been instituted to Kingston Pitney, a sinecure for the last 400 years, where, since there was no church, the ceremony of institution had to take place on a piece of wasteland opposite the local hospital. There was nothing sinecurish about his Whitchurch ministry. For 30 years he devoted himself to the affairs of the village and its institutions, as well as filling a number of roles in the church bureaucracy. A learned man and a scholar, he recorded some notes on the parish and its history which have proved useful to later researchers. Although gentle, kindly and tolerant by nature, he insisted on certain standards of behaviour and conduct. Towards the end of his life he undertook a long journey to visit his brother in Australia. Among the memories that he brought back was that of the young women passengers on board the ship, whose shorts, he

Above: *Allan Gerry, 1953–69.*

Above right: *Harry Kennen, 1970–77.*

Right: *Guy Warmington, 1938–52.*

Far right: *Ivo Morshead, 1978–91, with Mrs Morshead, having just baptised Kimberley Spray.*

felt, were far too revealing. He was a leading temperance advocate. His campaigning zeal as an abstainer did not, however, prevent him from exercising his business acumen, at least when it affected the church. An illustration of this occurred at a meeting of the Parochial Church Council on 22 February 1933. The vicar was in the chair. The following exchanges took place:

Captain England: I want to draw attention to the bill-posting hoarding outside the church.
Mr Chaffe: Do you mean the board with the advertisement for Guinness Stout on it?
Captain England: Yes.
Mrs Wollaston: It is horrible! It is an eyesore.
Admiral Wollaston: It is quite repulsive.
The Vicar: I bought the noticeboard from Mr Glanville, and I made an arrangement with the Whitchurch Inn whereby they give me £2 a year for the right to display advertisements on the board.
Mrs Wollaston: It is really horrible to have a hoarding displaying an advertisement for Guinness Stout opposite the church gate.
Mr Bull: Who gave the right to these people to put the thing there?
The Vicar: I did.
Sir James Stewart: Is it within our right to say we won't have the board there?
The Vicar: No.
Mr Bull: If the board falls down, who will replace it?
The Vicar: I shall.

The church tower, with its embattled appearance, houses six bells. The medieval church had a smaller peal, of probably three or four bells, but they were very large and threatened the masonry. The recasting, undertaken in 1786 by the Pennington Brothers, Cornish bellfounders, was carried out at a cost of £70. The first four bells were inscribed 'IP' and 'CP', these being the initials of the founders. The fifth bell carried the words: 'John Moor Knight Esq and John Berriball CW', the 'CW' being an abbreviation for 'churchwardens'. The sixth bell, the tenor, weighing 15cwt, bore the name 'Henry Pengelley, Vicar'. In 1912 the walls of the bell chamber were reinforced and, as the incumbent Mr Beebe put it: 'The bells were rehung, and quarter-turned so that after 126 years the clappers might strike on an undented surface.' Meanwhile, in 1897, the ringers had organised themselves into a society and had drawn up a list of rules. They were:

1. That this Society shall be known as the Whitchurch Guild of Ringers, and shall consist of not more than twelve members.
2. That the members shall meet one night in the week for practice, viz: on Wednesday, but during Lent on Tuesday evening, and shall ring twice on Sundays (morning and evening) at 10.30a.m. and 6p.m., and for practice from 7.30p.m. till 9p.m. That on Sundays during Lent the Bells shall be only chimed.
3. That there shall be a Captain and a Vice Captain of the Belfry to be elected by members of the Guild. Such office to be held for six calendar months, viz: from the first Wednesday in January to the first Wednesday in July, after which they shall retire, but are eligible for re-election.
4. That any young men wishing to become Probationers must give in their names to the Captain or the Vice Captain and be approved by them. Such numbers not to exceed six.
5. That no smoking, swearing, or drinking take place in the belfry, and that no stranger be admitted to the belfry during the ringing of the bells without the consent of the Captain or Vice Captain.
6. That the bells shall not be rung should any parishioner be known to be lying dead or dangerously ill within the vicinity of the Church.
7. That any presents of any kind shall be handed to the Captain for distribution.
8. That these rules shall be strictly enforced, and that any infringement of them shall be dealt with by a committee consisting of five members, viz: the Vicar, Captain, Vice Captain, and two of the members of the Guild.

The re-dedication of the bells following the most recent overhaul, 21 November 1965. The picture includes the captain, Harry Mudge (far right), Revd Gerry, and the Bishop of Plymouth, Rt Revd Guy Sanderson.

The idea of a surpliced choir was one of those issues that divided churchmen in the last part of the nineteenth century. In most parish churches the singing had hitherto been led by a small choral group gathered round the organ. The innovation involved distinctive dress in the form of cassocks and surplices

Choristers in c.1951, flanked by, on the left: *General Frederick Barron of Greystones (vicar's warden);* on the right: *George Chaffe of Anderton Farm (people's warden).* Left to right: *John Sellis, David Dashper, Robert Bucknell, ?, Jack Endacott, Victor Stacey, Clive Ruberry, Graham Stephens, Peter Sears (organist), Billy Barnes, Richard Sleeman, Aubrey Friend.*

The choir in the early 1960s. The identity of the three boys at the front has not been established. The others, left to right, are: Keith Jones, Kate Symons, Percy Richards, Margaret Mudge, Aubrey Friend, Mary Gerry, Jack Endacott, Pearce Richards, Revd Gerry, Revd Rae, Mr Lumb, Mr Chubb, Miss Pearce, Daphne Jones, Jill Bellamy.

The Whitchurch Ringers, 5 May 1924. Left to right, back row: *Messrs Headley, Lovell, Skinner, S. Sleeman, Cornish, Dawe, Toye;* middle row: *Messrs Roberts, Penhall, Symons (vice captain), Collins (captain), E. Sleeman, Friend;* front row: *Messrs Bickle, Mudge, Brewer.*

and distinct accommodation in choir stalls. The latter were installed at Whitchurch in 1875, the former a few years later when the new vestry was completed. The practice of employing a choirmaster predated these developments by at least a century. In the 1780s John Toop was being paid four guineas a year; he was still in the post 50 years later before handing over, successively, to a Mr Sortridge and a Mr Cox.

The work was sufficently demanding to justify the appointment of a deputy choirmaster. Mr Toop's assistant was Katherine Hughes. The quality of the music was considered to be of sufficient importance to justify, in 1817, the spending of £48 on 'a new singing gallery'.

The earliest form of musical accompaniment in the church was that of a small orchestra. We know that it included at least one violin, because there are frequent references in the churchwardens' accounts to its constant need for attention and repair. By the 1800s the harmonium had become the sole instrument. In 1882 a surplus in the fund for the restoration work to the church, supplemented by a gift from Montague Bere of Grimstone, made possible the purchase of an organ built by Hole & Son. It was rebuilt and enlarged 13 years later. The first man to play it was Harry Gaud, who was the organist in the years up to 1895. He was paid a salary of £25, the organ-blower receiving 25s. Mr Gaud was succeeded by John Chichester, who held the office until 1913.

He was followed by Ellen Walker, formerly of Walkhampton. In 1916 Martin Bodinner, a music teacher who lived at Fernhill Villas, took over the duties. He resigned in 1929 and died in the same year. His successor was Percy Richards, who had previously been the deputy organist at Tavistock Parish Church. Others who have held the post have included Peter Sears in the 1940s and '50s and Judith John and David Crocker in more recent times. But the scene through much of the twentieth century was dominated by Percy Richards and his son Pearce. Pearce Richards left in 1965 to become organist and choirmaster at Tavistock Parish Church.

One form of devotion which brought together various elements within the church community was the nativity play. The participation of members of the Sunday school, the choir, and the congregation combined to produce an annual occasion.

The Whitchurch churchyard is quiet and peaceful. It is, however, unlike many country graveyards, not secluded or unvisited. Its paths are much-used transits, not only to and from the church, but between parts of the village. It contains some features, such as the stocks and the war memorial, and some graves, such as those of Tom Balment, Marjorie Beaver, Edward Eyre, and Mary Metters, which will be featured in later chapters. Between the main gates and the south porch there is an octagonal socket-stone, similar in age and appearance to others

Above: *A nativity play in the 1950s.*

Left: *Old socket-stone with commemorative cross in the churchyard.*

Above and left: *Two views of Whitchurch Methodist Chapel.*

Below: *The stable in 2000.*

Above: *The former Merrivale Chapel in 2000.*

WORSHIPPING

Left: A presentation to Pearce Richards as he leaves for new responsibilities at Tavistock Parish Church.

Percy Richards receives a picture on his retirement. The choristers surrounding him are, left to right: *Alice Gully, Mrs Harvey, Mrs Mudge, Mr Stephens, Mr Percy Richards, Mr Bert Frise, Mrs Edith Richards, Mrs Beryl Stephens, Miss Jill Bellamy, Miss Kate Symons, Mrs Betty Perkins. The group includes four sisters, Mrs Gully, Mrs Harvey, Mrs Mudge and Mrs Symons.*

in the parish and beyond, which carry granite crosses, and which were erected as signposts, particularly between the religious houses of the area. In this case the socket-stone had been long parted from its cross. In 1981 it was given a replacement cross, the inscription on which reads: 'Erected in memory of William Henry Mudge 1981 by parishioners.'

Of the graves, there is much to be learned from the inscriptions about a range of historical subjects, including the changes that have taken place in the average age of death, the fluctuating fashions in christian names, and the shifting tastes in tombstone literature. Great fun can be had in trying to match the sentiments of the inscription with the supposed personality of the person interred. One example must suffice. The stone marking the grave of Roger Willcocks and his wife Mary, who both died in their eighties during the late-eighteenth century, has this parting shot:

> *Farewell vain world I've seen enough of thee*
> *And now am careless what thou say'st of me.*
> *Thy smiles I count not nor thy frowns I fear.*
> *My cares are past, my head rests quiet here.*
> *What faults thou seest in me take care to shun*
> *And look at home, enough there's to be done.*

Across the road from the church is the stable. In such a scattered parish, where for some parishioners attendance at a service required a journey of some miles, attention had to be paid to the need for stabling accommodation for Sundays and for other days when the church might be being used. Such a 'horse park' had certainly been available in the early-nineteenth century, although it was said in 1851 to have the double disadvantage of being dilapidated and being some distance from the church. In that year vicar Sleeman offered a half-crown to anyone who could come up with 'a plan and specifications' for a replacement. When it was erected, the new building was, for a short time, the subject of a dispute as to whether the vicar or the parishioners owned it. The matter was settled in the form of a compromise, in which it was agreed that the land was the vicar's but the building belonged to the parish. According to this agreement, made in 1878, the stable was to continue to be used 'for the purpose for which it was originally intended, that is for the use of the parishioners on Sundays and other days for putting up their horses.'

It is, perhaps, not a coincidence that the incumbency of Richard Sleeman, with his heavy responsibilities towards his large family, the cricket club, and the chase, was the period that saw a significant advance in the parish by the Nonconformists. From the 1850s there was, for some years, a Congregationalist chapel, although it is not clear where it was situated. *Billing's Directory* for 1857, for example, refers to 'a small chapel belonging to the Congregationalists, but no stated minister.' Presumably it was supported from the neighbouring Congregational Church in Tavistock.

The major breakthrough for the Nonconformists in the parish was, however, to come from another Dissenting tradition, that of Methodism. In the early years of the nineteenth century the Methodist Church splintered into a number of competing sects, partly on lines of doctrine and worship, and partly on the basis of regional variations. Among the strongest of these sects in the South West were the Bible Christians. They originated in Devon and gained a firm foothold in the area in 1828 with the establishment of a circuit based on Brentor. Following the opening of their chapel in Tavistock in 1847, Bible Christians in Whitchurch began to consider the possibility of having their own chapel, although the cost of such an undertaking, among what was essentially a working-class community, appeared for some time to rule it out. It was through the generosity of the Willcock family of Anderton that their prayers were answered. The family leased, and later donated, the land to a body of trustees who managed to raise the £70 required to erect the building. It was said that one reason why the cost was so modest was that 300-year-old ship's timbers were used for the roof supports. The building was opened

A Band of Hope parade in the early years of the twentieth century.

in 1850 and was called 'Unity Chapel'. When, on 30 March 1851, the national religious census was taken, it was reported that attendances at the two services in the Unity Chapel had been 90 in the afternoon and 80 in the evening, compared with a total of 80 for the two services in St Andrew's on the same day. The comparison, no doubt, explains why Revd Sleeman refused a request to make a return of the numbers in his own congregation; the recording had to be done by the local registrar. Over the next few years the Methodist congregation grew, and in 1861 a substantial addition to the building appeared in the form of a new chapel seating 198, nearly twice as many as the original Unity Chapel, which now became a home for the Sunday School. Major renovations were carried out in 1923 and in 1935. The former involved the installation of electric light and was celebrated at a reopening service by a congregation of 119.

The religious census also noted that 12 people attended an evening service on that Sunday in March 1851 in a building more than 50 years old, but which was described as 'not a separate building' nor one used exclusively for worship. They were members of the Wesleyan Methodist Association. Both Wesleyan and Bible Christian sects subsequently established places of worship at Moorshop, and, just outside the parish boundary, at Foggintor and Rundlestone. The Wesleyans also had a society at Moortown. Meeting-places tended to be schoolrooms and cottages rather than purpose-built places of worship, although the Moorshop Chapel flourished between 1907 and 1950. This Wesleyan chapel, now a ruin, is fondly recalled by Wesley Dingle, who was a Sunday-school student there in the 1940s. Its birth coincided with the appearance of a permanent chapel at Merrivale. Methodist preachers had been visiting Merrivale regularly since 1847, but it was 1901 before a room in the settlement, which could hold 80 people, was brought into use as a chapel. This was the 'Iron Chapel', designed to fill the gap until the permanent stone-built chapel could be erected. It served its purpose until 1962 and then stood, resilient but redundant, waiting for the replacement that never came.

Joyce Elliott, who as Joyce Hendy was brought up in Whitchurch, belonged to a 'chapel family'. She recalls that: 'the highlight of the Sunday school was the anniversary. We all had new clothes and the following day we had tea and sports and an evening meeting.' She also remembers being involved in the temperance movement. In Whitchurch this was a campaign in which the leaders of both church and chapel took prominent roles. There were frequent processions and demonstrations. Mrs Elliott recalls:

We also belonged to the Band of Hope and the Temperance Society. At the Band of Hope we had slides shown by the Vicar, Rev Beebe. I can see him now, standing by the screen with a long pointer and showing places on the screen; he would 'tap, tap' the floor for the next slide.

Chapter 6

CARING

During the reign of Elizabeth I Parliament passed a number of statutes which together constituted the Poor Law. The main principle of these Acts was that each parish should assume responsibility for its own poor. As far as Whitchurch was concerned the only help that had been available to the poor, apart from unreliable church donations and individual acts of charity, had come from Tavistock Abbey. The closing of the Abbey in 1539 had created a vacuum which was filled by the new law. The parish was now to be responsible for caring for its poor. Local Justices of the Peace were to work with local officials appointed by the Parish Vestry, the council representing those who owned property in the parish, in order to identify those who needed, and deserved, help. Support took the form of money or food, clothes or other goods.

The cost of providing this support was shared among the property owners in the parish. They were required to pay rates, the size of their bill depending on the value of their property. A further statute of 1662 offered a drastic solution to the problem of the poor who applied for help to the authorities of a parish to which they did not belong, either by birth or long-term domicile. The main targets of this legislation were vagrants and beggars. The solution was that such people could be returned to their parish of origin, as long as a removal order was signed by two JPs. The means used to effect the removals were not always sensitive. The following entry appears in the Mary Tavy Parish Register for 1691:

One William Warden was brought to the house of Richard Reddicliffe, one of the constables of this parish, on horseback by three men from Whitchurch with a testimonial under the hands and seal of Degory Polwheele, Minister, Stephen Chubb and Edmund Drake, Constables, and Richard Doidge and Richard Wickwell, parishioners of Whitchurch, certifying that he was openly whipped for a wandering rogue, the said 12th day of March, and was assigned to pass from parish to parish by the officers thereof, the nighe straite way to Cheston in the county of Hartford, where he confessed he was born. In six-and-twenty days next ensuing the said date, he died on horseback on Blackdown, as Roger Harris, John Scoble, and Thomas Harman were conveying him to the officers of Lamerton. He was buried the same day at night.

The Tavistock bench, whose responsibilities extended to such parishes as Whitchurch, found itself involved in much work as a result of the 1662 Act. When cases were brought before the magistrates the officials of the parish concerned would claim that the individual was not their responsibility, since he or she had been born elsewhere. Evidence would be taken from the pauper and from anyone else whose testimony might help to establish the facts, and the magistrates would then deliver judgement on whether a removal should be enforced.

In the early-nineteenth century, for example, the court decided, over a period of 20 years, that 19 paupers domiciled in Whitchurch should be removed to their native parishes. Fifteen of them came originally from neighbouring parishes, while the other four hailed from West Cornwall. There were 11 men and eight women. The oldest was 93 and the youngest 21. Only five of them were able to sign their names, the other 14 making their marks at the bottom of their statements of evidence.

Occasionally the bench took a different view of a projected removal. Susanna Odger, for example, at one point in her testimony, recorded that she had been offered a job in the village by Mrs Creber, a farmer's wife. The wage was to be £3 a year, but this would be reviewed at the end of a month, and, if things were going well, the appointment would be extended and the pay increased by 10s. The magistrates were content to await the outcome of the month's probation. There was a happy ending and Susanna, although not a native of Whitchurch, was allowed to stay.

There were, inevitably, examples where, from Whitchurch's point of view, the process worked in the opposite direction. In these cases, the testimony of those involved often included some interesting descriptions of their early lives in Whitchurch. Matthew Gloyne, for example, explained that he had been born in Whitchurch in 1773 and that:

.. when I was about seven years of age I was bound an apprentice by indenture to Charles Keagle of the parish of Whitchurch, yeoman, with whom I served until I was twenty-one, and then continued with him about six months afterwards as a weekly servant.

The following 37 years had been spent either at sea or moving between parishes for work. John Fuge explained that he had been born in 1767 in Whitchurch:

... where my parents then resided, although I believe they were settled in the parish of Petertavy. When I was very young I was placed with my grandfather, John Gee, who resided in the parish of Whitchurch, and I used to go to school when I was residing with my grandfather. When I attained the age of ten years I began to work with my grandfather at his quarry, called Brook Quarry in Sampford Spiney.

Sometimes, matters of settlement became rather complicated. Mary Reed was born in Whitchurch in 1806. Her case surfaced in 1835 when she was 26 years old. She testified:

At the time of my birth my parents resided in Whitchurch but their settlement was in Marytavy. When I was eighteen years of age I hired myself for a year to Mr Hamilton of the parish of Tamerton Foliot, and lived with him two years as a yearly servant. When I was about twenty years of age I was married to Richard Bale, who was legally settled in the parish of Sampford Spiney, by whom I had two children. About two years ago Richard Bale died, and at Ladyday last I was married to my later husband Robert Reed, who was legally settled in Walkhampton. I had only one child by Robert Reed, and she is aged three weeks. Robert Reed has died.

The Elizabethan legislation left to each parish the decision as to what form of relief they should offer their paupers. The alternatives were 'outdoor relief', under which deserving cases were able to receive support while remaining in their own homes, and 'indoor relief', the practice of offering help within the setting of a residential, all-embracing poorhouse or workhouse.

In the earlier years Whitchurch followed the general pattern, certainly among smaller parishes, of deciding that with the limited number of paupers they might expect to have to cope with, the former solution was the more practical one. The arrangements can hardly be described as generous.

During the middle years of the eighteenth century the churchwardens became so concerned about the number of apparently deserving cases that they allocated an annual sum of £1 from church funds to be distributed among 'those poor people of the parish who do not receive weekly relief.' It may be that, following a trend by which a large number of parishes turned to the more tough approach, the decision was taken in Whitchurch to apply the ultimate deterrent of the workhouse. The problem was, indeed, a growing one, as was evidenced by the fact that of those buried in Whitchurch churchyard in the last 17 years of the 1700s, 34 were paupers.

Local tradition has the workhouse as occupying the last-but-one building on the road out to Grenofen, on the left-hand side of the road. Its neighbouring cottage, almost attached to it, was, it is believed, the home of the master; throughout the twentieth century the latter was to be the Toye family home. Frank Toye was the occupant for much of this time. His grandfather, William Nancarrow, who had been born in 1867, always referred to the dwelling as 'The Master's House'. If local lore is right about this, then the picture changed in the 1830s. The tithe map of 1843 lists the 'workhouse' as a dwelling occupied by Thomas Bennett, and the 'master's house' as occupied by William Menheniot and known as Underhill Cottage. Major change came about with the passing of the Poor Law Amendment Act in 1834. Whitchurch was included in a Union of local parishes, centred on Tavistock. They were to share the provision of a workhouse, built at the top of Bannawell Street in Tavistock to accommodate the majority of paupers in the area. This building was opened in 1838. Of the existence of a workhouse in Whitchurch before that date, documentary evidence is awaited.

After the opening of the Tavistock workhouse in 1838 'outdoor relief' continued to be administered within the parish of Whitchurch, where this was considered appropriate. In 1851, for example, the only recipient of 'outdoor relief' was a 72-year-old widow in Middlemoor called Martha Easterbrook. At the same time there were six people in the Union Workhouse who had been born in Whitchurch. Two of these were children aged ten and four, who were with their widowed mother. For the rest of the century the census recorders, when they visited the workhouse, found no Whitchurch natives there in 1861, 1871, or 1881, and only two in 1891.

In Whitchurch 'outdoor relief' emerged as the preferred option in dealing with the small number of parishioners who needed help, and the workhouse solution was reserved as a last resort. It was not at all what the framers of the new law of 1834 had had in mind.

The twentieth century saw the end of the Poor Law, as public provision from the State and from county authorities replaced the more local agencies and deprived parishes of one of their oldest functions. Property taxes or rates have, however, survived as principal sources of local government finance, their yield having been diverted to other purposes.

The Poor Law represented the public side of parochial charity. On the privately funded side, there have been six major charities. The oldest was Pengelly's Gift. This dated from 1723 when Francis Pengelly, in his will, left an annual sum of £6 for a period of 900 years, to be devoted to:

... causing to be taught poor children of the parish to read, write, and cast accounts, and for teaching and

instructing such children in the Church of England catechism and in the principles of the Christian Religion.

In addition he gave £100, the income from which was to be spent in buying wool, which would be distributed each November among 'such industrious but poorer sort of the parish as should not receive alms or any allowance as poor from the parish.' The charity had ceased to operate by the early years of the nineteenth century, and the Charity Commissioners pulled the curtain down firmly in 1865. By then Peter Sleeman's Gift had also become a casualty. This had taken the form of a £10 bequest, the interest from which was to provide a small annuity for 'four poor widows'. It had lapsed by 1824.

In 1890 a London publisher called John Marshall made a gift of property in memory of his wife Ann, who was a native of Tavistock. The result was the appearance in Whitchurch of a range of six cottages, to be occupied by residents of the two parishes who 'from age, ill-health, accident, or infirmity, are unable to maintain themselves by their own exertions.' They were to be of good character, at least 60 years old, and single, although married couples without young children were also considered. The income from the 12 acres of Whitchurch property and from investments in stocks would be at the disposal of the 13 appointed local trustees to spend on maintaining the properties and providing the almspeople with small annuities. In 1905, with the scheme well into its stride, £62 was spent on repairs and improvements, and £85 was paid to the cottagers.

Michell's Charity was formed as a result of a £1,000 bequest by William Pryce Michell, the 'squire of Holwell', whose munificence also resulted in the construction of the Michell Chapel. The first call on the fund was to be the care of the graves of the families of himself and his wife, and of the surrounding areas in the churchyard. Thereafter, annual surpluses were to be distributed on Christmas Day, after Morning Service, at Whitchurch church. The recipients were to be 'the oldest and most deserving and destitute poor men and women of good character residing in Whitchurch, preference being given to such as reside near Holwell.' The vicar and churchwardens were to administer the fund, and to choose whether to provide support 'in coats, money, bread, or kind'.

The most modern of Whitchurch's charities, and one that is shared with seven other parishes in the immediate area, is the Tavistock, Whitchurch and District Nursing Association. Its object, as with similar associations in other parts of the country, was to try to fill gaps that were thought to exist in healthcare provision after the establishment of the National Health Service. The poor, if they fell sick, might now benefit from free hospital services. But what about the expenses that might be incurred by patients in their own homes? The State did not meet the costs of convalescence. Nor did it provide any of the small extras – items of diet or of clothing – that could make such a difference to the lives of people of limited means. Here was the identified area of need. The local association had its scheme approved by the Charity Commissioners in 1954. Some discretion

Marshall's Gift.

was to be left to the trustees in defining specific areas of need, but the scheme offered, as guidelines, three categories. The first was the supply of special foods and medicines, medical comforts, extra bedding and fuel, and medical and surgical appliances. Then there was the provision of domestic help. And thirdly the trust would wish to consider cases of expenses arising from convalescence. The governing committee has, since its foundation, met twice a year to consider claims brought to its attention, particularly by doctors, district nurses and clergymen. In the earlier years of the trust most of the grants were in kind: a pair of boots, a special chair, a delivery of coal, or a pair of blankets, with a generally observed limit of £10 worth of assistance in any particular case. By the 1990s grants of £30 had become the norm. By the end of the twentieth century the list of recipients numbered some 25.

On 25 July 1904 a deed was signed under which Joseph Lovell, farmer and owner of what later became known as The Old Vicarage on Church Hill, sold a piece of land for £20. The buyers were the vicar and churchwardens. The land was to house a parish room which would be erected 'in connexion with the church'. According to the agreement, the room would be:

> ... *forever thereafter used by the inhabitants of Whitchurch as a reading room, library, concert or dancing room, lecture room, or for any other good object which the trustees for the time being might think proper, but not for political meetings or other political purposes.*

The building was opened in 1905, when, on 31 October, the school was closed for the day and the village enjoyed, in the new room, a day of celebrations. It was the culmination of three years of effort, beginning in September 1902, when the vicar convened a public meeting to discuss the possibility of such a project. The usual range of fund-raising activities began, the breakthrough coming with the agreement over the site. A subscription list was opened and assistance was provided by parishioners like Benjamin Shires, who was an architect, and John Willcock of Anderton, who promised to provide some materials. Ten well-wishers agreed to give £10 each – they were Revds Chambers and Honey, Mrs Lampen and Mrs Spencer, Miss Rowband, and Messrs Argall, Coppin, Chichester, Priestley Shires and Pooley Martin. The tender for £500 for the construction, submitted by William Higman, the Tavistock-based builder, was accepted, and the result was the slate-roofed building of brick and stone close to the Whitchurch Inn. Six years after its opening, the new facility was enhanced by the construction of a gymnasium alongside, built to commemorate the coronation of George V. Opened with a flourish by Sir John Spear in December 1911, this latter provision was erected at a cost of £140, of which £50 was in the form of a single anonymous donation. Another early addition came with the purchase of a piano, which cost £40, a sum raised over a two-year period of hard work by a specially-constituted committee. The trustees, now established as the vicar, churchwardens, one nominee of the Easter Vestry meeting, and four representatives of the Parish Council, had the responsibility of running the new enterprise effectively and to general satisfaction. There were to be differentials in hire charging between parishioners and outsiders, and also between church occasions and other events. A basic private-hire charge of 10s. was enhanced by the use of the piano (5s.) or by an overtime payment of a half-crown if the event went on after midnight (this could not happen in the case of dances, which were to end at midnight). The caretaker's fee was sixpence, while sixpence was payable for each fire used and twopence per hour for each lamp lit. By such measures of careful accounting the trustees carried out their responsibilities under the 1904 deed. As the twentieth century wore on the smart little Edwardian building came increasingly to show its age. By the 1990s the issue had resolved itself into a straight choice between renovation and replacement. Replacement won the day. In 2002 the building was demolished, with the prospect of a new hall being built a few yards up the hill on a site next to the old stables.

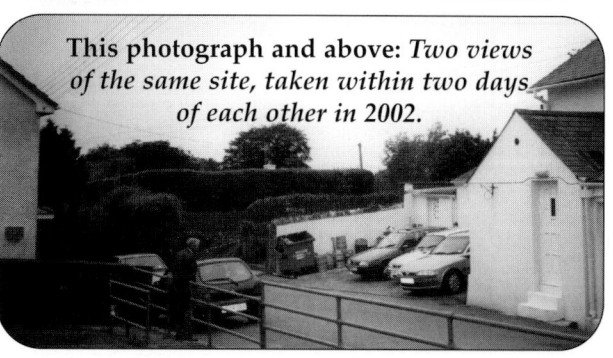

The Parish Room.

This photograph and above: *Two views of the same site, taken within two days of each other in 2002.*

CARING

Left: *Chollacott Nursing Home.*

Residential, nursing and caring homes have become well-established features of 'the caring scene', and of modern life generally, and there are a number in the immediate area. One such is Chollacott House, impressively situated overlooking the Whitchurch–Tavistock road. It was first advertised as a nursing home in the 1930s, when it was run by two sisters called Hamilton.

On 6 May 1953 the maternity home opened in premises on Whitchurch Road that had previously been 'Endmoor' and 'St Michaels'. At 6.15 on that evening Mrs Doreen Gedge became the first patient, and at 8.15 her daughter Elizabeth became the first delivery. By the end of the year there had been 87 births, and thereafter deliveries proceeded at an average of 15 a month for some time, increasing to a total of 222 in 1959 and 263 in 1960. The work was done by a staff of 19, nine of whom were nurses. The first matron was Mrs George. She was followed, in fairly quick succession, by Miss Dodd, Miss Halse and Miss Grills. The home survived periodic threats of closure before the axe finally fell in 1995.

The work of individuals in the 'caring field' in the parish could in itself fill a book. One example must do duty for a legion of people who have over the years devoted themselves to the welfare of others. Miss Dido de Blois Rowe of Bleak House and latterly of 105A Whitchurch Road was awarded the WVS Long Service Medal for work over 15 years as founder and organiser of the Tavistock Home Help Service.

A different aspect of the caring function is the concern to maintain law and order. Of the parishes in the immediate area, Whitchurch had fewer problems than other, more populous and concentrated communities, such as Tavistock or the Bere Peninsula. Before 1856, however, it was incumbent upon each parish to make its own provision in the light of its own judgement of needs and problems. The Whitchurch Parish Vestry would decide at its annual Easter meeting, usually in the light of advice offered by the local Justices of the Peace, how many officers would be required in the circumstances likely to prevail in the forthcoming 12 months.

In times of general contentment, with political stability, stable trade and decent harvests, two might be considered an adequate number to deal with the occasional act of violence, robbery or vagrancy. If there were rumours of unrest, threats of strikes or fears of unemployment, the property owners of Whitchurch might opt for a safer number, like six.

The post of constable was not one that was, as a general rule, actively pursued. It involved no qualifications or training and was generally viewed as one of those occasional duties that were bothersome distractions that had to be accepted as one of the obligations of being an active citizen. Allowances were payable for travelling and for such services as executing warrants, but paid constables remained a rarity before the middle of the nineteenth century. In Whitchurch the Vestry decided to introduce the principle of remuneration in 1843, when they paid John Creber and Richard Toop 10s.0d. each for their year's work. The sum constituted more a small honorarium than a wage. At the same time, four unpaid constables were appointed – James Blatchford, George Brown, John Tozer and George Warne. It may be that the duties of these four were of a lower order than those carried out by the two paid officers. It is more likely that the quartet were held in reserve, called into action only in emergencies, and serving in a capacity not unlike that of Special Constables in a later age.

Having two constables appears to have remained the norm in the parish until 1848, when the number was increased to three, at which level it remained until, in the next decade, the system of parish constables was swept away in favour of professional county forces. The new Devon Constabulary had an area headquarters at Tavistock, and one constable specifically assigned to Whitchurch. He was paid £1 a week. It is not clear who the first incumbent was, or where he lived. No police house is listed until 1878, in which year Constable Hilman moved into Marlborough House, which had been rented by the police authority from a family called Highman. The dwelling, 182 Whitchurch Road in 2003, continued to house the village policemen until 1926, one of its later occupants being PC Nankivell. John Nankivell, after working for the force, became a motor scout employed by the RAC. He died in December 1920 in a cycling accident at Lumburn at the age of 30.

Members of the Battery in 1914, recruited from the Devon Constabulary. PC Fred Connett is third from the left on the back row.

Below: *War reservist Fred Connett in 1942, pictured with his successor on the Whitchurch beat, PC Arthur Walters, and Inspector Derges of Tavistock.*

Above: *Local policemen join in the 1935 jubilee celebrations by marching through Tavistock. PC Connett of Whitchurch marches behind his inspector, Mr Barnicoat, with the Tavistock sergeant, Sgt Gale, to the right.*

CARING

The two police houses on Plymouth Road as they appear in 2003.

The first house – Marlborough House. *The second house – Crelake Corner.*

In 1926 the police authority had a new house built on the corner of Whitchurch Road and Crelake Park, and here Constable Ernest Bedford, Kennford-born former labourer and soldier, began his seven years of residence. This was the generation that had fought in the First World War and Bedford's successor was also an old soldier. He was Fred Connett. PC Connett had been a railway porter before joining the force at Paignton in 1913, had served during the First World War in the Battery recruited from the County Police Force, and had resumed a copper's life thereafter, finding himself assigned to Whitchurch in 1933. He was there until his retirement in 1938, after which the Second World War saw his recall as a reservist.

The Whitchurch beat, as it was trodden by men like Ernest Bedford and Fred Connett, was extensive. It included a number of scattered 'conference points', at which the policeman on duty was required to be at a certain time so that he could communicate his position to a superior officer. Given the nature of the roads and tracks in the area, and of the changeable weather conditions, it is not surprising that a constable, even if he knew his patch well, would sometimes get into difficulties reaching Merrivale Bridge or Warren's Cross at a late hour on a winter night. Moreover, it was during this period that the village of Lamerton was added to the Whitchurch beat. After Constable Connett came PC Arthur Walters, a Totnes-born former driver, who was of the first postwar generation. He was followed by Constable John Cuttle, the last of the men to make the Whitchurch beat their own. Soon after the Second World War it was absorbed into the Tavistock town section, and in the late 1950s the house was sold, bringing down the curtain on 100 years of professional, local policing in the parish.

Left: *Behind the Whitchurch Inn can be found the village stocks, with an 1809 date. They were repaired by the Women's Institute for the 1953 coronation, having previously for some time lain in forgotten seclusion in a barn.*

A Christmas party for the village children in the 1940s.

Members of the Townswomens' Guild Choir face the camera in the 1950s outside the Whitchurch Inn, after performing in the Parish Room.

Chapter 7

SHARING

In the early weeks of 1907 the *Whitchurch Parish Newsletter* reported that:

On January 3rd the Parish Room was crowded for the Sunday School entertainment and prize giving. Recitations were given by Maud Brewer, Emma Vanstone, Ethel Friend, and Albert Brewer; a song by Katie Lovell and pianoforte selections by Mary Southcombe and Veretta Doidge. The pantomime 'Cinderella' was excellently performed by Ethel Westcott, Polly Whitehair, Nellie Bickle, Kathleen Chubb, Albert Colwill, Jack Friend, Frank Vanstone, and by some of the younger children who impersonated fairies. The acting was arranged and superintended by the Misses Chambers, and the dresses prepared by Mrs Walkden. Ethel Westcott made a very charming Cinderella.

The Parish Room was at that time in only its second year, but it had already become the established venue for a range of activities. Groups of artists and musicians, some homespun, some from the town down the road, and others from further afield, found ready audiences there. Schools, churches, clubs and organisations found it a convenient centre in which to hold events. Classes and meetings of all kinds were conducted there. And for those for whom the golden age of their lives was the period in the middle years of the twentieth century, there was the regular round of dances and whist drives, the two key elements, surely, of the community life of any village during that era.

One of the star performers in the Parish Room and elsewhere in the early years of the twentieth century was a talented local lad called Henry Creber. Born in the village in 1874, in a house that, to him at least, had a better claim to having been the birthplace of Drake than had Crowndale on the other bank of the river, Henry later carved out a unique place for himself on the local scene by becoming Devon's best-known grocer. In the time that he had left after running the Brook Street business, renovating his Whitchurch cottage 'Sunnycot', campaigning for the Band of Hope movement, and raising a family, Henry threw himself into the study of photography, an art and science still, at that time, in its infancy. His displays of the possibilities opened up by the world of the camera amazed contemporary audiences. For example, in the Parish Church on the evening of Good Friday 1908:

Mr Creber displayed some magnificent slides illustrating The Passion on the huge screen across the chancel arch, the vicar giving practical addresses on each subject depicted on the screen.

At about the same time Revd Beebe was regularly throwing open the vicarage grounds for appropriate events, including May Day celebrations. This is what happened in 1909:

About 250 visitors were present. The programme commenced with a procession of children, the girls in white dresses and gaily coloured sashes and the boys in smock-coats and rush hats. They were greeted with loud applause. The maypole, some thirty feet high, was erected on the vicarage lawn, and made a brave show with its variegated streamer ribbons. Twenty-six took part in the maypole dances, accompanied by a small orchestra consisting of Miss Florrie Coppin (piano), Masters C and G East and Mr Knott (violin). A pleasing feature of the entertainment was the procession of village maidens to the chair of state, opposite which they lined up to enable the May Queen to pass between them. The Vicar announced that at a Royal Court held on the previous evening the maidens of the village had enthusiastically elected Louise Sleeman as Queen of the May. The Morris Dances were exceedingly well done. Prizes were awarded for recitations and songs. There was a sweet stall and a refreshment stall. Bertie Sleeman desported himself as 'Jack in the Green' and his antics caused much amusement. Total receipts exceeded £15, which went to the fund to provide a gymnasium. There were two

Anne Clifton, Rosemary Scantlebury and Stephanie Brown at a Parish Room dance in the 1950s.

Above: *A gathering in the Parish Room in November 1964 to celebrate a Tennis Club event. Left to right: Margaretta Mudge, Olive Robinson, Harry Mudge, George Perkin, Emily Angell, Ernest Mercy, Louisa Mercy, Betty Griffiths, George Pearse, Lily Robinson, Barbara Hambly, Ken Watkins, Flo Watkins, Marjorie Greening, Helen Hill, Jimmy Angell. The figures on the wall behind formed part of a mural, painted during the war by a serviceman of unknown identity who was stationed here. It survived for some years but is now sadly lost.*

Above left: *The 1992 Produce Show.*

Above: *The Whitchurch WI holds its annual Products and Handicrafts Show. Special guests on this occasion in 1965 included German visitors from Celle, Tavistock's twin town.*

Left: *The Christmas Bazaar in the Parish Room during the 1990s, displaying a European theme.*

performances, admission in the afternoon being sixpence and in the evening threepence.

The vicarage itself was also the venue for social gatherings of the church choir and ringers. Typical of such occasions was that of 1907 when, after a hearty supper:

Mr J.W. Daw of Walreddon astonished the party with tricks of conjuring and sleight of hand. These were very cleverly performed, and although the limited space put Mr Daw at a great disadavantage, we were only able to solve the mystery of those tricks which he himself explained to us. An exhibition was afterwards given by Miss J. Chambers of telepathy and thought-reading.

The openness with which parishioners were welcomed to events at the vicarage was to set a pattern which was maintained at the house during the next phase of its life, the 'Beaver era'. Other mansions in the parish, notably Walreddon and Holwell, were also to offer their grounds and facilities for events and causes with which the residents of the time were associated.

Please Book this Date.

WEDNESDAY, JULY 17th.

WHAT FOR?

A Garden Fete

WHERE?

Holwell, Whitchurch.

(By kind permission of Mr. & Mrs Frank Radcliffe).

WHY?

To Help the Blind of DEVON

The National Institute for the Blind and the Devon County Association for the Blind.

SOME of the ATTRACTIONS.

The Full Military Band of the Devonport Division of Metropolitan Police.

By permission of SUPT. O. WEBB.
Conductor: Mr. H. WILLIAMS, R.M.S.M.

Refreshments, Teas, Ices, Sweets, Produce, General, and many other Stalls.

Competitions Hoop-la, Clay Pigeon Shooting, Clock Golf, Treasure Hunting, Skittles, Cocoa Nut Shies, Penny Throwing, Aunt Sally, are among the goodly number you will find in the grounds.

EXHIBITION of DANCING, PLAYS, CONCERTS, etc., etc.

Any Kind Offers of Personal Assistance, Gifts for the Tea, Articles for the Stalls, gratefully welcomed by MISS D. M. SMITH, Home Teacher of the Blind, Marlborough House, Whitchurh.

The prospect of an afternoon out in the early 1930s.

A number of the organisations that thrived within the parish community in the early part of the twentieth century were connected with the church. There were, of course, the choir, the bell-ringers and the Sunday school. There were also three Bible classes, one for men, one for women and one for youths, and a Church history class. The Men's Guild, part-social and part-religious, offered a programme of meetings and speakers and a forum for the discussion of a variety of topics. Its counterpart was the Women's Social. The Mothers' Social developed into a branch of the Mothers' Union, which maintained a sturdy and significant presence in the parish. The Whitchurch branch of this national organisation was formed at an inaugural meeting on 8 June 1910. The guest speaker on that occasion was Mrs Perceval Jackson of Kingsteignton, whose talk was on the twin themes of the sanctity of marriage and 'the pernicious effects of bad literature upon the minds of the young.' The window in St Andrew's depicting the Madonna and Child was a gift from the branch in 2001 to mark the 125th anniversary of the national launch of the movement. Then there were the Temperance groups and the Band of Hope movements which straddled the otherwise deep sectarian divide, and under whose banners useful contacts could be maintained between Anglican and Nonconformist congregations.

For some years in the twentieth century there was a local branch of the British Legion. Leadership here was provided by the steady flow of retired Army officers who have followed tradition in seeking their final retirement home in Whitchurch. There was also, for a time, a thriving choral society. In the early years of Scouting and Guiding Whitchurch had its own packs. The girls' organisations seem to have been longer-lasting, due, no doubt, to the leadership of people like May Cranch. Miss Cranch, the daughter of the Deputy Registrar for Marriages for the Tavistock district, was always associated with Courtenay Cottage, just off the main road from Tavistock to Grenofen. Her involvement with the Brownies was to be followed by active participation in the Red Cross and founder membership of the Whitchurch WI. She will also be remembered for her efforts to keep alive the art of lace-work.

The Scouts had a small but active troop. In 1926, for example, J.C. Wilson of Caseytown, their recently-appointed scoutmaster, left this description of their summer camp:

On July 31st one rover scout and eleven scouts marched to Princetown, making tea in the grounds of Eggworthy House en route. On arrival at Princetown we put up in the headquarters of that troop. On August 1st a short service was held by Rev Woolcombe, scoutmaster and assistant curate of Princetown, and the rest of the day was spent in bathing, camp duties, and visiting friends. On August 2nd the rover and two of the scouts were

As the picture suggests, the Guilders cloak their ceremonies in elaborate ritual. This is, as far as is known, the only picture ever taken of them. For legal reasons, details of names, ranks, date and place are withheld, and can only be supplied at the cost of a round of drinks.

The Annual Dinner of the Whitchurch Branch of the Royal British Legion at the Whitchurch Inn, 1962.

SHARING

Whitchurch Guides and Brownies in 1926. Left to right, back row: Doris Martin, Win Tickle, two Miss Northeys; third row: Ethel Bolt, Emily Westlake, ?, Joan Willcock, Nora Hendy, Elaine Freethy, Marjorie Martin, Amy Mudge; second row: Hilda Crocker, Phil Sleeman, Margie Mudge, Miss Stewart (Homedown House), Miss Slater (Brookfield), Miss Beebe (vicarage), May Cranch, Kate Symons, Marjorie Sleeman; front row: Mary Thomas, Edna Martin, Joyce Hendy, Hilda Martin.

Whitchurch Brownies, 1928. Left to right: *Veretta Wallace, Iris Vogwill, Ruth Hawkins, Brown Owl May Cranch, Joyce Hendy, Joyce Westlake, Muriel Mitchell.*

Below: *Margaret Mudge (the WI) and Bill Sully (the Council), share a thought and a seat in 1965. The plaque reads: 'Presented by Whitchurch WI in commemoration of the National Federation's Golden Jubilee 1915–1965'.*

Above: *In 1976 the Ladies' Open Group held a tenth-anniversary dinner at Whitchurch House, the home of one of its founder members, Marjorie Beaver, who is sitting on the right.*

Left: *WI members preparing ploughmen's lunches, 1993.*

Left: *Members of the Open Group on an evening walk in 2000.*

Right: *Members of the Rifle Club share an evening at the Whitchurch Inn with friends from the Tavistock Rifle Club. The date is 1954, and the occasion, the centenary celebrations of both organisations.*

compelled to return owing to having to get back to work by Tuesday morning. The remainder marched ten miles to Hannaford, lunching at Dartmeet. We were fortunate in the weather and a safe, pleasant bathing pool was found. On August 7th the return home was made by lorry.

The Colts and Guilders are a group of predominantly middle-aged men recruited largely from the business community of the area, the centrepiece of whose activities was a ceremony conducted on a Sunday each year in March. Tradition dictated a journey, on foot if possible, from Whitchurch village to the Dartmoor Inn at Merrivale. Arriving for noon allowed for a two-hour lunch stop there, before the pilgrimage continued with a walk to the Peter Tavy Inn for 'tea'. Thereafter, the last port of call was the Buller's Arms at Mary Tavy, where dinner was taken before a coach returned the party to its home base, the Union Inn in Tavistock, for a well-earned drink. The dual purpose of enjoying each other's company and raising money for worthy causes is upheld throughout.

The Ladies' Open Group was founded in 1967 as a society to bring together women of the parish of different ages and beliefs to consider a range of contemporary issues. They hold fornightly meetings and an annual fund-raising event for charity.

In November 1927, 12 years after the first branch was established in Britain, the Whitchurch Women's Institute was founded. The 50 founder members who attended the first meeting were given a demonstration of basket making. Over the years this organisation has not only provided itself with a programme of meetings, events and visits, but has been responsible for many activities that have involved, and have benefited, the wider community. For many years its members organised an Annual Fair each summer, with a variety of stalls, and a Produce and Handicrafts Show. Its drama group assembled productions, initially for the enjoyment of fellow members at their Christmas parties, but also for the pleasure of wider, local audiences, and, in some cases, for entry in the WI County Festival of Drama. In 1965, to celebrate the 50th anniversary of the movement in Britain, the local branch produced an excellent book of pictures and information about Whitchurch called *Our Village Today*. This remains an invaluable source for anyone who wishes to understand more about the local community. At the same time, to mark the anniversary, a seat was presented. Originally intended for Church Hill, it found its way finally to Whitchurch Road. It continues to represent one of the positive marks on the local landscape which we owe to the WI. Another is the lime tree at Anderton Corner, planted to mark European Conservation Year 1970. At that period, with membership nearing 100, it was decided that the branch should divide into two, one group continuing to meet in the afternoon and the other, consisting mainly of younger members, forming an 'evening branch'. This was done in 1984. In 2002 members celebrated their 75th birthday with a lunch at the Two Bridges Hotel. The WI remains one of the most active and durable organisations in the parish.

Almost all the clubs, organisations and societies in Whitchurch had one feature in common, and one that they shared with comparable associations in other places. No organised society could feel that it had become firmly established until it had entered into its calender of events the summer trip. When the twentieth century came in it ushered in the age of the annual 'treat' or 'outing'. For an early example we can turn to the outing of the Mothers' Social Group on Tuesday 30 June 1908:

It was a memorable day. A large party of over 50 closely packed in two wagonettes left Whitchurch Corner at 9.30a.m. The outlook was doubtful, but all was well until we crossed the Tamar. Ascending the steep hill at Gunnislake the clouds rolled up ominously and a smart shower fell. At Callington a halt was made for lunch at the Temperance Hotel. About half an hour after starting again, a storm suddenly burst over our heads with great violence, flashes of forked lightning, loud thunder claps, and drenching rain startled the horses, made children cry, and blanched many a face with fear. By God's providence we all had a wonderful escape, though two heifers were killed in a field not far away. The heavy rain played havoc with hats and dresses, head gear especially suffering. By the time we reached Saltash the sky was clear again and the sun shining brilliantly. Without further mishap we reached Plymouth at about 3.30 in good time for an excellent tea at Sleeman's Restaurant. The return drive by way of Roborough Down was made at 8.15, and home was reached soon after 10 o'clock, all arriving safe and sound, thankful, and more or less hungry.

Whitchurch WI members in 1987, as they might have looked if they had been founder members of the branch in 1927.

Residents of Merrivale leaving for a trip to the seaside in the early 1920s.

Members of Whitchurch Methodist Chapel, on an outing, pause in Bedford Square.

Chapter 8

LEARNING

It all started with Francis Pengelly's will, which came into effect in 1723. His bequest of £6 a year for 900 years was intended to provide the children of the poor of Whitchurch with a basic education covering religious instruction, reading, writing and arithmetic. A charity school was founded, administered by a Trust. It continued to operate for 70 years and then, in 1793, for some reason payments from the Trust were stopped. Legal action was taken and the vicar of the day, Revd Henry Pengelly, a descendant of the benefactor, who was himself one of the trustees, stepped in to keep the school going by appointing a mistress to care for the pupils, then said to number between eight and ten. The length and complexity of the legal case meant, however, that this could be no more than a temporary expedient, and in 1794 the school was discontinued. The law took a further 26 years to decide that the charity was no longer operative. When the settlement came, in 1820, the school was reconstituted, no longer as a charity institution, but as a subscription school, with voluntary contributions from parishioners forming the basis of its operation. This was the period when dame-schools were cheap and popular, particularly in villages, and the school that was reborn in Whitchurch in 1820 was one such. The 'dame' was a lady who, although unqualified, offered to provide some elementary teaching. The quality of any such instruction, as well as the levels of care and discipline and the nature of the general atmosphere, was bound to vary greatly according to the personality and gifts of the dame. The poet George Crabbe described one of the worst examples:

> *Yet one there is, that small regard to rule,*
> *Or study pays, and still is deemed a school;*
> *That where a deaf, poor, patient widow sits*
> *And awes some thirty infants as she knits,*
> *Infants of humble, busy wives, who pay*
> *Some trifling price for freedom through the day.*

We have little evidence on which to judge whether Crabbe's picture, drawn in the 1820s, was a fair description of Whitchurch School at that time. Nor do we know whether the 'humble busy wives' whose children were put in the care of the dame made a contribution, a 'trifling price', towards the cost of running the school, to go alongside the subscriptions of philanthropic patrons of the establishment. We do, however, know a little about the 'dame' who guided the school through 31 years from the time of its reconstitution in 1820. She was Kitty Hughes and she had been born in Bere Ferrers in 1771. She was also known to do a bit of curing on the side, repeating charms over an inflamed wound before sending the patient off to her friend Jane Squires at Mill Hill, who completed the cure with a little ointment. Recognisable always by the ever-present little old hat, Kitty took her school duties very seriously. Her regular method of carrying out the wishes of her patrons, for example, was to line up the pupils at the close of school each day and require them, before they were allowed to leave, to repeat their catechism. When vicar Pengelly complained to her on one occasion about the manners of the children, Kitty responded by instructing her charges that if they happened to be on the roadside when the vicar rode by they were to take off their caps or curtsey. The following day a group of boys found themselves in this situation and dutifully lifted their caps. This action so alarmed the clerical horse that it reared and nearly unseated its ageing rider. Mr Pengelly thereupon persuaded Kitty to amend her advice, so that in future a touch of the cap was considered a sufficient act of courtesy.

The 'dame era' lasted for a generation or so. It ended in 1851, when Kitty reached the age of 80. In that year the vicar, Richard Sleeman, considering that a change was necessary, arranged for her retirement and replacement by a master. John Doidge had been born in Mary Tavy and was a member of a family with roots in that parish going back to the sixteenth century. The Doidges had been associated with mining enterprises in the area, but John had other ambitions. Appointed the village schoolmaster at Whitchurch, he and his wife Mary were to live, for the next 25 years, in the building that since 1820 had been part-school and part-home. Kitty moved out, went to live in Buckland, and died there at the age of 87. The modest building that passed to the Doidges still stands at the time of writing, immediately opposite the church. The fact that it was then, as it has continued to be, in the ownership of the church, meant that it was both available and suitable for the

A picture taken in 1926 between the departure of Frank Lapthorne and the arrival of Edith Henry. Miss Nancarrow, later Mrs Toye, is in charge. Pictured are, left to right, back row: *Henry Jope, Henry Daw, Reg Cruse, John Luscombe, ?, ?, George Munday;* third row: *Miss Nancarrow, Beatrice Penhall, Winnie Hicks, Phyllis Abel, Iris Patey, Eileen Mitchell, Barbara Hall, Muriel Mitchell;* second row: *Arthur Thomas, Peter Thomas, Cicely Cox, Joyce Hendy, Mabel Hicks, Edna Martin, Evelyn Lavers;* front row: *Ralph Toye, Claud Cruse, Freda Cox, Master Mudge, Francis Daw.*

The pupils in 1933.

John Doidge and his home and school, as it appears in 2003.

purpose to which it was put in 1820. Significantly, the school was at that time described as a 'parochial school' and was managed by the vicar. Annual income from subscriptions amounted to about £20, this amount being augmented slightly by small charges, the so-called 'children's pence'. In 1870 there were said to be between 60 and 70 pupils, of both sexes. Mr Doidge and Miss Henwood shared the teaching duties.

One feature of the long period of John Doidge's mastership was that he was answerable to no one, except the vicar, for any aspect of his conduct of the school. This was to end in 1874 when Whitchurch took the option, offered in the 1870 Education Act, to establish for itself a School Board. This five-man body, elected triennially by the ratepayers of Whitchurch, was to run elementary education in the parish from 1874 to 1903. The first board consisted of W. Pryce Michell of Holwell as chairman and H.F. Pengelly Spry of Sortridge as vice-chairman, along with W.H. Chichester of Grenofen, J.W. Willcock of Anderton, and the vicar, Revd George Johnston. They appointed a clerk, the Tavistock-based lawyer Robert Luxton, and paid him £10 a year. Their first decision was that they should assume responsibility for Whitchurch School and should aim at the speedy replacement of the building, pending which Mr Doidge and Miss Henwood should be asked to continue, on their existing salaries. Philip Blowey of Buckland was then commissioned to build, for £800, a new school immediately adjacent to the existing one.

It was completed in time for the new master to take up his duties at Christmas 1876. The board appointed Joshua Hooper of Bridestowe. He was to have a salary of £50, together with half of the grant that was received from the Government and half the 'school pence'. The latter fees involved a complicated table in which the father of a child under the age of five would pay a weekly charge of one penny, or twopence or threepence, depending on whether he was a labourer, a mechanic or a farmer, these being considered the only possible potential parents of elementary schoolchildren. For children older than five the charges were twopence, threepence and sixpence. Increases were triggered if or when the child reached a certain standard of attainment, while reductions took effect in the cases of large families. Joshua Hooper also had the use of a rent-free cottage in the village, provided by the vicar, and his wife was appointed as sewing mistress at a salary of £20. As he took over, his predecessor John Doidge 'retired' to Pennington Farm with four volumes of Macauley's *History of England* under his arm, a present from his former pupils. He farmed for the next 28 years, but continued to play an active part in the life of the school for much of that time. He finally retired in 1904 and died two years later at the age of 74.

The new school opened in January 1877 with 100 pupils, the board having exercised its right to enforce compulsion before it became universally applied. Under the new regime regular visits and reports were made by inspectors and they were quick off the mark. Within a month they were reporting that:

The building is a nice one and probably in another year the children may do fairly in an examination, but the school has been at work too short a time to afford a satisfactory test. The master needs some efficient help. Ball Frame, Object Cards, and Form and Colour Boxes are wanted for use with the infants, and there should be at least two sets of reading books for each standard.

Unfortunately, Mr Hooper's performance was soon seen to fall below the expectations of the board. He showed some impatience with slower children, a number of whom, although as old as 11, were, because of the introduction of compulsion, in the first year of their school life. It was recorded that 'several unpleasantnesses have occurred', and that the board, 'having had to complain on more than one occasion', felt that 'it would be desirable for all parties that a change in the mastership should take place.' He was replaced by Richard Sharpe, who was offered similar terms to his predecessor except that the salary was increased to £60 and a pupil-teacher, Agnes Parratt, was engaged. Pupil-teachers were children who were among the brighter pupils in elementary schools and who, at the age of 13, were formally apprenticed to their head teachers as a preliminary, five-year-long stage towards qualification as a teacher. At the same time Thirza Penhall was employed as the new sewing mistress. The inspectors decided, in December 1879, that 'the school has steadily continued to improve. The children are orderly and well-behaved and do their work, for the most part, well.'

Mr Sharpe was a firm disciplinarian. The girls shared a drinking cup. One day Mary Nicholas broke it. The master ordered her to bring in, on the following morning, the cost of its replacement. Either Mary could not bring herself to confess her crime to her parents, or they were told what had happened and could not afford the bill. The fact was that Mary did not attend school for three weeks. It required the intervention of the vicar to get her back and to have the debt cancelled. The following week the master taught the children a new song that began with the words 'Be not swift to take offence'.

The idea of compulsory education was a novelty, locally and nationally, in the 1870s. Many people, including some parents and prospective employers, saw it as an unwelcome limitation on the rights of parents. Mr Sharpe, who was required by the board to enforce attendance, conducted a ceaseless campaign against the twin problems of absenteeism and chronic lateness. In one of innumerable entries on this theme in the school's log-book he noted, in May 1879: 'I kept in several children who came late. Those who live at Grenofen are the worst offenders.' Timekeeping was a problem, because you had to try to distinguish between genuine lateness caused, for example, by snow on the moor, and wilful tardiness that disrupted classes. Carrots and sticks provided the answers: oranges were favoured in the first category, detention in the second.

But a far greater problem was caused by parents who refused to accept their obligations under the new regulations on compulsion. The motives were mixed. Some claimed to be expressing their natural rights as freeborn Englishmen to do what they wanted with their own children. Fathers needed sons and daughters to help in the fields or in the workshop. Mothers with large families needed support in the home. In some cases sheer hardship played its part. It was not always possible to find the twopence that was due to the school, let alone to provide the shoes for the child to wear to get there. These kind of problems proved difficult, frustrating and time-consuming for Mr Sharpe and his successors over the years. At least some of the cases were straightforward. On 22 June 1883 'several children absented themselves to visit Mr Wombwell's Travelling Menagerie at Tavistock.' To his intense relief the master was, in 1886, provided with an attendance officer, who could chase up recalcitrant parents. The abolition of fees in 1891 also had an effect. Mr Sharpe was still, however, left with major problems. The only help he had in trying to cope with a school of between 60 and 100 pupils came from a sewing assistant and a pupil-teacher. The solution to this difficulty was as far beyond his control as were the two phenomena that brought occasional, albeit sometimes prolonged, closures – namely weather and epidemics. In 1895 the inspectors submitted a report that contained the sentence: 'The school cannot be considered to be in a satisfactory state as regards the educational standards attained.' Mr Sharpe decided to retire, becoming the first master of the school to draw a pension. He was succeeded by William Newton.

It is common practice for a new incumbent in any post to denigrate the work of his predecessor, so as to produce a benchmark against which his own magnificent achievements can be measured. Mr Newton's first impression was that the school was 'in an extremely bad state both as regards work and discipline.' The Newton priorities lay in the field of discipline. Within one week 11 separate offences had been punished by caning. They were: constant misbehaviour, talking, inattention, taking advantage of the master's absence with another class, impudence, disobedience, idleness, comparing sums, repeated carelessness in arithmetic, lateness and truancy. When the parents of Alfred Southcombe complained about their son being hit, the master explained himself thus to the board:

During a drill lesson the boy kept making mistakes, and, as I thought that he was doing it deliberately, I struck him with the cane. The boy then stopped altogether and would not move. I again struck him, when he fell down. I thought it was temper.

Mr Newton was warned about such conduct, but he survived. Her Majesty's inspectors noted that 'a wonderful improvement has already been effected in the order and mental agility of the scholars.'

The first assistant mistress, appointed to teach the infants, came in 1897 in the form of Bertha Dawe, a former pupil-teacher. Pupil-teachers continued to be engaged at the school; they helped with the teaching and attracted an annual grant of £5. At Whitchurch during this period there was always one, and sometimes two, pupil-teachers over whom the master was required to keep careful supervision. On 22 January 1897 he noted 'I heard the Senior PT give a very fair lesson on 'The Cow' and the Junior PT a fair one on 'The Dog'.' In 1903 the Whitchurch School board, which had also for some years been responsible for the school at Horrabridge, was dissolved, its powers passing to Devon County Council. The last campaign of the old board was to grapple with the most intractable of all school problems, that had once again been brought to their attention:

There is an offensive smell emanating from the closets. The office arrangements are not satisfactory, especially as regards the urinal on the boys' side; the seats in the offices should be divided by partitions.

And so, with a sigh, the board passed on to others the insoluble problem of the closets, along with a cheque

LEARNING

for £2.8s.3d., the balance of their accounts.

William Newton's 20-year reign ended with his retirement in 1915. Miss Laura Ball was appointed, but fell ill after a few months and had to resign. Frank Lapthorne took on the job temporarily, and, as is the case with so many appointments that originate in short-term stop-gap decisions, it proved markedly successful. In his nine years he was responsible for a number of innovations. HMI referred to some of them in their 1923 report:

The headmaster gives freely of his own time for the benefit of the scholars, who appear to be very fond of him. He is also arousing the parents' interest in the school by means of annual concerts and by the reports sent home in connection with the periodic examinations. An open day is about to be held... In singing a sweet tone has been procured... The small garden, which is under cultivation, and the woodwork done by the older boys, are interesting features. The infants are bright, happy, and perfectly natural in demeanour.

There followed educational trips, field work, a library and a piano. And then, in 1926, Mr Lapthorne took his abilities, and his ideas, to Lewtrenchard. Miss Edith Henry then took over. Over the next ten years she noted faithfully the events that affected her and her school:

The attendance not so good, owing to whortleberry picking.
The books of Iris Patey, who recently died of diphtheria, were burned.
Miss Cocksedge presented a large doll for the girls to dress and five shillings for a fund to be spent on the boys.
Miss Cocksedge presented thirty books, an aquarium tank, and a model of the 'Queen Mary'.
The temperature was so low that, even though the fire in the stoves was as big as could be kept in, the ink froze in the inkwells.

Miss Henry was popular and effective. The decline in numbers was due mainly to the change that occurred in 1928 when the Dolvin Road School in Tavistock became a senior school, and senior pupils who had hitherto stayed on at their elementary schools in the area were now to attend that school. Whitchurch became exclusively a junior school, or, to embrace its last change of name, a county primary school. Frederick Stoyle saw the school through the years of the war and the period immediately following, and after his retirement in 1949 came Mabel Alford.

Numbers over the following years hovered between 30 and 50. A number of 'firsts' were registered, such as the first student on teaching practice in 1951, the pioneer portable gramophone in 1952, and, in 1965, the first mealtime assistant, who was required to encourage children 'to eat, particularly, green vegetables and salad, and to avoid waste.' The most taxing spell of Miss Alford's 17 years in the post must have been the winter crisis of 1963, when the school had to close for four weeks, with the lavatories frozen and the water-supply suspended. For one week the juniors, with the head teacher, moved in with Tavistock County Primary School. A plan to do the same with the infants was aborted when the children turned up in their old classroom ready to move, to discover that their teacher was holed up in Plymouth.

John Foxhall, who became headmaster in 1967, had been born in Cork in 1921. His father was a soldier, and his mother's family had included a number of teachers. He took the Whitchurch job after 14 years as deputy head of Tavistock County Primary School. He was later to claim that one of the most significant innovations in his 17-year reign was one of the first, the establishment of the Parents-Teachers Association. Mrs Beaver, who was also chairman of the managers, was its first president. Mr Foxhall was also justly proud of his efforts to make his pupils aware of the Dartmoor heritage around them. In sport and music the school quickly developed strong reputations. Numbers doubled within five years and burst into three figures in the mid-1970s. By 1970 the school had a staff of 12. They were:

Headmaster	Mr J.W. Foxhall
Qualified Assistant Teachers	Mrs L.R. Lethbridge
	Mrs A. Stein
Permanent Supply Teacher	Miss H. Drake
Musical Instrumental Teacher	Mrs E. Kilpatrick
Cook Supervisor	Mrs M.I. Youldon
Kitchen Helpers	Mrs I.D. Toye
	Mrs H.W. Munday
Mealtime Assistants	Mrs F.A. Watkins
	Mrs P.M. Craze.
Caretaker/Cleaner	Mr J. Endacott
Secretary	Mrs C.M. Foxhall

The dramatic increase in numbers, over which Mr Foxhall and his successor presided, is illustrated by the following figures of the numbers on the roll in the January of the year indicated:

1968	*38*	*1980*	*160*
1972	*75*	*1984*	*180*
1976	*113*	*1988*	*232*

In January 1971 it was announced that:

... planning is being sought for up to 400 houses in the area between the Whitchurch–Tavistock road and the A386, and that a reservation of a site for a new school in the same area is now being considered.

From that point the campaign for a new school got under way. A short-term solution to the problem of

The school in 1965. Left to right, back row: Sally Jackman, Ian Chappell, Linda Cox, William Seager, Judith Hitchon, Ronald Whatton, Andrew Seager, Veronica Larson, Paul Williams, Susan Toye, Paul Perkin, Teresa Mudge, Mrs West; third row: Miss Alford, John Rowe, Valerie Toye, Jeremy Bartlett, Mervyn Burridge, Shirley Jackman, Roger Denshaw, Wendy Toye, Derek Cruze, Ann Seager, John Haytor, Wendy Toye, Mark Williams, Martin Roberts, Peter Heath; second row: Michael Burridge, John King, Clare Haytor, Andrew Watkins, Sandra Bray, Philip Maker, Wendy King, Stephen Seager, Shirley Toye, Graham Burridge, Linda Toye, Tim Larson, Angela Larson, Scott Eslick, Geraldine Perkins, Ian Doidge; front: Frances Brewer, David Rowe, Christine Cox, Sandra Burridge, Kevin Bartlett, Janet Watkins, Ian Denshaw, Shirley Burridge.

*The school music group in 1968.
Left to right, standing: Stephen Colman, Linda Toye, Christine Cox, Sandra Burridge, Natalie Wilton; sitting: Janet Watkins, Helen Perks, Tim Eslick, Neil Foley, Kevin Bartlett.*

rising numbers was found in the provision of temporary classrooms, of which there were eventually three. A crisis situation was reached in 1978, when some parents on the Bishopsmead estate were denied places at the school for their children. The publicity that ensued undoubtedly served to give greater priority to the Education Authority's plan for a replacement building. In the meantime every expedient, such as the use of two rooms in the original school building next door, was grasped. This latter provision proved an ideal venue for small-group activities and for the music for which the school had become renowned. In 1975 a violin quartet, with Ellen Fraser, John Fraser, Jeremy Dixon and Jonathan Kilpatrick, was awarded a Certificate of Distinction at the Plymouth Music Festival.

Ten years elapsed between the commitment to provide a new school, in 1973, and the realisation of the project, in 1983. Finally, on 22 July 1983, Pickfords moved in. The new school opened its doors on 6 September. The transfer was, however, to be phased, and for some time the old building continued to be used. In the new building were the headmaster, three classes with their teachers (Mrs Dickson, Mrs Brock and Mr Portman), two cleaners, and five cooks and kitchen helpers. In the old school were the deputy head, Mrs Kelly, with three staff (Mrs Foy, Mrs Portman and Mrs Symes), two infant helpers and two cleaners. Shared between the two were three mealtime assistants and one crossing-patrol officer. The two sites were half a mile apart. Each Wednesday they gathered for a 'get together', an all-school assembly. One of John Foxhall's last contributions to the school was to grapple with the problems of a split-site school, but the solutions had to await his successor. He retired in 1984 and was succeeded by John Marks.

The moment of reunion came in 1990, when the old building was finally vacated and the infants moved down the hill to join their older colleagues. Under John Marks, Ricci Achillini and Angela O'Shea-Warman the school has continued to exploit its natural advantages, to develop features, such as an IT suite, that would have been considered unrealisable just a short time ago, and to continue to foster relations with parents and with the world outside the school gates. What a contrast with the world of Kitty Hughes, or even with the picture painted in the mid-twentieth century of a small village school! And yet certain features persist. In 1930 the inspectors, when describing the general atmosphere, used words like 'caring', 'pleasant' and 'friendly'. What the recent history of Whitchurch School has demonstrated is that you can grow bigger whilst still retaining these qualities.

The provision of elementary education in the parish of Whitchurch has predominantly been the responsibility, thoughout the years, of the village school. There have, however, been occasions when

Heads of Whitchurch School From 1820

1820–51	Kitty Hughes
1851–76	John Doidge
1877–78	Joshua Hooper
1878–95	Richard Sharpe
1895–1915	William Newton
1916–17	Laura Ball
1917–26	Frank Lapthorne
1927–37	Edith Henry
1937–49	Frederick Stoyle
1950–67	Mabel Alford
1967–84	John Foxhall
1985–92	John Marks
1992–2000	Ricci Achillini
2001–	Angela O'Shea-Warman

other establishments have shared the duties. There was, for example, a board school at Horrabridge, which drew some of its pupils from the southern part of the parish during a period when the parochial boundary left some of Horrabridge village in Whitchurch parish. Then there was Merrivale. Here was an area that belonged to Whitchurch but which, compared with other parts of the parish, found the village school less accessible. Some of the children there attended schools in the Foggintor and Rundlestone areas during the nineteenth century, although these were beyond the parish boundary. In 1912, with the closure of the Foggintor Mission School, a school was opened at Merrivale Quarry. It operated for three years, under the leadership of Mrs Lucy (or Louisa) Jewell, the wife of a Royal Marine, a Roman Catholic, and the mother of five small children. She noted, in her log-book, at an early stage in the life of her school that:

The work of the school is being conducted under great difficulty. A large traction is engaged drawing and shifting heavy truck-loads of granite outside the windows, and it is almost impossible to hear either teacher's or children's voices at times.

In 1915 a new school was opened up the hill, which was known as Walkhampton Foggintor School. Mrs Jewell was asked to head it, but she declined, pleading the need to see more of her family. She moved away and later resumed her teaching career, as so many women have since, when her children were older. The post was then offered to Frederick Stoyle, who was later to move to Whitchurch School. The Merrivale School closed after a life of only three years.

At various times there have been a number of private schools in the parish, most of them single-sex, some of them offering boarding facilities, and all of them small. A Miss Coffin, for example, ran one for

Above: Tavyside School in 1960. At the time the school was owned by Marjorie Kelby and Elsie Elsby, and was the largest independent school in the parish. The picture was taken during the school's occupancy of The Priory.

Left: Whitchurch School in 1967. John Foxhall had just taken over as headmaster when this picture was taken, and he is standing to the right of the group.

LEARNING

Two homes of Whitchurch School pictured in 1990.

Left: *The new building in its setting.*

Below: *A front view of the old building.*

Bottom right: *A rear view of the old building.*

Below left: *The new building.*

a time on the road between Grenofen and Horrabridge. Jane Elizabeth Carpenter, the daughter of James Carpenter, the mine captain at Anderton, opened a school at her home, Anderton Cottage, in the early 1880s. Advertised as a 'Ladies Boarding and Day School', it survived for some 20 years. During the same period Helena Fox ran a ladies' boarding-school at 2 Church Park Villas. For boys at that time John Honey Gaud operated a private school, with boarding facilities, at 4 Fern Park Villas. In the early years of the twentieth century Mabel Duncan opened, and quickly closed, a girls' school, and Harriett Ashwin's enterprise was equally short-lived, in spite of a vigorous advertising campaign which offered a 'High Class Boarding and Day School for Girls' at St Alban's House. Henry Brewer opened up in Chollacott Villas in 1906, and was prepared to take both girls and boys, but he had turned his attentions elsewhere by 1910. Bleak House appears to have offered educational facilities of some kind between the wars. St Michael's School for Girls, housed in the building on Whitchurch Road which was later to provide a home for the maternity hospital, was established by Miss Annie Raymond during the First World War, and lasted longer than many of its contemporaries.

The school with the choicest setting was undoubtedly the Tavyside School. Originally housed on Mount Tavy Road in Tavistock, this enterprise was moved to The Priory in 1957 by its owners, Marjorie Kelby and Elsie Elsby. It was subsequently sold to Mr Frank Bye. In the 1970s there were over 40 boarders, who lived at The Priory; the day-school meanwhile operated in Russell Street in Tavistock. The Priory has since reverted to private residential accommodation.

The Playgroup Movement got under way in the 1960s and in 1968 a group was formed in Whitchurch, the leading pioneers being young mothers Pat Eslick and Thelma Bishop. Initial problems in the use of the Parish Room were gradually overcome and the group established a unique position in the landscape of village activities. Meanwhile, the old village school on Church Hill, with its memories of a century of successive generations of Whitchurch children, was adapted to accommodate a kindergarten. The end of the twentieth century saw it housing a school based on Montessori principles.

The Whitchurch Inn, in its village setting, in the 1870s.

Crossways Stores in the 1920s. Stephen Toye, who had recently bought the property, is seen here carrying out some major alterations.

Chapter 9

TRADING

In most villages the Post Office occupies a key position, not only as a commercial centre but as a social hub. Whitchurch is no exception. Its original Post Office was a small building on the Horrabridge Road, which opened for business in the 1880s. Before that the nearest office was in Tavistock, although there was a letterbox at Moortown from the mid-1870s. The first sub-postmistress was Miss Amelia Willcock, a member of that remarkable Anderton-based family. Her sister Melon shared the premises, selling groceries, while her brother John ran the farm. Letters arrived, via Tavistock, each day at 7.05a.m. and 4.20p.m., and post was despatched daily at 7.10a.m. and 5.25p.m. During this period a further letter-box was added at Grenofen. Miss Willcock was able to provide most postal needs; she could, for example, issue postal orders, although she was not empowered to cash them. In the early years of the new century the office was re-sited in a new building near the crossroads, where it has remained until the time of writing. By 1919 further postboxes had been sited in the parish, at Grimstone, Moorshop, Walreddon, Middlemoor and on Whitchurch Road. At about that time Essie Willcock took over from her Aunt Amelia as the sub-postmistress. Her brother Joseph ran a butcher's shop on the same premises. They continued in business until 1956, by which time both brother and sister were in their seventies. Sadly, both died within a very short time of the shop being sold.

The Post Office and Stores in the 1990s.

The business came to the Wilton family, who had previously run the shop known as Crossways Stores. Bryonie Wilton took over as the sub-postmistress, with her husband Vernon running a grocery shop alongside. The family ran the Post Office for 20 years until 1976, so that for almost a century the service was provided by just two families.

There was, for a short period in the early years of the twentieth century, a small Post Office at Merrivale. Run successively by two sisters, Florrie and Martha Knowling, the office accommodation was little more than a domestic room with a table.

In September 1913 it was reported that:

During the past month, post office employees have been busy erecting additional poles along the Whitchurch Road, up Church Hill, and along the Down Road, terminating for the present at the gate to the vicarage drive. The vicarage, and many other houses, will now be in direct touch with Tavistock and the postal telephone system. The comfort and convenience of this is inculculable [sic], especially on a wet day.

And so it came to pass that Revd Beebe was the first person in Whitchurch to put an end to wet-day misery. By 1927 he had been joined by Charles Allen, Sophie Barrington, Robert Barter, Harold Bellamy, George Bittleston, Frank Bolt, Edward Brown, Kenneth Brown, Hugh Coleridge, Bridget Cordner, Richard Doble, John Dunn, Lucy Freeman, Alice Innes, Elizabeth Lovell, Frank Radcliffe, Ernest Shakerley, Benjamin Shires, Helen Spender, William Stephens, James Stewart, Wilfred Thomas, Charles West, Walter Willcock and William Williams. Ten per cent of households in the parish were now on the telephone network.

The building on the crossroads, across the neck of Anderton Lane from the Post Office, has most recently been known as Pooh Corner. A century ago it was a grocer's shop. For some 30 years, between the 1880s and the First World War, the proprietor was Maria Creber, the widow of Walter Creber, the Crowndale farmer. She was the matriarch of the Creber grocery dynasty. Her style of working in the Crossways Stores, which was the accurate, if prosaic, name of her shop, was based on the need for precision and accuracy, and if this meant bisecting a caramel sweet

Above and right: *The Whitchurch Inn in the nineteenth century and in 2003.*

Below and left: *The Dartmoor Inn between and wars and in the 1960s.*

TRADING

so as to produce the exact measure, so be it. She was followed by William Nancarrow, who, in the late 1920s, sold the property to Stephen Toye. He was a professional mason and he made a number of alterations to the building, including raising its roof.

In 1937 the Wilton family took over the business, adding newspaper deliveries to the other services that a rural grocery was expected to provide. Martin Beaver was later to explain that the regular despatch of bills was not one of the strengths of the business; he recalls his mother at the end of the Second World War, having not received a bill for newspapers for the last five years, being driven to sending a cheque based on an estimate of what the costs might have been. Mr Beaver has another vivid recollection of the family, which concerns the son, Vernon:

Vernon, delivering the newspapers, would toil up the hill to our house with his bike. What happened then became folklore. He would use the return journey to test his own daring. He seemed to lead a charmed life as he sped down the hill, judging the traffic at the crossroads.

Vernon it was who, following war service in the Royal Navy, returned to take over the store from his mother, who was in ill health. In 1953 he married a Cornish girl, Bryonie Knight, and they buckled down

Right: *Bob and Linda Elliott in the Halfway House in 1961 with their son Dean, a future captain of the Whitchurch Cricket Club.*

Below and bottom: *The Halfway House, c.1955 and c.1905.*

together to the task of selling everything from paraffin to toothpaste. Then in 1956 the Post Office came on to the market, and Vernon and Bryonie bought the property, moving across the road, he to run a grocery department which had previously been a butcher's shop, and she to work as the sub-postmistress. Altering the premises to produce one large L-shaped area, the Wiltons continued for the next 20 years to run an emporium which was general store, haberdashery, greengrocery, stationery shop and Post Office. Meanwhile, the building across the road that they had vacated reverted to being a private residence and emerged as Pooh Corner.

The main outlet for dairy products for many years was the farm on Church Hill. Close by was Mr Westlake, the obliging village cobbler. It is also thought that the village at one time supported a sweet shop.

Young Kathleen Giles, as she then was, who was growing up in Middlemoor in the 1930s, remembers the kind of services provided for those, like her family, who lived in the more remote parts of the parish. There was the daily visit from the milk float, pulled by a particularly friendly horse, and the weekly delivery of groceries by the Tavistock Co-op. But Kathleen's most vivid memories are reserved for an enterprising family of Middlemoor farmers called Wallace. Robert and his son ran the business and built a new home for the family called Tregortha, on the right-hand side of the road as you enter the hamlet from Whitchurch village; other cottages were built on the farm site in the mid-1930s. Butter and cream were kept in a container suspended in a box-well nearby. Using a large canvas-sided lorry, the Wallaces developed a delivery service. Kathleen remembers:

They did regular visits to the outlying moorland settlements, with paraffin, crockery, vegetables, and so on. In fact they ran a mobile ironmongers and greengrocers combined. We bought from them our oil and anything that we didn't grow in our own garden.

Of the two garages that once did business in the parish, the older one, built close to the Tavistock/ Whitchurch parish boundary on the A386, is Waterways. Hugh Brian Cooke was a Lincolnshire man who trained as a wheelwright and motor mechanic and took to spending holidays in Devon. When he bought Waterways in 1935 he had begun trading in Morgan three-wheelers. The premises and immediate area surrounding his new acquisition had had a variety of functions in recent years, including those of bone-mill, furniture repository, hand laundry and ginger-beer factory. It was now to sustain a Shell-selling garage, a tin-shed-like structure, and a three-storey house, reduced to two by fire. The introduction of petrol rationing in 1939 brought closure, but, unexpectedly, the business reopened in 1943 when the large number of American forces, then beginning to gather in the area in preparation for D-Day, realised that they needed a fuel depot for their vehicles. Fully operational again in 1945, the garage was now equipped with a 2,000-gallon storage facility, which from 1950 held Esso fuel, the franchise going in that direction following the introduction of competition. The old garage building was demolished in the early 1960s and, at the end of that decade, Hugh retired to nearby Brook Mill Farm. The house at Waterways passed through a brief but interesting period as the Virtuous Lady public house, but was demolished in the 1990s. The garage, meanwhile, changed hands a number of times.

Waterways in 1957.

In 1954 Francis and Winifred Martin, who lived at Hunson Villa on Whitchurch Road, built a garage on land which adjoined their house and had previously been an orchard. Their son Raymond, who had served an apprenticeship at Bond's Vigo Bridge garage in the 1940s, proceeded to run the business for 26 years following its opening in 1956, selling fuel and offering repair and service facilities. The premises were sold in 1982 to a Mr Hamil, who ran the business for three years before selling the property for housing development.

In 1850 there were only two families in Whitchurch who could be said to earn their living from the 'hospitality industry' – that is running inns, hotels or guest-houses. In 1870, 1890 and 1910 these numbers had risen to four, seven and twelve respectively. Featured particularly were the parish's three inns, the Whitchurch Inn in the centre of the village, the Dartmoor Inn at Merrivale, and the Halfway House at Grenofen.

Of these, the Whitchurch Inn is by some distance the oldest. Its ownership by the Church and its position close to St Andrew's and within a day's journey of three monastic houses that attracted pilgrims and other visitors, all indicate that this was a medieval hostelry offering accommodation, hospitality and shelter to weary travellers. Its parallel function was that of a parish hall where members of the local community would meet, and where events such as church festivals or village weddings could be celebrated. The first tenant whose name has come down to us was Thomas Lightfoot. In 1702 it was recorded that, in addition to the tenancy of the inn, renewable annually, for which the level of rent payable to the vicar and churchwardens was specified, 'the parishioners also gave him (Lightfoot) lease to make use of the parish stables in the course of the week, but to keep them clean and clear of everything on Sundays.' The need to insist on the last provision was because on Sundays the parishioners themselves would require the use of the stables to park their horses during their attendance at church services. A century later Thomas Foot was agreeing to a contract containing identical words. The rest of the agreement, reached with Mr Foot on 5 June 1792, read:

We, Walter Willcock and George Radford, churchwardens, and other of the parishioners of the parish of Whitchurch, and Thomas Foot, innkeeper of the said parish, do consent and agree that the said Thomas Foot should hold the public house at Whitchurch for the term of seven years at a yearly rent of £8.10s, and to pay his rent quarterly. The said Thomas Foot to repair, and keep in repair, the glass of the windows and to yield up the same in good repair at the end of the term, and to pay and discharge the window and house tax and all other taxes that may be imposed.

The longest-serving tenants of the Whitchurch Inn in the next era were Walter Toop from the 1840s to the 1860s, William Mashford from 1878 to 1900, and Herbert Avery from 1900 to 1915. Postwar hosts have included Arnold Wade, Gordon Foden, Brian Jones, Geoff Bradford and Rachel Newphry. For many years the procedure was that the parishioners, at their annual Lady Day meeting, would consider applications for the tenancy, if the contract had expired, and make decisions. The going rate for the annual rent in the nineteenth century was £10, and this is what William Mashford paid in 1878 after the appointment, for the first time, had gone out to competitive tender. For much of the twentieth century the inn was leased to brewers, who installed the tenants. For a time in the 1930s it came within the control of the People's Refreshment House Association Ltd. More recently independent landlords have run it as a free house.

The building contains a number of interesting features which suggest that there have been major reconstructions and refurbishments throughout its history, a recent one being carried out in 1999. There is a medieval bread oven. As a guidebook has it: 'Oak beams, open fires, and a tithe room, all contribute to the feeling of being in an old place.' A particular feature on display in the wall of the bar is a nineteenth-century shoe, with some explanatory notes:

This shoe was found in one of the walls during extensive renovations. It was probably hidden in the wall in about 1860, following the custom dating from the thirteenth century of deliberately concealing shoes in buildings, near doors, windows, and chimneys, in order to ward off evil spirits which could possibly enter through the openings. The shoe, a good luck symbol, would have been well-worn, so that it contained the spirit of the wearer and would therefore be more effective against evil spirits. Such symbols are not supposed to be removed from the building as bad luck inevitably follows. This may well explain the significant problems and setbacks experienced during our renovations, as the shoe was removed and taken to Plymouth Museum for identification. In returning the shoe, we hope its presence will bring about a more settled future.

To which, having in mind the inn's continued close connection with the church, it is surely appropriate to say 'Amen'.

The origins of the Dartmoor Inn at Merrivale lie in a row of seventeenth-century cottages, probably built to house quarry workers. As an inn, its life appears to have begun in the early years of the nineteenth century, when it first offered stabling and other coaching facilities on the new turnpike road across Dartmoor. Richard Leamon was the landlord in 1825 and through the 1830s and '40s the place was run by John and Jane Jobe. Their successors over the next 100 years were, in turn, John Harding, Peter Hannaford, John Lillicrap, Frederick Harding, Samuel Dawe, George Pursey, George White, Robert Drunsfield, William Bickell and Georges Pigache.

There were major extensions between the wars when the stabling block was added to the west and the other cottages to the east of the original inn, which was the largest of the original cottages. In 1912 William Crossing, in his *Guide to Dartmoor,* had written of 'a roadside house of entertainment called the Dartmoor Inn', and, while it is not clear what exactly entertained the good Mr Crossing, there is no doubt that the place has charmed many generations of visitors. This is partly due to the setting, but also to such attractions as the featured crockery collection and the friendliness of the ghost, whose name is Mary.

During the 1970s, when Peter and Sheila Plumb were running the business, a room and breakfast at the Dartmoor Inn would set you back to the extent of £1.50, with early-morning tea adding 5p to the bill. Their brochure advertised, in particular, the proximity of a variety of sporting opportunities, including fishing (permits obtainable at the inn), shooting (snipe, pigeon and rough shooting by arrangement with local farmers), golf (moorland courses at Yelverton and Tavistock), and hunting (caps sold at the inn for 50p).

The ghost at the Halfway House at Grenofen is anonymous, but is said to be frisky. As an inn this is the youngest of the three in the parish.

Remarkably, from its beginnings in the 1860s until the 1960s it remained in the hands of one family. It all started with John and Mary Bolt. Both born in Whitchurch, they became domestic servants, he at Walreddon Manor and she at Anderton Farm. The day before they were married, in 1859, John's father was killed in an accident at Heckwood Quarry. The young couple lived in one of the cottages at Grenofen Cross, opening a small grocery shop there in the 1860s. Soon after that come the first references to the Halfway House, with John usually listed as 'beer house keeper'.

Mary was a person of extraordinary vigour and energy. She raised 12 children, tended the horses of visitors, ran the grocery store, and kept livestock in an adjacent field. And this pattern she maintained after John's death in 1900 right up to the time of her own demise in 1919 at the age of 80.

The business then passed to Mary's eighth son, Frank, who ran it until 1945. It then came to the third generation of the family in the persons of Frank's daughter, Muriel, and her husband, Reginald Elliott. At this point the grocery shop was closed, and, together with the old kitchen, it became part of the public area. Bob Elliott and his wife Linda inherited the pub in 1960 and ran it for three years before it was sold at auction to John and Gwen Ashby. The adjoining cottages were subsequently demolished and the car park extended. Since the closure of the railway line it is no longer possible to experience the rumble of a train passing beneath your feet through the tunnel that extends immediately underneath the inn, but no doubt the antics of the playful ghost make up for that. It has been generally assumed that the name of the inn indicates a location midway between Tavistock and Horrabridge, but just as likely must be the explanation that it is halfway between Plymouth and Launceston.

A mystery remains. *Billing's Trade Directory* for 1857 contains the following entry in the Whitchurch list: 'Nicholas Jane, beer retailer, 'Alma Arms''. In 1866 there is a listing for 'Henry Nicholls, beer retailer', but no reference to premises. Henry may well have been a brother, or at least a close relative, of the William Nicholls who was running the Whitchurch Inn at that time. It seems at least possible that the Jane of 1857 and the Henry of 1866 were close, and perhaps 'Nicholas' is a misspelling of 'Nicholls'. The question remains as to whether there was at one time an 'Alma Arms', and if so where it was. It cannot have survived very long otherwise it would have become part of local folklore, and there appears to be no lingering folk-memory of an inn of that name. During that particular period 'Alma' was a popular title to bestow on a new public, or for that matter private, building, since it commemorated the first major engagement of the Crimean War, the Battle of Alma, fought in 1854. Alma Cottage, on Church Hill, dates from this period. Could the cottage have been, at least for a brief period, a public house, run by the same family that had the Whitchurch Inn, a few doors up the hill?

The lounge bar of the Dartmoor Inn in the 1960s.

Chapter 10

TRAVELLING

Among the well-known features of the Dartmoor landscape are the granite crosses that marked the routes taken by medieval travellers. These early signposts were designed particularly to help those undertaking journeys to, from, or between the main religious sites in the district, notably the monastic houses at Tavistock, Buckland, Plympton and Buckfast. Four remain in Whitchurch parish, in whole or in part. The descriptions given are those provided in Masson Phillips' classic 1937 study, *Medieval Stone Crosses*.

Churchyard

Near the south entrance to Whitchurch churchyard is a stone cross dedicated in 1981 to the memory of William Henry Mudge. It was placed on an old socket-stone that had occupied this site for many years. Its original position, and the circumstances in which it lost its cross, are not recorded.

An octagonal socket-stone with hollow-chamfered top edge. The socket-stone is nearly square, and is unusually shallow.

Green Lane

The second of the parish's granite signposts stands by the roadside in the north-west corner of Whitchurch Down, near the Golf House and near the top of Green Lane.

A roughly-shaped socket-stone sunk in the turf, with a square socket-hole penetrating the stone, bears a modern stumpy shaft, on which is mounted the ancient head portion with arms of a cross of rough rectangular section. On each face, between the arms, there is an incised cross. The 'restoration' of this cross in 1934 is an example of well-meaning but sadly misguided endeavour.

Pixie Cross, pictured on a postcard from 1904.

Windypost.

The new shaft is absurdly short and much too thick; in fact the only thing that can be said in its favour is that the head of the cross is now safe from removal.

Pixie Cross

The third of the crosses is near the centre of Whitchurch Down, close to the road to Tavistock and about one mile north-east of Whitchurch village. Legend has it that the name, Pixie or Pixie's Cross, by which this monument is known, derives from the experience of the clergyman who, sitting on it to avoid the attentions of a bull, presented a pixie-like appearance. The alternative name, Gibbet Cross, suggests a more sinister, although hardly a more likely, history.

A tall, very rudely-shaped cross of rough rectangular section, with peculiarly mis-shapen arms. There is an incised cross between the arms on one face.

Windypost

The fourth of the parish crosses is on Whitchurch Common. North of Pew Tor and close to Feather Tor, it is known as either Beckamoor Cross or Windypost.

A tall cross of octagonal section, leaning slightly to the west. The shaft is straight and does not taper. The square corner of a broken stone (a socket-stone?) is visible at the base of the cross, partly hidden by turf.

An ancient trackway crossed Whitchurch Down and led, via Moortown, to Windypost, where it forked. One branch crossed Beckamoor Water at Feathertor Ford, and proceeded, round Vixen Tor, to Merrivale. The other crossed the Walkham at Long Ash. The two were reunited at Merrivale, from where the route proceeded in an easterly direction across Dartmoor.

The socket-stone in the churchyard.

The roadside cross near the top of Green Lane.

Milestone at the top of Green Lane.

Another old track took a south-easterly direction from Warren's Cross to Huckworthy Bridge, and then on to Plympton Priory. A north–south route, from Peter Tavy to Horrabridge, crossed the parish at Moorshop, Pennycomequick and Plaster Down. Two old milestones indicate distances on these roads from Plymouth. On a grassy bank at the top of Green Lane, on the east side of the road, is a rectangular granite block with the corners chamfered at the back and with incised lettering on the face, reading '14 miles to Plymo'. The north side has the inscription '1/T' (i.e. one mile from Tavistock). At Pennycomequick, on the eastern side of the road leading up to the Down, close to the point where a lane branches off to Moortown, there is a stone inscribed '13 miles to Plym'. Both these stones were removed in 1940, in accordance with wartime emergency measures designed to confuse an occupying force. They were subsequently replaced close to their original positions.

William Marshall wrote in his book, *The Rural Economy of the West of England*, in 1796:

The roads of West Devonshire are, at present, most remarkable for their steepness. Less than half a century ago they were mere gullies, worn by torrents in the rocks; which appeared in steps, as staircases, with fragments lying loose in the indentures. Speaking with little if any latitude, there was not, then, a wheel carriage in the district; nor, fortunately for the necks of travellers, any horses but those which were natives of the country. At length, however, good turnpike roads were formed, between town and town, throughout this quarter of the island, and most of the villages have carriage roads open to them; though many of the byroads, as yet, are narrow, and abound with steeps.

Marshall was pointing to the fact that, until the middle of the eighteenth century, responsibility for roads rested with the individual parishes. There were several reasons why this arrangement led, in many cases, to neglect. Whitchurch is a good example of the situation that obtained in countless parishes in the area. The parochial authorities, and their ratepayers, would find it very expensive to maintain conscientiously all the roads within the parish boundary. In the cases of the moorland tracks, perhaps it was not necessary to pay much attention. With the roads that crossed the parish linking places like Tavistock and Plymouth, a certain amount of maintenance was, however, necessary. It was paid for in two ways. The able-bodied men of the parish would be enlisted to make a contribution by offering their direct labour on a certain number of days each year. And local property owners would, through the payment of rates, help to purchase material and possibly employ additional labour. Both methods proved unpopular among parishioners. It was a common complaint in Whitchurch that the inhabitants were being required to pay to maintain roads that were predominantly used by outsiders. If the citizens of Tavistock and Plymouth had nothing better to do than to travel between each other's towns, then at least they should pay the cost of repairing the road that they used, and not rely on the good nature and honest toil of the men of Whitchurch who had the ill-fortune to live between them. The result, unsurprisingly, was that such work as was done on the roads was minimal and was performed grudgingly, and therefore with little attention to quality. We can suppose that up to the middle of the eighteenth century the roads in Whitchurch ref-lected very accurately William Marshall's description.

Turnpike Trusts, of which 380 had been formed in different parts of the country by 1770, provided at least a partial answer. These were companies formed by businessmen, landowners and professional people with a special interest in the improvement of local communications. Their practice was to decide which roads in the area were sufficiently important to the local economy to justify investment in them. Given parliamentary approval, the Trust would then make themselves responsible for those roads and for the employment of labour in repair and construction work. Costs would be recovered, and profits made, by charging the road-users tolls, to be collected at gates by suitably-housed toll-keepers. In 1761 the Tavistock Turnpike Trust was formed. As far as Whitchurch was concerned there was only one route in the parish that was considered to be of sufficient economic importance to justify it being taken over. The Trust agreed to assume responsibility for the Tavistock–Plymouth highway. All other roads in Whitchurch would remain in the custody of the parish.

The road that the Turnpike Trust took over in 1762 went through the village of Whitchurch. It had been described as leaving Tavistock by the old town bridge and then passing:

> ... through St John's Lane, by Ash Farm House and Sortridge Gate, to the north-east end of Horra Bridge, and from the south-west end of the said bridge by certain places called Rock Jump, Knacker's Hole, and Manadon Gate, to a place called Old Town Gate in Plymouth.

It was a well-established route, one reputedly taken by Catherine of Aragon after her arrival in Plymouth in 1501 on her way to her wedding with Prince Arthur. The Trust provided a new bridge at Tavistock to take their road over the Tavy, Abbey Bridge, and installed three turnpike gates at which tolls would be collected, at Abbey Bridge, Horrabridge and Crownhill. Whitchurch people, and anyone else who wished to use the road, would be required to pay a toll at each gate, according to the following scale of charges:

Passenger transport
Drawn by 6 or more   18d.
Drawn by 4   12d.
Drawn by 2   6d.
Drawn by 1   3d.

Goods transport
Drawn by 4   24d.
Drawn by 3   8d.
Drawn by 2   6d.
Drawn by 1   3d.

Beasts of burden (per animal)   1d.
Droves of cattle (per score)   10d.
Droves of other stock (per score)   5d.

Left: *A milestone on the turnpike road above Merrivale.*

The success of their enterprise in its early stages (in one of the first weeks of their operation, 672 horses passed through the Tavistock checkpoint) encouraged the Trust to construct a new road from Tavistock through the northern part of Whitchurch parish, past Taviton and Moorshop, to Merrivale, where there was a toll-gate, and beyond. The new road, opened in 1773, was well provided with milestones, which still survive at the time of writing.

Meanwhile, the turnpike road from Abbey Bridge along Whitchurch Road and through Whitchurch village to Horrabridge and Plymouth was, after a promising start, increasingly giving the Trust concern. It failed to generate the kind of income that was anticipated, and since the management did not believe that this one uneconomic route should be subsidised by the remaining profitable ones, the result was that the level of maintenance was reduced. Measures like the withdrawal of concessionary rates to some local farmers and the doubling of tolls on Sundays were introduced, creating more discontent without contributing substantially to a balancing of the books. The route also appeared to suffer, more than most, from physical obstructions which recalcitrant landowners refused to do anything about. It took, for example, a long time and a lot of money to get rid of the pig house in Whitchurch that jutted out dangerously into the road. The Trust finally threw in its hand and abandoned the road. It was now generally agreed that a solution could only come in the form of a new road. And this could only be done by persuading the Plymouth-based Turnpike Trust, the Plymouth and Tavistock Trust, which already controlled the stretch of road between Plymouth and Horrabridge, to take an interest in such a project.

Given wider borrowing powers, this Trust picked up the pieces and what finally emerged was a brand-new route. The old road had left Tavistock by Abbey Bridge and passed through Whitchurch, Sortridge and Horrabridge. The new route was to exit the town via West Bridge and to follow the left bank of the Tavy before rising to Grenofen and then descending to cross the Walkham at the newly-built Bedford Bridge. It would then link with the Trust's existing highway at Horrabridge. The new stretch was formally opened by the Duke of Bedford, after whom the new bridge was named, on 12 June 1822. The

Plymouth and Dock Weekly Journal reported that:

The trustees of the Plymouth and Tavistock Turnpike, being met at two o'clock by His Grace the Duke of Bedford and a large party of gentlemen, went in procession over the new road, which presents a variety of picturesque scenery. The carriages preceded by nearly 150 persons on horseback, with the Dock Cavalry bringing up the rear. At the entrance of Tavistock the procession was met by the inhabitants and received with acclamations.

John Bayly, a 13-year-old schoolboy, was taken by his uncle to witness the scene on that memorable day. He wrote:

You have a much better view of the country from the new road than you had from the old, and the ride is much more pleasant, besides avoiding Horrabridge Hill and other steep but short hills between Horrabridge and Tavistock. We arrived at Tavistock about 4 o'clock and found all the town out to see the Duke.

Master Bayly's otherwise interesting day was marred by the lack of organisation at the celebration dinner. 'It was a complete scramble', he wrote, displaying that special brand of indignation peculiar to 13-year-olds.

The first turnpike gate after West Bridge on the new road was sited at Grenofen. A survey of the traffic passing the gate over a three-week period in October 1852 gave the following statistics:

People	
On Foot	2,627
On horseback	835
In two-wheeled vehicles	2,899
In four-wheeled vehicles	5,105
Total	11,466
Goods	860 tons
Animals	
Cattle	645
Sheep	1,191
Pigs	46

The old turnpike road via Whitchurch village, now facing redundancy, became neglected. Rachel Evans, walking along Whitchurch Road in the 1840s described it as 'dry in winter, shady in summer, radiant with some kind of verdure at every season of the year.' There was, indeed, no shortage of verdure. But as a thoroughfare it became secluded and rather neglected. The old road was to await the arrival of the motor car before it could regain the noise and bustle of a busy artery.

Left and below: *Traffic-free days: The road to Grenofen beyond the village when Thelma Bishop walked it with her children in 1960; and a stretch of Whitchurch Road, c.1904, looking north from the entrance to The Priory.*

TRAVELLING

The two turnpike trusts that served parts of the parish of Whitchurch had both disappeared by the end of the nineteenth century. The Tavistock Trust's operation of its road from Tavistock to Moretonhampstead ended in 1867 when the business was wound up. The Plymouth and Tavistock Trust, running the highway through Grenofen and Horrabridge to Plymouth, staggered on until 1884. Responsibility for the roads reverted briefly to the parishes, the latter now being grouped in districts, each with its Highways Board. In 1889 the new County Councils assumed these duties.

The death of the turnpike trusts was not suicide but murder. And the assassin who wielded the knife was the railway. In 1859 the South Devon Railway Company, later to be incorporated into the Great Western Railway, opened its branch line between Plymouth and Tavistock. The line entered the parish of Whitchurch when it crossed the Walkham atop Brunel's great viaduct. This fine edifice, 367 yards long and 132 feet high, comprised 15 spans of 66 feet each. Tall stone piers supported a superstructure constructed of Baltic timber. Steel replaced wood in 1910. The line then entered the Grenofen Tunnel, 374 yards long, emerging for a final stretch that took it via a raised embankment and a bridge across Anderton Lane, on to a course that ran more-or-less parallel to Whitchurch Road until it entered Tavistock. A passenger on the inaugural trip on 21 June 1859 recorded his impressions:

No line in the country of double the length is so rich in its attractive features. At every point along the line where there was a sign of human habitation the train was received with glad welcome, old and young turning out in holiday attire to do honour to the occasion. Rapid as was the pace at which the train proceeded, there was time enough to catch sight of the pleasure-beaming faces of joyous rustics, who made the welkin ring with their cheers.

We may assume that nowhere were the rustics more joyous, and nowhere did the welkin ring more loudly, than in Whitchurch. It took, however, 47 years for the village to be recognised by the GWR by the installation of a station. Whitchurch Halt, or Whitchurch Down Halt as it came to be called, was opened on 1 September 1906. Its positioning, midway between the village and the principal routes up to the Down, indicated clearly that the company was hoping that this new facility would be equally popular among resident villagers, needing to visit town or city, and visitors, intent on a day out in the countryside. Anthony Kingdom, in his book on the line, described the halt as it appeared in the 1950s, the last decade of its life:

It consisted of a long straight platform capable of serving long excursion trains. It was brick-faced with slab edging and a tidy chipping surface. At its centre, adjacent to its large cast iron on wood nameboard, was its entrance leading in onto a paved section on which stood a square corrugated waiting shelter. No less than five standard lamps were placed along its length. Two either side of the shelter were of cast iron and fitted with swan neck extensions carrying gas lamps. The others were similar fittings mounted upon wooden posts immediately in front of the timber and wire fence that bordered the rear. Onto the fence also bordered the back gardens of houses situated in Whitchurch Road, and as a result it was adorned with many fine rambling roses.

For most of its life the halt was manned by a porter, in the latter years by George Pring. From 1956 it was unstaffed. It had a fair number of commuter customers who constituted a regular core of users. Among them was the dentist with the Whitchurch Road practice, who programmed himself to respond immediately to the sound of the approaching late-afternoon train, which took him home every day. It is said that more than one patient was, at the sound of the tell-tale noise, left abandoned in the chair, open-mouthed and speechless. The most popular train of the week was the 'Woolworth Special', which offered a half-day on Saturdays in Plymouth during a time when shops in the city were open on Saturdays until eight o'clock. The excursion fare was sixpence.

It was claimed by those who campaigned against the closure of the line that the halt was still doing brisk business right up to the end. The end was, of course, the Beeching axe. It fell on 29 December 1962. Ceremonies and mock funerals were planned. The last down-train bore a large floral wreath on its smoke-box door. The platform was packed with sightseers, determined to mark the end of an era. Sadly, the ceremonial had to be abandoned when a blizzard lifted the curtain on the harshest winter on record. The railway that had been launched with so much colourful celebration and enthusiasm quietly expired. It had come in with a roar of self-confidence; it disappeared with little more than a snowy whisper.

Within a short space of time the track had been lifted and the land sold off, much of it, including the site of the halt, to residents, who were thus able to extend their gardens. The one dramatic moment that symbolised the finality of these proceedings came in November 1963, when a large deposit of dynamite was laid at the foot of the Walkham viaduct, and Brunel's century-old masterpiece was summarily demolished.

The first half of the twentieth century was the period when Whitchurch was best served by public transport. It was not only the age of the halt, but also the era when bus services began. Devon Motor Transport began its life in 1920, and in its first year was including Whitchurch in its original north–south route. The DMT was sold to the Western National

Above: *The GWR line exiting Whitchurch en route for Grenofen.*

Right: *Whitchurch Down Halt.*

Below: *The GWR line near Grenofen Manor.*

TRAVELLING

Company in 1927. Meanwhile, some small operators began to ply local routes. In the 1920s Bert Cole of Peter Tavy had a 14-seater Crossley charabanc called 'Eddystone Belle', which had bench seats and a canvas hood that could be open or closed according to the weather. Its regular Friday route between Peter Tavy and Tavistock took in Moortown and Moorshop. In 1929 it was replaced by a Chevrolet christened 'Peter Tavy Blue'. Giving way, in turn, to a Bedford 20-seater, it did sterling work during the war, carrying, among others, military personnel. In 1949 the concern was sold to White & Goodman's, who adopted the name 'Sunshine Coaches'. They launched, in 1949, a new service between Tavistock and Huckworthy that was carried on, after 1953, by Pridham Brothers of Lamerton. Single fares from Tavistock were:

Whitchurch Inn	4d.
Middlemoor	5d.
Caseytown	6d.
Moorshop	7d.
Pennycomequick	8d.
Moortown and Warren's Cross	10d.
Oakley Cross	12d.

The explosion of motor-car ownership in the last part of the twentieth century has had social effects far beyond the impact on public transport. The following figures are from the censuses of 1981 and 1991:

Households with:	1981 no.	per cent	1991 no.	per cent
0 cars	10	6	12	6
1 car	73	47	98	50
2 cars	58	37	70	36
3/+ cars	15	10	16	8

Whitchurch ended the twentieth century with a traffic problem. As the new century dawned new ideas were still needed on how to moderate speeds on Whitchurch Road and a radical attempt to redesign the road to Grenofen had proved controversial. Meanwhile, residents, whose modest request was the right to cross the road in safety somewhere near the Crossways, looked to the authorities for sympathetic support and practical solutions.

Below: *Brunel's viaduct.*

Clockwise from above: *Two images of the stones marking the boundary between Tavistock and Sampford Spiney. They are reminders of the controversies of the 1830s and '40s;* the ancient boundary stone on the bridge at Horrabridge; the old boundary, the Honour Oak, on Whitchurch Road; and the old boundary-stone near the top of Down Road.

Chapter 11

GOVERNING

The people of Whitchurch, or at least those with the necessary qualifications, could, in theory, participate, from 1295, in the periodic election of knights to represent the county of Devon in the national Parliament. In practice the limitation of the franchise to those owning a significant amount of property, the so-called 'forty shilling freeholders', together with the normal convention under which certain well-placed county families monopolised the nominations, meant that contests were rare, and that it was not until the late-nineteenth century that Whitchurch experienced anything resembling a democratic election. Moreover, the selected representatives, unless they belonged to families like the Russells or the Courtenays, would probably have no local connections or concerns. In the 1850s the parish, with a population of between 1,100 and 1,200, had 32 voters.

Subsequent Reform Acts, in 1884, 1918 and 1928, extended the franchise in stages to all adults, and at the same time steps were taken to introduce the principle of constituencies of equal population. From 1885 Whitchurch formed a part of a large, mainly rural constituency, known as Tavistock until 1974 and thereafter first as West Devon and then as West Devon and Torridge. The representatives over that period have been:

1885–86	*Lord Ebrington*	*Liberal*
1886–92	*Lord Ebrington*	*Liberal Unionist*
1892–1900	*H.C.F. Luttrell*	*Liberal*
1900–06	*J.W. Spear*	*Liberal Unionist*
1906–10	*H.C.F. Luttrell*	*Liberal*
1910–18	*J.W. Spear*	*Liberal Unionist*
1918–22	*C. Williams*	*Conservative*
1922–24	*M.R. Thornton*	*Liberal*
1924–28	*P.P.K. Slaney*	*Conservative*
1928–31	*W.D. Wright*	*Conservative*
1931–42	*C.M. Patrick*	*Conservative*
1942–66	*H.G. Studholme*	*Conservative*
1966–74	*M.R.D. Heseltine*	*Conservative*
1974–87	*P. Mills*	*Conservative*
1987–95	*E. Nicholson*	*Conservative*
1995–97	*E. Nicholson*	*Liberal Democrat*
1997–	*J. Burnett*	*Liberal Democrat*

There was no elected council with responsibilities that covered Whitchurch until the late-nineteenth century. The Devon County Council, which was to take over such duties as education, roads, social services and the police, was created in 1889. At the next level, district councils were established five years later. Whitchurch became part of the area covered by the Tavistock Rural District Council, with functions related to housing, planning and refuse disposal. The Rural District Council, which embraced 22 villages in the area but excluded the town of Tavistock, was subject to reorganisation in the last part of the twentieth century, the unit that emerged being the West Devon Borough.

But long before these democratic innovations Whitchurch was affected by political authority in some form. In the Middle Ages one such source was the lord of the manor. He was the principal landowner, who, through his administrative staff and his manorial court, could enforce local laws and customs relating to such matters as agriculture, boundaries and tenure, and to the status of individuals who might occupy any one of a number of points on the scale between freemen and slaves.

Tristram Risdon, one of the earliest historians of Devon, has Sir Robert Giffard as lord of the manor of Whitchurch in the middle of the twelfth century, and he appears to have been followed by his son Gervaise, and then by his grandson Walter. The title then passed via Walter's daughter, Emma, who was said to be 'not sound of mind', to her husband Sir Robert Denham, whose lordship occupied the middle years of the thirteenth century. Over the next 200 years the manor passed through the hands of such families as Le Abbe, Trewin, Deynsell, Fortescue and Gilbert. It was quite common for a geographically large parish, as Whitchurch was, to be composed of more than one manor. Thus Walreddon was a separate manor, the lordship of which might, or might not, rest with the same family at any particular time. In the nineteenth century the Bulteels held the lordship of Whitchurch and the Courtenays the lordship of Walreddon. During that period Whitchurch Down was divided, in terms of ownership and manorial rights, between Thomas Bulteel, a banker who held the manor of Whitchurch, and his Tavistock opposite number, the Duke of Bedford.

A second source of authority within the parish was the Church. The vicar and churchwardens were empowered by statute to impose on all property owners a tax 'for repairing the Church and Church House and for other necessary occasions.' The costs of maintenance of the fabric accounted for the bulk of the expenditure, together with the expenses involved in cleaning the building, caring for the churchyard, digging the graves and providing the wine. But there were wider considerations. The 'other necessary occasions' might include any of a whole range of situations, from offering hospitality to travellers, to rewarding the culling of foxes, badgers, hedgehogs, wild cats, or similar threats. In levying rates for these purposes, all owners of property were required to contribute. In 1723 this meant a total of 74 people, of whom exactly half were resident in the parish and the other half were absentee landlords. During the nineteenth century opposition to the principle of Church Rates grew, as Nonconformists became increasingly resentful of an arrangement by which they were required to give financial support to a Church to which they did not belong. The law was changed in 1870, and thereafter the Church had to rely on voluntary contributions, and particularly on offertory collections.

The parish is the oldest unit of local administration in England. Existing in the Middle Ages with functions that were largely confined to church matters, parish government had fresh life breathed into it during the Tudor period, when its powers were widened. A whole range of law-and-order responsibilities, from drunkenness to the enforcement of the game laws, was dropped into the parochial lap. So were highways and the Poor Law. Parish officials, such as churchwardens, overseers of the poor, constables and highways supervisors, were appointed by the 'parish parliament', known as the Vestry since that is where it normally met, at its Easter AGM. Whitchurch also had a parish clerk. The last two to hold that office, before the changes brought about by the formation of the Parish Council, were John Doidge and George Finzell.

Some of these officials were paid. In 1843, for example, Thomas Spry received a salary of £12 a year as overseer of the poor, while John Frost was given £2 for the, presumably, less arduous task of collecting the national taxes on incomes and property. James Willcock was soon after appointed to a new job as 'Inspector of Nuisances', for which he received an annual payment of £3. He soon found himself busy dealing with complaints about the activities of gypsies encamped on Plaster Down. On a number of matters these officers were required to work alongside the local Justices of the Peace, who also found their workload expanded, to encompass such matters as enquiring into broken bridges, licensing alehouses, regulating apprenticeships and carrying out certain police duties.

Over the years more and more duties came the way of local government. The creaky old parochial system could cope with some of them. For some others, ad-hoc bodies had to be established. School boards and Turnpike Trusts fall into this category. It all happened in a typically English way, with a series of unconnected responses to the emergence of particular needs.

It was not until the reforms of the 1880s and '90s that the arrangements became more logical and systematic, as well as more responsive to the people. A clear pattern emerged from these reforms, with councils at three levels – county, district and parish. The birth of parish councils introduced the concept of the civil parish – a civil parish might, or might not, cover the same area as the older ecclesiastical parish with which it shared a name. Since councils were also springing up at county and district levels, civil parish authorities were left with very limited powers. The first Whitchurch Parish Council described its functions as 'to provide and maintain monuments, playing fields, footpaths, and churchyards, and to administer local charities.' In 1974 the councils of the two neighbouring parishes, Whitchurch and Sampford Spiney, came together so that, while the two parishes retained their separate identities, they shared a first-tier council known, so as not to promote one of the partners over the other, as the Plaster Down Grouped Parishes Council.

When, in 1992 and again in 2000, a beating of the bounds took place, it was purely a ceremonial occasion. The first of these ritualistic beatings was held in 1925, when a group of 30, led by the Parish Council chairman and including one participant aged 75, did the whole boundary in one day. Earlier perambulations had, on the other hand, had severely practical purposes. They had been undertaken to affirm and assert boundaries that might have been questioned or challenged. When the civil parish was born in 1894 its boundaries were the same as the ecclesiastical parish. These boundaries have, however, been the subjects of reviews and controversy at various stages.

It is difficult to discover who lit the fuse that caused the explosion in 1833 which led to a long drawn-out boundary dispute between Whitchurch and Sampford Spiney. On 14 May of that year a group of residents of the latter parish, with a point to make, described only as 'the ladies of Sampford Spiney', undertook a perambulation of their bounds. They were 'attended' by William Courtenay, lord of the manor of Walreddon, who feared that any 'encroachment' by Sampford Spiney would reduce the scale of his own jurisdiction. He protested that the line the ladies were taking, particularly in the Pew Tor/Plaster Down area, was not the correct one. On 10 September he organised his own 'beating' with the help of a number of Whitchurch parishioners. They took a different line in the disputed areas from that taken by the militant ladies of Sampford Spiney. Representatives of the latter were present and were said to have made their protest, though it is not clear what form any such demonstration might have taken. Courtenay now strengthened his case by obtaining a statement from Edward Carter to the effect that the line taken by the Whitchurch group 'exactly corresponded' with the one that had been followed at a 'beating' in 1779 that Edward recalled having participated in as a young man. Some accommodation appears to have been reached over the next year, because in July 1834 it was decided that a series of stones would be erected along an agreed line marking the boundary, these stones to be marked 'WB' on the sides facing Whitchurch and 'SB' on the sides facing Sampford Spiney.

Nine years after the supposed agreement, William Courtenay suddenly announced that he had known nothing of the erection of the stones, and that they did not correspond with any agreed line. The Sampford Spiney Vestry responded that the lines drawn by the positioning of the stones:

... are the ones handed down to them by their ancestors as the correct and proper boundaries of this parish from Whitchurch, and this vestry will not consent to any alteration whatever being made.

It was an impasse. Both sides were convinced that they had right on their side, and since both sides were confident of the outcome, they agreed to submit the issues to arbitration. A body called the Tithe Commissioners appointed one of its number, a James Jerwood, to investigate and adjudicate. His judgement, delivered in May 1845, took the form of a suggested compromise in which the disputed area would be partitioned, Great Pewtor being declared to be in Whitchurch and Little Pewtor in Sampford Spiney. This accommodation was accepted by both sides and prepared the way for a gesture in which Whitchurch ceded to her smaller neighbour a rectangular area of land on Whitchurch Common as common grazing land. This salient, surrounded by alien Whitchurch territory, together with the narrow 'corridor' through which it was reached, continues in being at the time of writing. It makes a curious and interesting feature on contemporary maps, but it hardly revolutionised the economies of either parish. It is, indeed, not easy to understand the emotions that the dispute evoked at the time. Rights of tenure and issues of common grazing were involved. So were mineral rights, real or potential. William Courtenay, in taking up cudgels for Whitchurch, was defending his own, because he could not enjoy manorial rights on land outside the parish. But the most intriguing aspect of the whole affair was the role played by the 'ladies of Sampford Spiney'. Sadly, their story lies beyond the scope of this book.

The decision to include Sortridge in Whitchurch parish was essentially administrative tidying up. In March 1885 Local Government Board Order 15033 effected the transfer. Sortridge had previously been in the anomalous position of being part of, but physically detached from the rest of, the parish of Peter Tavy.

There were much more serious repercussions a generation later, when, down the road from Sortridge, Horrabridge was given parochial status. Up until 1950 this village had been divided between three parishes, Whitchurch, Walkhampton, and Buckland Monachorum. The bridge over the Walkham, which gives the place its name, was historically the boundary point. Built into the western parapet at the centre of this ancient bridge is a boundary stone. A round-headed rectangular granite block, it fills the whole thickness of the parapet and bears a sunken cross on its face.

The establishment of the new civic parish of Horrabridge in 1950 (it had been an ecclesiastical parish since 1867) had an obvious effect on the geographical size of Whitchurch and on the size and balance of its population. The change was, however, seen as logical, sensible and fair. When it came to the other major boundary alteration of the twentieth century, none of these descriptions seemed to apply, at least not from a Whitcurch viewpoint. This was the dramatic and controversial proposal to re-draw the boundary between Whitchurch and Tavistock. In March 1884 the editor of the *Tavistock Gazette* wrote:

If the erection of dwelling houses between the picturesque little village of Whitchurch and the town of Tavistock continues to be carried on with the spirit that has marked building enterprises in that locality of late years, the town and the village may eventually be united by an almost unbroken line of habitations.

He went on to recall that:

About a decade ago the only houses between Crelake and Whitchurch village were Mr Toye's house and two cottages. Since then Mr Chilcott has built his commodious mansion, and Chollacott Villas and Ferndale Villas have emerged.

It was in the 1890s that a particular term began to be used to describe the evolving relationship between Whitchurch and Tavistock. In 1892 a petition requesting an extension of the footpath on Whitchurch Road beyond the existing limit at Crelake used the argument that 'Whitchurch is now becoming a suburb of Tavistock.' Three years later the *Tavistock Gazette*, which had made this issue a matter of editorial policy, claimed that 'Whitchurch has become a suburb of Tavistock, from where it largely draws its supplies.' The vicar, Revd Beebe, pitched in with a talk delivered in Tavistock Town Hall in 1910, in which he said:

I have many interests in your beautiful town. In fact I cannot get on without coming several times a week into your town. If I want any money I have to come to your banks. If I want any drapery, any forage for my horse, any implements for my garden, and for many other purposes, I find it absolutely necessary to be continually in touch with the good people of your town.

In a similar setting some four years later Mr Beebe developed his theme:

Our parish is now practically a suburb of Tavistock, being connected with it by an almost continuous line of houses. Before many years have passed, the two places will have become amalgamated for civic purposes, and, indeed, the first step towards this has been taken in the present year by the extension of the Tavistock water-supply into the village, which will be shortly followed by the extension of gas or introduction of electricity from Tavistock into the village.

Shortly after the vicar had delivered himself of these views someone produced a copy of his words and they were widely distributed. When they reached a wider public they contained an interesting slip. In the second sentence the word 'years' appeared with a 't' instead of a 'y'. Or was it a slip?

One of the issues that came to dominate the agenda in this developing debate was that of the drainage and sewerage arrangements. According to the *Tavistock Gazette*: 'The rise in the population of Whitchurch has been so rapid that it has outgrown the limited sanitary arrangements which prevailed when it was a mere village.'

The Tavistock Urban District Council took up the matter in 1907, when it 'considered the question of some kind of amalgamation with Whitchurch, or a portion of it, for sanitary and other purposes.' By then the prediction, first made in the 1880s, that 'the town and the village may eventually be united by an almost unbroken line of habitations', was well on the way to realisation. It was not, however, until 1928 that the UDC made a formal application to incorporate part of Whitchurch parish. The application went to Devon County Council and a public enquiry was held in Exeter, as a result of which the bid was rejected. The passing of the Local Government Act in the following year did, however, alter the context of such operations by encouraging suitable takeovers to produce larger, and supposedly more economic, units. In 1931 the County Council responded to this national initiative by launching a full-scale enquiry. Among other suggestions it wrote to its smaller district councils to ask them whether they should consider joining a neighbouring authority. The Tavistock UDC was one of these smaller units. It wanted to retain its autonomy. The way to do it, its members decided, was to revive the case for enlarging itself by swallowing part of Whitchurch. It would then be large enough, in both area and population, to fend off any challenges to its independence. In the early months of 1931 the UDC told the County Council that:

This Council is prepared to take into the Urban District of Tavistock such portions, or the whole, of the two adjoining parishes of Tavistock Hamlets and Whitchurch, as will make for the most convenient, efficient, and economical administration of local government, and be mutually advantageous to all concerned.

In November of the same year a special committee of Devon County Council held a four-hour enquiry. The two cases were presented by the clerks to the two councils directly concerned, the Tavistock Urban District Council and the Tavistock Rural District Council. Both were solicitors, the former Martyn Wivell and the latter Kenneth Johnstone. Wivell outlined two options, one of which would transfer the strictly urban portion of the parish, and the other which would be based on the main services provided by Tavistock. The first would involve the transfer of 209 acres, 139 houses and 560 people. If the second solution were favoured the respective figures would be 336 acres, 200 houses and 800 people.

The 'Tavistock case' rested on the arguments that the UDC was already supplying Whitchurch with water and gas and could provide an improved system of refuse disposal; that Whitchurch people enjoyed Tavistock facilities, such as schools and shops; that the area in question was essentially urban in character; and that no natural boundaries, such as rivers, were involved. On the last point Mr Wivell argued that 'You can't tell where Tavistock ends and Whitchurch begins.' Johnstone's defence of the status quo hinged on the claim that the Rural District Council was doing a good job for Whitchurch, that the boundary that was now threatened was an historic one, and that the proposals for change would have the effect of amputating healthy limbs from the body of a living community. It was suggested both that the existing arrangements had the support of the people of Whitchurch and that the only reason why Tavistock wished to expand was to save itself from losing its status. These issues had by now been the subject of debate for some time and positions had become entrenched. It was clear on all sides that the matter could only be resolved by a full enquiry conducted by the relevant Government department, the Ministry of Health. This opened in Exeter in June 1933. Barristers had been briefed by both sides and over the next months arguments were presented, witnesses were called, and maps and documents were pored over. Finally, in April 1934, came the report. It was a bombshell. Whitchurch had braced itself for the loss of much of the Whitchurch Road ribbon development and most of Whitchurch Down. What was not anticipated was the Ministry's decision to transfer the centre of the village itself, including church, school, parish room and inn. These changes were more radical than either Tavistock had requested or the County Council had recommended. The transfer of the 'suburban area' alone would have caused disappointment, ill-feeling and resentment, but much of that would, in all probability, have evaporated over time. But the loss of the 'heart of the village' was destined to engender deeper, and more abiding, emotions. Martyn Wivell did not help matters by launching an attack on the Rural District Council. As an example of the inefficiency of that body, as he saw it, he quoted a case of the RDC giving approval for the construction of a bungalow which the County Council immediately ordered to be demolished. 'Whitchurch' said Wivell, 'should be very happy at having got away.' He went on:

> *The fact is that Whitchurch was sadly neglected, and now that Tavistock has come to the rescue the transferred areas will pay less and receive more, having finished with rural ideas and become urbanised.*

In other words, the villagers ought to be grateful that they had been saved from the clutches of a silly authority and delivered into the arms of a sensible one. It is unnecessary to add that things were seen rather differently from Whitchurch, and that such words only served to add a layer of bitterness to an atmosphere already characterised by suspicion.

There persisted in Whitchurch, after these changes had been implemented in 1935, a strong feeling of resentment. Goliath had won, but at the cost, it was felt, of ignoring the wishes of the people and of tearing apart a viable community. Some people pointed to the absurdity of all the main symbols and institutions of the community – church, school, inn, parish room, Post Office – now all lying in another parish. It had produced, at the very least, an anomalous position. For some, the matter was even more serious. Over the years efforts were made to reopen the boundary question (although the Boundary Commission's confirmation of the changes was not challenged).

The best organised and most determined of these efforts came in the 1970s, spearheaded by William Dallmeyer, the chairman of the Parish Council. Petitioning, canvassing and the holding of a public meeting all suggested strong support for the campaign, which concentrated very much on the theme of the need to recover 'the heart of Whitchurch'. Meanwhile, the Tavistock Council assembled a formidable case. The argument for a change in the boundary to restore to Whitchurch much of what had been lost in 1935 was dismissed as 'feeling whipped up in certain quarters and based on nostalgia for the past rather than on the real situation that has existed over the last fifty years.' The roles had become reversed and it was now the voice of Tavistock that was arguing for the status quo. Their submission to the Boundary Commission ended with the words of Lord Falkland in 1641: 'When it is not necessary to change it is necessary not to change.' The 'heart of the village' campaign received some support from the infant West Devon District Council, which decided that 'Whitchurch is an identifiable community separate from Tavistock, and the majority of residents appear to favour its return to Whitchurch Parish.' The West Devon Council solution was therefore 'the return of some of the area of land transferred in 1935 back to the parish of Whitchurch, but with a more appropriate boundary.' The Boundary Commissioners were unimpressed. They found the Tavistock Town Council case a strong one and preferred the Town Council and Lord Falkland to the West Devon Council and Captain Dallmeyer.

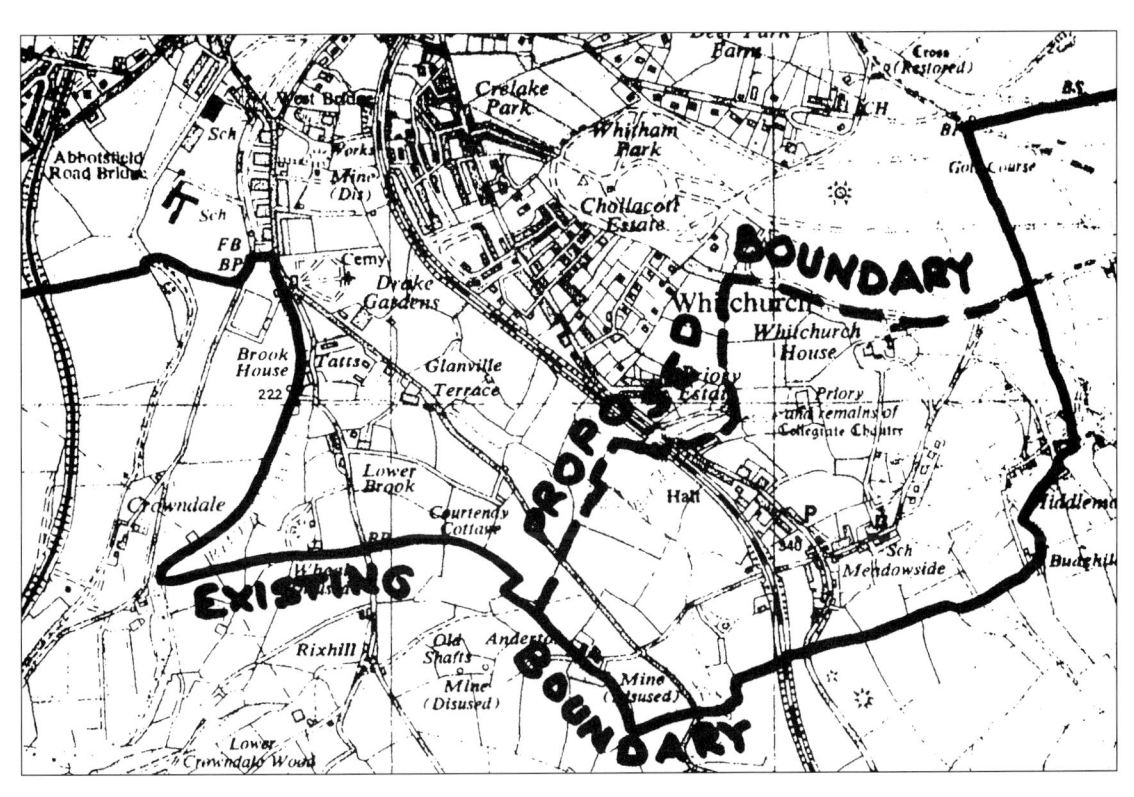

Left: *Map showing 1935 settlement (existing boundary) and the 1978 proposal that was rejected by the Boundary Commission.*

Above: *YMCA camp on Whitchurch Down, 1909.*

Left: *The Boys' Brigade, founded in 1883, was the pioneer of the uniformed church-affiliated youth organisations. A local branch had been formed in 1905, in which year it organised this camp on Whitchurch Down.*

In 1909 permission was given for a Territorial Army Camp to be held on Whitchurch Down. The Commoners' Association insisted on a set of strict conditions, and the Army was faced with a bill for £3 for a two-week camp, together with costs of 12 shillings for the supervision of the commoners' cattle and five shillings for tidying up afterwards.

Chapter 12

CONFRONTING

We know nothing of the possible involvement of Whitchurch men in wars before the twentieth century. Nor does any evidence exist to suggest that the civilian population at home was much affected by such conflicts. Given the importance that both sides in the Civil War attached to both Tavistock and Plymouth, it must be assumed that during that war troops passed through the village at regular intervals. Whether the local people were able to distinguish between the Royalist and Parliamentary armies was another matter, and we shall never know against which it was more necessary to lock up your daughters. Subsequent wars, against the Dutch in the seventeenth century and the French in the eighteenth, produced occasional fears of invasion, when parishes along the prospective 'invasion coast' were put on alert and required to take emergency measures. Whitchurch, in the middle of the French Revolutionary and Napoleonic Wars, in 1799, was, like other parishes in the area, told to appoint two officials for special duties. The instruction was that:

They be young men, quick-sighted, bold riders, and from their occupations or amusements accustomed to know the parish roads and country adjacent. That they be mounted on hardy horses habituated to the roads and stoney lanes. That each person be provided with a light fowling piece, a few bullets, and a powder horn, a hatchet or bill-hook, and a pointed case-knife. That he have also a blanket with eyelet holes at each corner which being staked out may serve if necessary in a wood or under a hedge for a tent. That he bring with him in the place of rendezvous three days' provisions and corn for his horses.

The 'rendezvous' point was Roborough Down. The chosen pair would each receive five shillings a day to cover the expenses of himself and his horse. The parish was responsible for providing the essential equipment.

In the nineteenth century there must have been a steady flow of recruits from the parish to the Army, and, given the Drake connection and the nearness of Devonport, to the Navy also. Others joined the Tavistock detachment of the Volunteers, the organisation of part-time soldiers charged with supporting the regular forces by providing a last line of home defence. The Volunteers were a product of the Napoleonic Wars. Disbanded in 1815, they were revived in 1859 to combat the supposed threat from another Napoleon. Their role was to be taken over in 1908 by the Territorial Army. The people of Whitchurch would probably be well aware of these voluntary organisations, because, between the 1880s and the 1920s, they tended to use Whitchurch Down as the venue for their occasional camps. A typical camp would last a fortnight and involve up to 2,000 men.

News of the outbreak of the First World War in August 1914 was greeted in Whitchurch, as in thousands of parishes all over the country, with a mixture of emotions. There was an outbreak of patriotic fervour, a firm belief in the justice of the cause, and a conviction that, like other recent European wars, it would have a quick and decisive outcome. Within a month 17 parishioners had volunteered for service in the Navy and 27 in the Army. A number of retired officers who had settled in the parish were recalled to duty. The vicar found himself without a churchwarden when both Major Hext and Colonel Coleridge returned to the colours, and no sooner had a replacement been found in Colonel Bittlestone than he was similarly recalled. By Easter 1915 the number of parishioners in arms had increased to 80. By the end of 1916 the introduction of conscription meant that the number of men in one or other of the services was 130, and the final total was 149. They included ten men who had been in the local Territorial Force before the war, who enlisted immediately and were posted to India. They were Corporals F. Bray and S. Hunt, Wheeler Corporals R.P. Sleeman and C.S. Sleeman, Gunners J. Copp, A. Toop and H. Westcott, Drivers P. Chapple and J. Friend, and QMS G.E. Donaldson. Four of them were to see action in other theatres – R.P. Sleeman (who was to return home as a Staff Sergeant), Gunner Copp, Driver Chapple and Driver Friend going on to serve in, respectively, Afghanistan, Palestine, Mesopotamia (Iraq) and France. Gunner Westcott died in India.

The ladies of the parish set up a working party which, over the period of four years that the war lasted, produced 49,000 articles which were distributed via the Plymouth War Hospital Supply Depot. Included were dressings, items of clothing, food parcels, bedlinen, sphagnum moss, blankets,

Above: *Former Territorials march through Whitchurch in 1914, on their way to the war.*

Left: *The war memorial in 2003.*

Below: *The scene at the unveiling of the war memorial on 23 May 1920.*

sandbags and bandages. The chief organisers in this effort were Lady Walker and Mrs Beebe, the wives of, respectively, General Walker and the vicar. They also ran a series of fund-raising events, which overall realised £800 for various aspects of the war effort. A War Savings Certificates Association was formed, the secretary of which was Mr G.S. Newton of Chollacott Park. A subscription list was prepared to provide support for a family of Belgian refugees, named Maes-Corluy, who were offered accommodation at 'Cheverel', a house belonging to Mr Walter Webb. Hospitality also was arranged for the large number of servicemen who were stationed in the area. Marines were billeted in the village at an early stage of the war and were quickly followed by 100 members of the Royal Naval Air Service.

The most decorated of Whitchurch's war heroes was Major-General Sir H.B. Walker KCB, KCMG, DSO, CB, KCB, KCMG, Croix de Guerre, Order of Savoy, Croce de Guerra. He commanded an Australian Division at Gallipoli, where he was twice wounded, and then led troops on the Western Front at Ypres and the Somme. The end of the war found him in Italy, in command of the 48th Division, the first division to set foot on enemy soil. Captain J.F.P. Nash, a veteran of the Boer War, was awarded the DSO for a number of deeds of heroism, notably at Festubert in May 1915, where 'he repaired the telephone wires personally under very heavy fire.' Corporal F.E. Veale of the Royal Fusiliers received the MM 'for bravery in action', and Corporal G. Jeffery of the Duke of Cornwall's Light Infantry was similarly honoured. Major E.L. Hughes, the son of Dr Hughes of Downhouse, was severely wounded on the Marne, at one of the first battles of the war. He was awarded the DSO and returned to the Front. Sergeant Burchmore was invalided out after suffering disabling wounds. The holder of the British DCM, the French Croix de Guerre, and the Russian Order of St George, he spent the last part of the war working as Revd Beebe's chauffeur.

Hostilities ended in November 1918 in an atmosphere of almost numbed relief. There followed a period of cost-counting and waiting for the boys to come home. Celebrations followed the signing of the Peace Treaty in the following summer. On 6 July 1919 Whitchurch participated in the national day of general thanksgiving. The flag of St George flew from the church tower and the porch and entrance gate were both festooned with flags. A special service began with the National Anthems of the Allies and ended with the Hallelujah Chorus. A triumphal arch had been constructed at the crossroads, and there were flags and bunting everywhere. The bells rang, the children gave displays and sports were held in Great Coulson Meadow, lent for the occasion by Henry Blake. (This particular site, behind the school, was to be the venue for a number of festive occasions over the course of the following century.) In the evening there was a tea, more sports, and then, to round off the day, a concert and dance in the Parish Room. To pay for the day 250 subscribers had contributed £78. Since only £57 was spent on the day's festivities, it was decided that the balance of £21 should be held over 'until all our men return from India and other fronts.'

Commemoration was to take a number of forms. In September 1920 a three-panelled oaken tablet was unveiled in the Parish Room. It listed, in six columns, the 138 names of parishioners 'who had served overseas'. The vicar and the school board were keen to ensure that due attention was paid to the need to remind the new generation of parishioners of the sacrifice that had been made. In May 1921, for example:

Revd Beebe unveiled a picture in the school depicting a Memorial in France to the 2nd Battalion Devonshire Regiment. The children were marched to the playground and sang a few patriotic songs, and the ceremony concluded with the saluting of the flag.

Interestingly, the annual observance of Armistice Day with the two-minute silence is an event which generations of children will still recall from their school experience.

The centrepiece of the parish's programme of remembrance was to be a war memorial. On 25 November 1918, within two weeks of the armistice, a meeting of churchwardens and sidesmen decided that 'a brass memorial tablet recording the names of the fallen be placed in the church.' Subscriptions were invited. A meeting of subscribers subsequently resolved that there should also be a granite cross in the churchyard bearing the names of the fallen. The decision was confirmed in May 1919, when a site was selected close to the roadside and the local mason, J.S. Rogers, was commissioned to do the work. The monument was unveiled on 23 May 1920. It was Whit Sunday and a brilliantly fine day. At noon a procession left the church by the west door, led by the choir and church officers. A short service was conducted jointly by the vicar and Revd Luxton, a United Methodist local preacher. The unveiling was then performed by Colonel George Bittleston of Ashleigh, churchwarden and war veteran. Wreaths were laid.

Right: *The grave, in the churchyard, of Driver R.G. Donaldson, who died aged 16.*

THERE ARE 20 NAMES LISTED ON THE MEMORIAL AS FIRST WORLD WAR CASUALTIES, ARRANGED BY RANK. IN THE ORDER IN WHICH THEY DIED, THEY ARE:

<u>15 September 1914: Cecil Howard Ker.</u>
The only son of Mr and Mrs George Ker of Moorland House, he was a captain in the 1st Battalion, Bedfordshire Regiment. Killed in one of the earliest battles of the war, the Battle of the Aisne, he is buried in the Vendresse British Cemetery in France. He left a young widow and an infant son.

<u>4 November 1914: Robert Peyton Hughes.</u>
At the beginning of November 1914 a joint British-Indian force launched an attack against the German colony in East Africa, later to form part of Tanzania. There was stern fighting for the port of Tanga. British and Indian losses were heavy. One 26-year-old officer who died was Robert Peyton Hughes, a lieutenant in the 101st, Indian Grenadiers. He lies buried in the Tanga Memorial Cemetery. His parents were Robert and Laetitia Hughes of Downhouse.

<u>20 August 1915: Reginald George Donaldson.</u>
At 16, Reggie Donaldson was the youngest of the casualties listed on the memorial. He had been a Driver in the Royal Field Artillery, responsible for carrying ammunition supplies. His parents, George and Eliza, had been living in Whitchurch at the time of his birth, but had since moved to St Austell.

<u>8 March 1916: Reginald Wilson Fox.</u>
Colonel Fox had lived at Grimstone for some years before he was recalled to duty in 1914 in the 6th Battalion, Devonshire Regiment. He was 49 years old when he died in operations in Mesopotamia (present-day Iraq) against the Turkish forces. His name is one of 40,000 recorded on the Basra Memorial.

<u>23 April 1916: John Foster Paton Nash.</u>
Captain in the 5th Battalion, Canadian Infantry, John Nash was a veteran of the Boer War. His wife, Eleanor, lived at 2 Church Park. Recalled for service in 1914, he served on the Western Front and died at Ypres, where he is buried in the Railway Dugouts Burial Ground. He was 50 years old.

<u>4 August 1916: Percy Beauchamp Astley-Cooper.</u>
The Thiepval Memorial to the Missing of the Somme, designed by Sir Edwin Lutyens, contains more than 72,000 names. One of them is Private Astley-Cooper of the East Kent Regiment. The son of Loftus and Florence, who finally settled in Bath, he died at the age of 40.

<u>11 August 1916: Charles Richard Philp.</u>
The Bouzincourt Communal Cemetery Extension holds the graves of some 600 First World War casualties who died in action around the nearby town of Albert in Northern France. Charles Philp is buried here. To the army he was Private Philp of the Army Service Corps. To the folks back home he was 'Char', son of Mary and John Philp of 1 Church Park Cottages, Whitchurch, and brother of Jack, Susy, Emm, and Will. He died a few days short of his 33rd birthday.

<u>18 February 1917: George Henry Rooke.</u>
Lance Corporal Rooke of the 8th Battalion, Prince of Wales Volunteers, died, possibly as a result of 'friendly fire' in an engagement at Ploegsteert, in Flanders, and is buried nearby. His family had lived at Merrivale for some years, his parents, John and Ada, having assumed an unofficial position of some authority in that small community. George enlisted at 18, and was 19 when he died.

<u>10 April 1917: Vere Raymond Bennett.</u>
Lieutenant Bennett of the 3rd Battalion, Sherwood Foresters, on attachment to the Machine Gun Corps, died at Arras in Northern France and is buried in the Cojeul British Cemetery near that town. He was the younger son of Henry Bennett of 1 Broad Park Villas and was 33 years old when he died.

<u>25 April 1917: James Trethewey.</u>
Killed in the fighting around Arras, Private Trethewey lies buried in the Duisans British Cemetery. His mother, Jessie, lived at Glendower in Whitchurch. He himself was a talented violinist who had spent some years in Canada. A private in the Army Service Corps, he drove an ambulance. He died at 37.

<u>May 1917: R.J. Ash.</u>
Private Ash of the Australian Infantry was killed in action at Vimy Ridge in May 1917.

CONFRONTING

16 August 1917: George Edward Mudge.
George Mudge was the son of Charles and Emma, who farmed Higher Collaton. A private in the 1st Battalion, Oxford and Bucks Light Infantry, he died in the Battle of Paschendaele, has no known grave, and is commemorated, along with 35,000 others, on the Tyne Cot Memorial.

14 October 1917: Hamilton Shirley Vincent.
Private Vincent was serving with the 2nd Regiment, South African Infantry, when he died at the age of 18, another victim of the killing fields of Paschendaele. With no known grave, his commemoration is on the Menin Gate Memorial at Ypres. He was the only son of Captain John Vincent and his wife Beatrice, who had been Whitchurch residents for some time, but who had moved to Plymouth by the time of their son's death.

24 November 1917: John Reginald Gilbert.
John and Maud Gilbert lived at Rose Cottage, Whitchurch, John earning a living as a builder. Their son, John Reginald, signed up when the war began in the 5th Battalion of the Devonshires. He died three years later at the age of 20, in Palestine, and was buried in the Jerusalem War Cemetery. His Whitchurch vicar was to recall his membership of the Sunday school and of the Band of Hope, but, most of all 'his bright, happy face'.

3 December 1917: Samuel John Creber.
The 16th Battalion of the Devonshires, to which Samuel belonged, was the Yeomanry battalion of the county regiment. Samuel died in the Palestine Campaign at the age of 26, and, having no known grave, is commemorated on the Jerusalem Memorial. The Commonwealth War Graves Commission describes him as 'son of C.W.R. and Mary Maria Creber, of Weastrim Cottage, Whitchurch.

23 April 1918: Alexander Allen Cordner.
Major Cordner, of the Royal Marines, was 38 when he died. He left a widow and a young daughter. Their home was 2 Fern Lea, Middlemoor. He lost his life in the daring raid on Zeebrugge, conducted on St George's Day 1918. His body was brought back home for burial in Whitchurch churchyard.

11 May 1918: Sidney Claude Friend.
The Friend family lived in the variously spelt Paisy or Paisley Cottages on Church Hill. William had been at the Front for nine months when he died, at the age of 20. It had been an eventful time, in which he had been wounded and then captured. His escape was followed by a period of exposure and other privations that took their toll on his health. Hospitalised at Rouen, he died there and was buried in the city's St Sever Cemetery.

31 October 1918: Eric William Compton-Lundie.
Stow and Maria Compton-Lundie had lived at 3 Fernhill Villas for some years before the war. Their son, Eric, became a soldier and served in the Boer War. He appears to have settled in South Africa and joined the 2nd Regiment, South African Infantry, in 1914. He died of wounds in the No. 2 Canadian General Hospital, and was buried in the military cemetery at Le Treport. His death, at the age of 35, occurred within days of the armistice.

8 November 1918: Harry Westcott.
There have been Westcotts at Rixhill for a long time. At the beginning of the twentieth century Henry and Florence lived there, bringing up their son Harry. The young man was to spend the war years in India and to die in a hospital at Bangalore three days before the signing of the armistice. He was 24.

12 November 1918: William Westaway Daw.
Hostilities ended on 11 November 1918. On the following day William Daw died in France, to be buried in the British Cemetery at Wimille. Thirty-five years old when he died, he was a Second Lieutenant in the 171st Tunnelling Company, Royal Engineers. His parents, John and Fanny, lived for some years at Walreddon Manor before moving, at the end of the war, to Torquay.

Three other men with very strong Whitchurch connections were among the fallen of the First World War, although their names appear on the Tavistock, rather than the Whitchurch, memorial. Henry Pengelly was born at Moorshop in 1893 and later moved with his family to Taviton. He died on the Somme in February 1917 and was buried at the Plantation Cemetery. Frederick Perkin was one of a family of 13, brought up in Whitchurch after a Sampford Spiney birth. He was 29 when he died in August 1917, yet another victim of Paschendaele. He is buried in the Brandhoek Military Cemetery near Ypres. Able Seaman William Holman was 30 when he went down with his ship, HMS Tornado, when it was mined off the Dutch coast. He was born in Plymouth, but his mother hailed from Rixhill. Both his parents appear to have died during his long years at sea, and the Tavistock Gazette obituary, in December 1917, described him as 'the only grandson of Mrs Hill and the late John Hill of Rixhill'.

The Second World War broke out on 3 September 1939. By then most people in Whitchurch, as elsewhere, had increasingly become resigned to the inevitability of conflict with Germany, and a range of precautionary measures had been taken. These plans were obviously speeded up and intensified once war had been declared. Some extracts from the Whitchurch School log-book will give an indication of how one village institution prepared for, and then confronted, the crisis:

11 October 1938: Children taken to the Parish Room to be fitted for their gas masks.
8 May 1939: The Chairman of the Managers paid a visit to discuss the recent Air Raid Precautions (ARP) suggestions.
7 September 1939: Special Meeting of Managers ref site for trenches.
8 September 1939: Examination of the fitting of the children's gas masks.
14 September 1939: Fire and gas mask drill.
20 September 1939: Discussion on the adaptability of the shed as an Air Raid Shelter.
27 June 1940: During Drill lesson, children were taken to the ARP site in the adjoining field.
4 July 1940: Air Raid Warning. Children taken to cover. [The shelter was normally in a copse in Coulson Meadow.]
17 July 1940: Windows treated with splinter-proof composition.
3 September 1940: Sandbags supplied.
25 September 1940: Presence of hostile aircraft – children taken to ARP site.
10 October 1940: Several evacuees admitted.
16 June 1941: School Savings Group subscribed £28 to War Weapons Savings Week.
19 March 1942: During the night the Military utilised the school premises.
26 November 1942: American Thanksgiving Day: Special History lesson and BBC broadcast.
3 February 1943: Wellington boots received, the gift of the American Red Cross Society via the WVS.
22 June 1943: The school's target of £30 for a Tommy Gun has been passed this morning.
22 December 1943: All the children attended a Christmas Party given by the American Military Police.

Air-raid precautions in the parish included the identification of 'Report Houses'. These were homes with telephones, whose occupants were required to communicate to a central point 'reports of bombs or other matters of interest from small, isolated communities.' The village was designated one of four Voluntary First Aid Points in the area. It had its quota of wardens, who would warn of raids, or order the donning of gas masks, by using their hand-rattles or hand-bells. Stirrup-pumps and sand dumps were provided to deal with fires. The Pimple was occupied by members of the Royal Observer Corps, who manned a lookout post on it. Around it, the Down, considered to be a potential landing site for enemy paratroops, was patrolled by the Home Guard. Near the entrance to Holwell House a concrete base was constructed, it is thought for a barrage balloon. Kathleen Evans (née Giles) was an eight-year-old child living in a Holwell Cottage at Middlemoor when war broke out. She recalls:

During the war the army camp spread from Down Road to our cottages. We had to walk right through it and often collected letters to post on our way to school in Tavistock. The flat, gorse-free area in front of our cottages was used as a parade-ground and for bayonet practice. The mess huts etc were long, rectangular buildings, mostly on the Tavistock side of the Whitchurch to Caseytown road. Hundreds of bell-tents covered the rest of the Down. The camp vanished overnight a few days before D-Day.

Whitchurch Home Guard, under the command of Captain Marrison.

CONFRONTING

THE WAR MEMORIAL CONTAINS THE NAMES OF TEN PARISHIONERS WHO WERE AMONG THE FALLEN OF THE SECOND WORLD WAR. THEY ARE, IN CHRONOLOGICAL ORDER OF THEIR DEATHS:

<u>17 December 1940: James Edward Halsey Coleridge.</u>
The son of Colonel Hugh and Mrs Kathleen Coleridge of Langstone, Moortown, Lieutenant Coleridge was 24 when he was lost with his ship, HMS Acheron, in December 1940. He is commemorated on the Portsmouth Naval Memorial. In his memory, his family presented the altar rails in St Andrew's Church.

<u>19 December 1941: William Edwin Geoffrey Waycott.</u>
Commemorated on the Plymouth Naval Memorial, Lieutenant Waycott died aboard his ship, HMS Stanley, at the age of 23. His parents, Cyril and Edith Waycott, lived at No. 4 Fernhill.

<u>3 July 1943: Keith Alan Thurston.</u>
Private Thurston of the 6th Battalion, Dorsetshire Regiment, was 20 years old when he died. He was the only son of Christopher and Blanche Thurston, and is buried in Whitchurch churchyard.

<u>27 November 1943: Herbert Dashper.</u>
Craftsman Dashper of the Royal Electrical and Mechanical Engineers died at the age of 23. He lies buried in the Kanchanaburi War Cemetery, which holds the graves of prisoners of war who worked on the construction of the notorious Burma–Siam Railway. He left a widow, Doris, who lived at Middlemoor.

<u>11 April 1944: William Hugh Waycott.</u>
Flight Lieutenant Waycott of 550 Squadron, Royal Air Force Volunteer Reserve, a holder of the Distinguished Flying Medal, is buried in Achiet-le-Petit Cemetery in Northern France. At 22 years old when he died, he was a cousin of Naval Lieutenant William Waycott, who died in December 1941.

<u>11 August 1944: Ronald Clifford Sanders.</u>
Plymouth Naval Memorial carries the names of almost 16,000 who were lost in the Second World War. One of them is Leading Stoker Sanders, who died at the age of 27 aboard HMS Albatross. He was the son of William and Florence Sanders. The family lived in Gem Cottage for some time after the war.

<u>22 October 1944: Maurice John Eustace Keast.</u>
Canteen Assistant Keast, Royal Navy, died in a road accident while on leave, and is buried in Tavistock Cemetery.

<u>6 December 1944: Leonard Barrington Curgenven.</u>
Lerwick New Cemetery on Shetland is the final resting place of Lieutenant Curgenven. His ship had been HMS Eclipse. The son of Engineer Captain and Mrs Curgenven, he left a widow, who lived at Bournemouth.

<u>3 May 1945: John Bone.</u>
The Bones lived in Whitchurch and moved to Lamerton after the war. John served as a Flight Lieutenant in No. 3 Squadron, Royal Air Force Volunteer Reserve. He died five days before VE Day, in a flight over Kiel, and is buried in the war cemetery there. He was 22 years old.

<u>18 March 1946: Anthony Bone.</u>
The younger of the Bone brothers, Sergeant Anthony Bone was 20 when he died. He was an Air Gunner. He is buried at Whitchurch.

The graves of Keith Thurston and Anthony Bone.

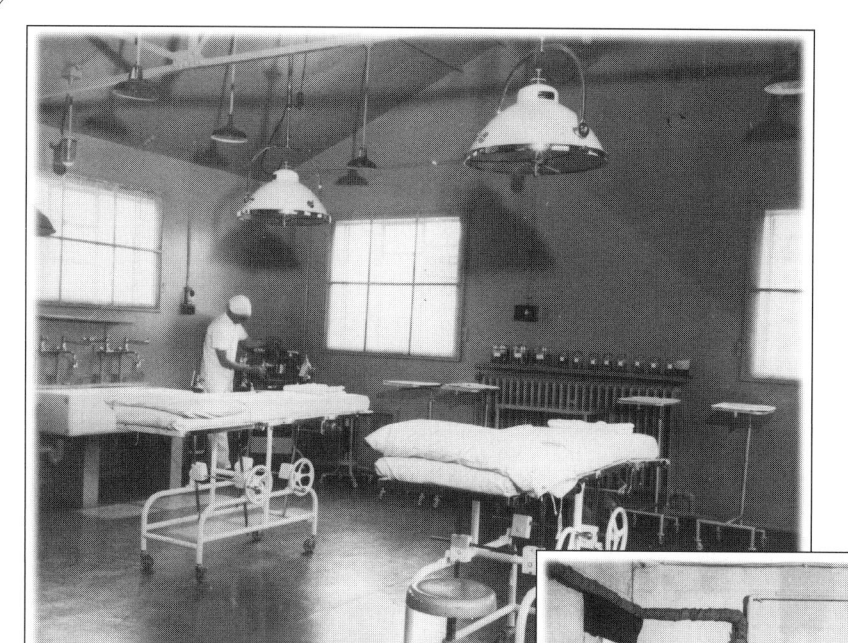

The 115th Field Hospital Unit, US Army, at Plaster Down, 1943–45

Left: *Operating theatre.*
Below: *Physiotherapy.*
Below left: *Patients' mess.*
Bottom: *Headquarters.*

CONFRONTING

Left: *Dental clinic.*
Below left: *Chapel.*
Below: *Nurses' Day Room.*
Bottom: *Laboratory Staff Christmas Dinner, 1944.*

For the benefit of the large number of troops stationed and billeted in the area, social events were organised at such venues as the Parish Room and Whitchurch House. The Sunday school room at the chapel was pressed into service as a canteen, operated by local people and with a piano player to go alongside the gallons of sweet tea.

From 1940 onwards evacuees arrived in steady numbers. They came in two varieties. Those here 'officially' were children, who, with or without their families, had been moved down through the official channels, particularly from London and the Home Counties, to find refuge with local families. The 'unofficial evacuees' came from Plymouth in spontaneous, unplanned flight from a city that seemed to be disintegrating around them under the weight of enemy bombs.

Whitchurch was hardly a prime target for enemy bombers. Such raids as occurred, like the dropping of eight bombs on Pew Tor, which killed some ponies, were the result of either navigational misjudgements or an eagerness, for some reason, to shed a load prematurely. There were, not surprisingly, a number of aircraft accidents in the area. An RAF Bomber, returning from a mission, came in on one moonlit night over Nutley Farm, lost height, took the tops off trees and hedges, and crash-landed near Little Down Plantation. Crashing into a mew of unthrashed corn, it scattered the corn over a wide area. The Polish crew escaped serious injury. While the aircraft was being salvaged the RAF commandeered the Moorshop chapel as a billet for their staff. The crew of Liberator FK242, that crashed near Fullamore Farmhouse in October 1942, were not so lucky.

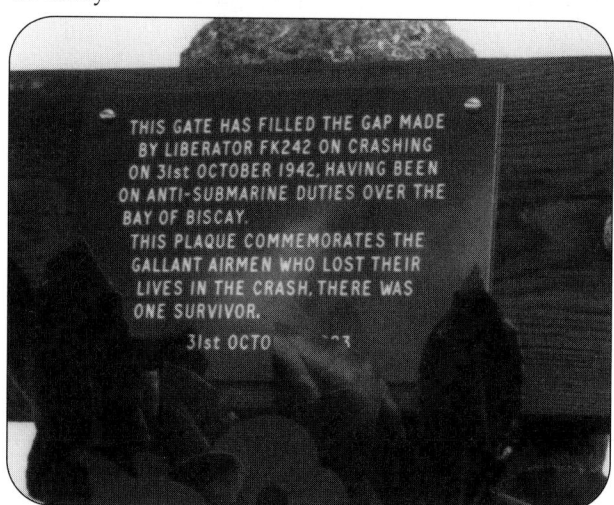

Sign on a gatepost on Fullamore Farm.

The build-up of the presence of American forces became very obvious in the last part of 1943 and the first part of 1944. On Whitchurch Down, where Caseytown Cross represented a dividing line

Right: *Three GIs chat with young Jim Cooke and his mother near the Waterways Garage that the Americans used to refuel their vehicles.*

between whites and blacks in a segregated army, a supply camp was maintained. The parking areas constructed alongside for their lorries have survived, and are still sometimes referred to as 'The American Car Parks'.

In July 1943 the US Army moved its 115th Field Hospital across the Atlantic and into accommodation that had been prepared for it by British contractors at Plaster Down. The 750-bed complex initially served as a hospital for American servicemen in the general area. By D-Day, 6 June 1944, the capacity had doubled. Between then and the spring of 1945 the resources of the enterprise were fully stretched, as regular train-loads of casualties arrived from European battlefields. It was said, for example, that 279 patients arrived at Tavistock Station on Christmas Day 1944 (514 having arrived over the previous 11 days) and that:

They arrived at the railhead on a cold night after a rare heavy snowstorm. Local householders helped the hospital ambulances to gain traction in the snow and ice leading up from the town to Plasterdown by applying the cinders and slag from their own fireplaces to the roadway.

In the last months of the war the number of receptions at Plaster Down declined as field hospitals were opened up in mainland Europe. On 22 April 1945, 22 months after its opening, this extraordinary triumph of American will and ingenuity became redundant. At the end of the war the camp buildings were put to various temporary uses, including the housing of Polish refugees and German prisoners of war. Thereafter they were used temporarily by various Army and Territorial units including the WRAC, who received a visit from the Princess Royal in July 1962. The military finally abandoned the premises in the early 1970s, and Plaster Down's last duty was to serve as a transit camp for Asian refugees thrown out of Uganda in 1973. Subsequent attempts to assign a function to the 230-acre site, including temporary housing for the homeless and a school, did not go beyond the drawing-board. In 1974 there was a sale of the remaining contents and in 1976 the buildings were demolished and the area reverted to natural moorland. Few traces now remain of an establish-

CONFRONTING

Top: *Plaster Down Camp.*

Above: *The sale at Plaster Down Camp in 1974.*

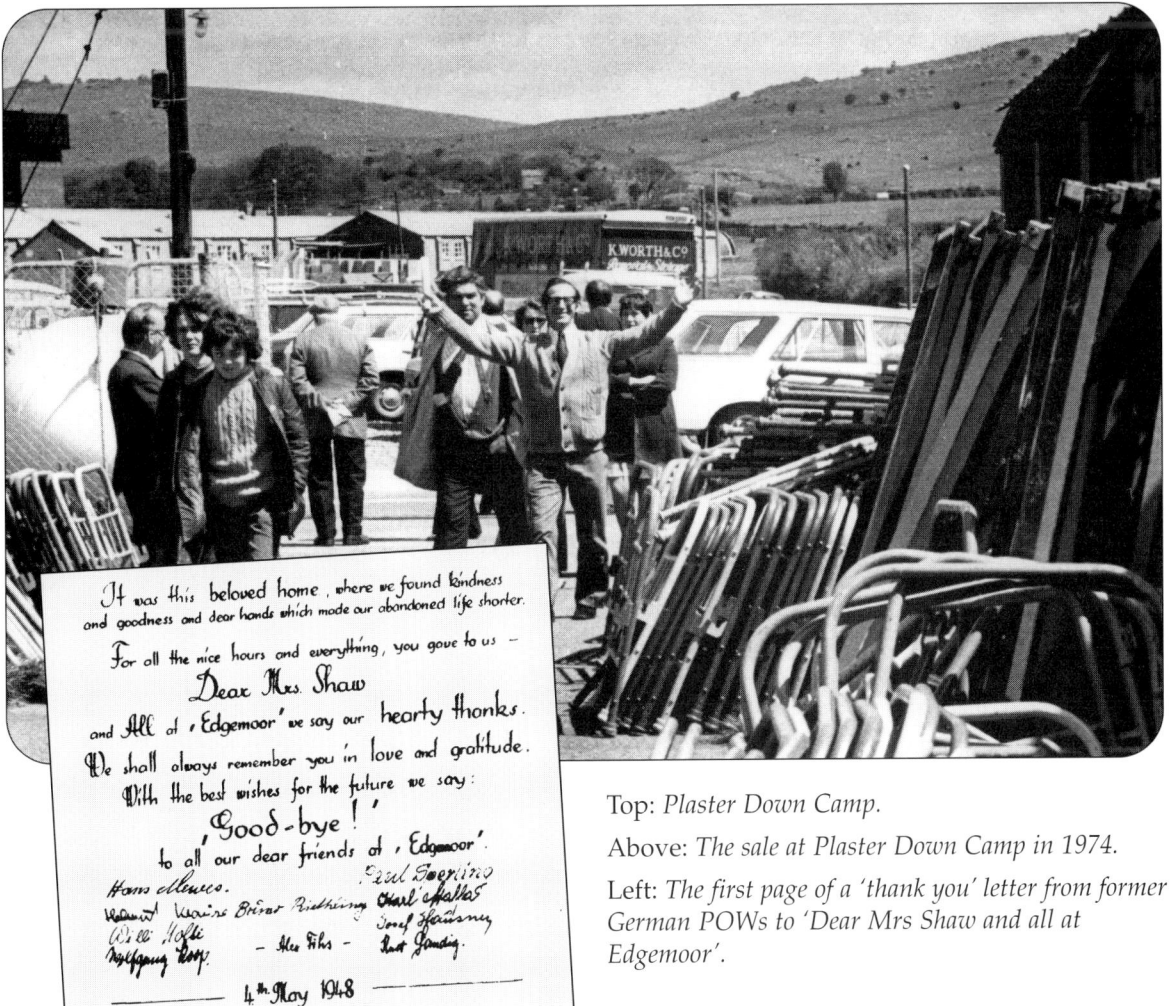

Left: *The first page of a 'thank you' letter from former German POWs to 'Dear Mrs Shaw and all at Edgemoor'.*

ment about which a former soldier, who had spent two years there, wrote: 'Hardened soldiers used to cringe at the thought of spending a winter there. Unless you've been there at night in midwinter you can't understand what cold is.'

One of the immediate postwar functions of the Plaster Down Camp was to house German prisoners of war. Prior to their release, some of these prisoners became involved in the local community in one way or another, and were employed, for example, in getting in the first two or three postwar harvests. Some of them formed lasting relationships with local families. One group benefited from the hospitality offered by the Shaw family, who lived at 'Edgemoor' in Middlemoor. In 1948, after their final release and return home, this group sent to Mrs Shaw a two-page 'thank you' letter, one page of which contained a contemporary photograph of 'Edgemoor'.

139

Above: AD2000 – *beating the bounds.*
Left: AD2000 – *planting the millennium oak.*
Below: *Awaiting the eclipse, 11 August 1999.*

Chapter 13

CELEBRATING

Douglas Jerrold, the nineteenth-century author, once wrote that: 'If an earthquake were to engulf England tomorrow, the English would manage to meet and dine somewhere among the rubbish, just to celebrate the event.' There have certainly been some interesting situations that have given rise to local celebrations in communities like Whitchurch. It was the cholera outbreak, or rather the feeling of relief that it may have passed, that produced a carnival atmosphere in the village in 1833. The epidemic had raged through the area. Attempts to check it by trying to restrict movement across parish boundaries had failed. Families left their Plymouth homes and, in a strange rehearsal of what was to happen in 1941, encamped on the edge of the moor in parishes like Whitchurch and Meavy. They felt that they were fleeing the scourge; the moorland folk believed that they were spreading it. The explosion of relief when it appeared that the plague had abated was rather premature; it re-appeared with full intensity in 1848 and again in 1866.

Other events of local importance have been marked by the holding of a special service, the ringing of bells, the planting of a tree, or a special ceremony of some kind. Such occasions might have been the result of locally engendered occasions or achievements, such as the realisation of a Parish Room or of a new school. Equally, they could have been responses to national events.

The ending of the two world wars brought, in both cases, well-organised displays of joy and relief. In 1919 there were bells, mugs, tea and sports. Such rejoicings had both a national and a local dimension. On the one hand the parish was participating in a countrywide celebration of a victory to which all parts of the kingdom had contributed. At the same

Left: *VE Day at Chollacott Close. Mary Jaggs is in the foreground.* Mothers, standing, include: *Mrs Stephens, Mrs Scantlebury, Mrs Jaggs and Mrs Smith.*

Left: *A mid-twentieth-century Whitchurch wedding. Vicky Shaw and Geoff Fox emerge from St Andrew's Church. The date is 29 December 1962, the day the 'Great Snow' began. The Shaws were a well-known family who lived at 'Edgemoor' in Middlemoor.*

Below: *An early-twentieth-century Whitchurch wedding. The couple, Florrie Lovell and Jack Bickell, are seated, flanked by the surviving parents and Harold Lovell, brother of the bride, who gave her away. The family members who also appear include Florrie's three sisters, two of them with their husbands. The Lovells of Home Farm were one of the best-known dynasties in Whitchurch in the first half of the twentieth century.*

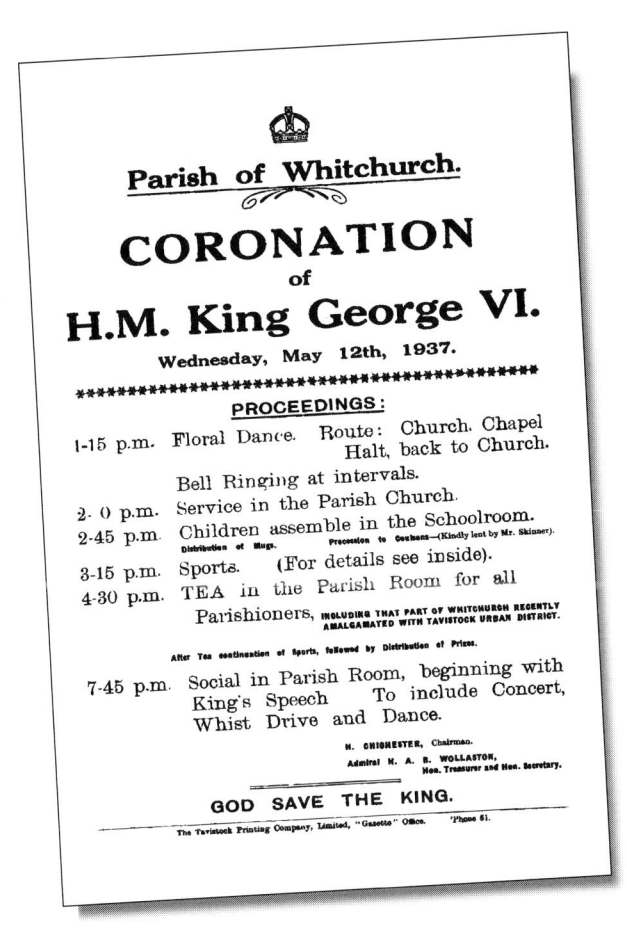

> **Parish of Whitchurch.**
>
> **CORONATION**
> of
> **H.M. King George VI.**
> Wednesday, May 12th, 1937.
>
> PROCEEDINGS:
>
> 1-15 p.m. Floral Dance. Route: Church, Chapel Halt, back to Church.
> Bell Ringing at intervals.
> 2-0 p.m. Service in the Parish Church.
> 2-45 p.m. Children assemble in the Schoolroom. Distribution of Mugs. Procession to Coxhams—(Kindly lent by Mr. Skinner).
> 3-15 p.m. Sports. (For details see inside).
> 4-30 p.m. TEA in the Parish Room for all Parishioners, INCLUDING THAT PART OF WHITCHURCH RECENTLY AMALGAMATED WITH TAVISTOCK URBAN DISTRICT.
>
> After Tea continuation of Sports, followed by Distribution of Prizes.
>
> 7-45 p.m. Social in Parish Room, beginning with King's Speech. To include Concert, Whist Drive and Dance.
>
> H. CHICHESTER, Chairman.
> Admiral N. A. B. WOLLASTON, Hon. Treasurer and Hon. Secretary.
>
> **GOD SAVE THE KING.**
>
> The Tavistock Printing Company, Limited, "Gazette" Office. 'Phone 61.

time there was a purely local focus to the occasion, with relief at the arrival back of our own lads and the dignified sorrowing at the loss of relatives, neighbours, friends and fellow villagers. VE Day, 8 May 1945, produced an outburst of rejoicing. Street parties were a feature of the occasion. David Gordon, home at Whitchurch House after coming down from Cambridge, describes 'a celebration gathering to mark the end of the war':

On that occasion Whitchurch people combined to make a day to remember. I rashly agreed to organise the main events. We had grown accustomed to sharing Whitchurch House, so that was to be the centre for many hours. With a band of helpers I set out to make entertainments for all ages. It was to be a bit of a fair, a romp for kids, and masses of good food made by our renowned WI, and generous gifts of produce from our farmers. A small marquee was set up near the house, really a tight squeeze on a hot day with smart serge suits. The music, provided by the Salvation Army Band, attracted a lot of unusual fans; our South Devon cows came to stand on the edge of the ha-ha, some with their heads lying on our rough lawn. For the main event I made a version of an army assault course, with triple-bars, a water jump, old tyres suspended from branches, scrambling nets, a canvas tunnel, and wooden ramps. The winner would get a silver cup. It was a time for the men to show off. We all knew that Courtney Rowe was the favourite; he was a keen crosscountry runner. The starting pistol was fired and off they went across the nearest field, across the stream, and into the big field, Courtney leading. Now came excitement. He slowed, then hopped, and then limped out of the way of his rivals. Then we knew that the fault was mine! In honour of the day, and to make a neat course, I had topped the grass. But Courtney ran in bare feet, and there were hundreds of cut thistles, which, when they dry, are agony for feet. And so the great race was tarnished. A women's race followed, with skirts tucked into knickers. A big crowd cheered them on, and it became the main event. That evening there was a dance in the Parish Room. Hundreds came. As a Gordon, I danced the Highland Fling in the Interval, having been piped into the Hall by a Royal Marine piper. And so ended a special day, which had helped to bring about a revival of belief in our village and a renewal of friendships.

Royal occasions have provided the opportunities for other festivities. The two coronations of 1937 and 1953 and the two silver jubilees of 1935 and 1977 were marked by programmes of activities and events which were quite similar to each other in their purpose and content.

The similarities between the proceedings on the occasions of these twentieth-century royal happenings need cause no surprise. The models were the earlier celebrations of 1887, 1897 and 1902, marking, respectively, the golden and diamond jubilees of Queen Victoria and the coronation of Edward VII.

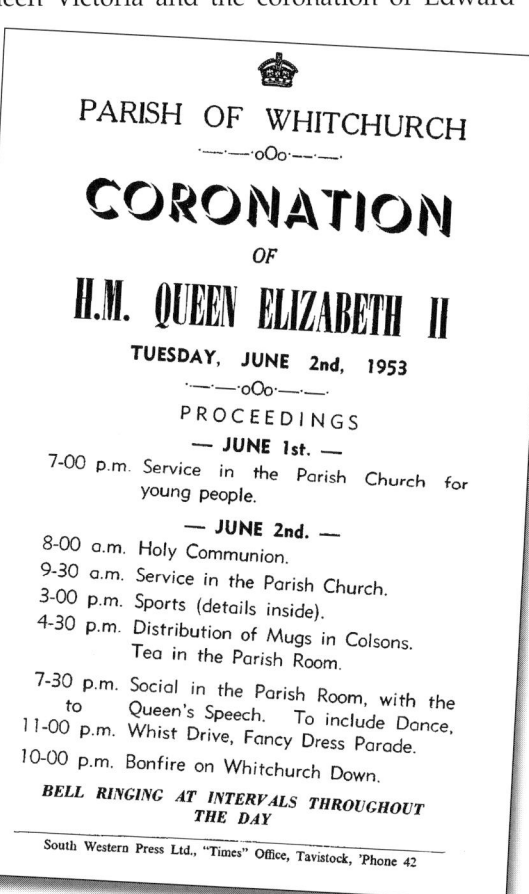

> **PARISH OF WHITCHURCH**
>
> **CORONATION**
> OF
> **H.M. QUEEN ELIZABETH II**
> TUESDAY, JUNE 2nd, 1953
>
> PROCEEDINGS
> — JUNE 1st. —
> 7-00 p.m. Service in the Parish Church for young people.
>
> — JUNE 2nd. —
> 8-00 a.m. Holy Communion.
> 9-30 a.m. Service in the Parish Church.
> 3-00 p.m. Sports (details inside).
> 4-30 p.m. Distribution of Mugs in Colsons. Tea in the Parish Room.
> 7-30 p.m. Social in the Parish Room, with the to Queen's Speech. To include Dance,
> 11-00 p.m. Whist Drive, Fancy Dress Parade.
> 10-00 p.m. Bonfire on Whitchurch Down.
>
> **BELL RINGING AT INTERVALS THROUGHOUT THE DAY**
>
> South Western Press Ltd., "Times" Office, Tavistock, 'Phone 42

Coronation street party at Chollacott Close, June 1953.

Here is the *Tavistock Gazette's* report of the celebrations in Whitchurch on the latter occasion:

The authorised form of coronation service was held at eleven o'clock, and a short address was given by the vicar. At 1.15 the children assembled at the gate of The Priory, when medals, given by the Celebration Committee, were distributed under the direction of Mr Newton and Mr Mallett, teachers. A procession was then formed, and headed by the Calstock Band, marched to a field kindly lent by Mr J Lovell, where a long programme of sports was successfully carried out. At four o'clock an adjournment was made to the school-room for tea, to which the children with their parents first sat down, and afterwards the other parishioners. Owing to the free tea having been held on the original date, a charge to defray expenses was made to all adults. [The date of the coronation had been postponed from an earlier date because of the illness of the King.] *After tea, sports were resumed, and concluded about eight o'clock. The prizes were distributed by Mrs E. Coppin, the wife of the Chairman of the Celebration Committee. After the sports, dancing on the green was carried on till ten o'clock. Music was provided by the Calstock band, which gave every satisfaction.*

One other element which became a feature of such celebrations was the joint enterprise with Tavistock which resulted in a mass exodus at the end of the day, from both town and village, to Whitchurch Down where a bonfire was lit, sometimes as part of a chain of such fires covering long distances. In 1887, for example, the bonfire associated with the celebration of Queen Victoria's golden jubilee was said to be 50 feet high, and to have included seven tons of old ship timber saturated with 200 gallons of tar. It was lit at ten o'clock, along with 26 other fires stretching from North Hessary Tor in the east to the Cheesewring on Bodmin Moor in the west.

It was not only on royal occasions that Victorian Whitchurch enjoyed its bonfire on the Down. The annual Guy Fawkes junketings, which were often preceded by a carnival in Tavistock, would invariably end with the ritual burning of the Guy and with the sights and sounds of fireworks. Another annual occasion on which Whitchurch Down proved to be a magnet was Good Friday. For just one day the whole area became a huge picnic site. Inevitably, facilities followed the crowds. Stalls sprang up, offering refreshments. Donkeys and ponies could be hired for rides round The Ring. Bob Norman manned an ice-cream cart. George Ball installed swings for the day. Such were the scenes and enticements that greeted the large crowds, intent on a half-day of fresh air and fun in the early 1900s.

As with every community the great majority of celebrations over the years have not been those that marked the great national festivals or occasions, or even those that were associated with organisations, societies, or institutions. Rather, they were personal and family affairs, baptisms, birthdays, reunions, retirements, anniversaries and, above all, weddings.

Chapter 14

MURDERING

A homicide is an unusual event in a small, quiet community, and murder has never caught on as a pastime in Whitchurch. When such a rare crime occurs in such a place it is likely to remain in the communal memory and in the public imagination for a long time. So it was with the Budghill murder.

The year was 1815, a significant year in the history of Britain. Wellington defeated Napoleon at Waterloo and brought the long French Wars to an end. The Corn Laws were passed prohibiting the import of cheap foreign corn. John Macadam's method of road construction was officially adopted, and Humphry Davy invented his safety lamp. George III's long reign was approaching its end, while Lord Liverpool's tenure as Prime Minister still had 12 years to run. In Whitchurch all these momentous events were overshadowed by the news of what happened on a local farm on 16 February.

Budghill Farm, lying between the village centre and Shorts Down, was traditionally part of the Walreddon estate. It was tenanted in the nineteenth century, successively, by John Metters, John Goddard, John Bickle and John Skinner. It remained in the occupation of members of the Skinner family from 1870 until 1940, when Frank Skinner, as the sitting tenant, bought it when the estate was broken up and largely sold off.

The tombstone reads:

In remembrance of Mary Metters who was barbarously murdered by her servant Sam Norton with a billhook. Of Budghill in this parish. Leaving a disconsolate husband and five children to mourn her untimely end.

Mary, the 45-year-old wife of a local farmer and the mother of five children, died on Thursday 16 February 1815. Her husband was attending Plymouth Market on that day. He had left at dawn. Norton, who was employed as a general domestic and farm hand, had expected to accompany him, but at the last moment his master had told him:

Samuel, it is a wet morning, and it is not worth while for two to go through the rain. I shall therefore leave you at home to take care of the cattle, and if you want further employ you can find it in the barn.

Soon after Mr Metters's early-morning departure the four younger children left for school, presumably in Tavistock, since the dame-school in Whitchurch was not established until 1820, and in 1815 the nearest school would have been in the town. The eldest child, Elizabeth, who was 16, had planned to spend the first part of the day shopping in Tavistock. She was to recall seeing Norton at eight o'clock in the morning, before she left the house. She also recollected, at the trial, that at that time he had been ostentatiously sharpening a billhook, but she had given the matter little thought at the time.

When she returned home at the end of the morning she found the house in disorder. Boxes had been broken open and articles scattered around, while her mother's bonnet lay in a corner. There were traces of blood here and there. She raised a neighbour, whom she called Thomas. This would probably have been either Thomas Rowe of Lower Statford Farm or Thomas Whitehair of Higher Pennington Farm. He searched the premises and found Mrs Metters' body in a stable. Close by, covered with hair and blood, was the hook which Elizabeth had seen Norton sharpening earlier in the day. The servant had struck his mistress repeatedly on the head, and had then dragged the body out of the house and into the outbuilding in which it was found, where he covered it with loose straw. His victim had probably made no effort to defend herself. Why should she? Norton was a servant who was around the house much of the time. She had no reason to fear him, or to anticipate a threat.

Having moved the body, Norton went through the house and took some money and some other belongings, including silver spoons and his master's watch. He also took some of Mr Metters' clothes. He was wearing them when he was apprehended in a public house at Princetown. An arrest and a confession followed quickly. Norton was committed to the Lent Sessions of the Exeter Assizes. Some details of his background were to emerge at the trial. He had been born in Tavistock 23 years before. He had escaped justice following what appears to have been a series of robberies, in which he was involved as a teenager, by joining the Marines. He then deserted and joined the Army, which, preparing itself to launch a Spanish campaign against Napoleon, asked

145

few questions of prospective recruits. After service in the Peninsular War he was discharged, when the Napoleonic Wars came to an end, and found himself back in his home town looking for a job. Mr Metters, who needed an extra hand to work in and around the farmhouse, took him on, knowing of his reputation and background but believing that he could be reformed. It appears that, up until the time of the murder, the servant had proved honest and reliable. Mr Metters could recall only one occasion when trust had been broken, and that had been when Norton had returned from Plymouth Market one evening having sold farm produce valued at £8, but without a penny in his pocket. At the trial it became very clear, as everyone who knew the family had known, that Norton was very slow-witted. A sharper operator would, for example, hardly have hung around to collect spoons or paraded himself in a local pub within a few hours of the murder wearing his master's clothes. He relished being, for however short a time, the centre of interest and attention, an experience that he had never had before. He seemed to enjoy recounting to an attentive audience how the first blow with the billhook had not been effective, and how he had had to strike his mistress repeatedly before she fell lifeless. Throughout the trial procedure he showed no remorse. On the contrary, he proudly announced that the murder was only a small part of his cunning plan to dispatch, on that morning, all the children, along with their mother, a scheme only frustrated by the children leaving the farm early to go to school, or, in Elizabeth's case, to do some shopping. This again reveals his simple-mindedness. There was no cunning plan. He cannot have been surprised, knowing the family's routine, that the children would have been absent. And he had himself expected until breakfast time that he would be spending the day in Plymouth. It was all the boastfulness of the simpleton. Poor Sam. It impressed neither public nor judge nor jury.

There was little delay following a trial which became a formality. Within six weeks of the murder the *Plymouth and Dock Herald* was reporting, on 1 April, the public execution that took place in front of the County Gaol at Exeter. It was reported:

The conduct of the hardened wretch during his confinement exhibited the most brutal depravity of mind. But, it seemed, the gallows were enough to chasten even the strongest of villains. On ascending the fatal drop, his courage foresook him and he appeared dreadfully agitated, and met his fate with fear and trembling.

The 'hardened wretch' was to face a second penalty. The mason responsible for Mrs Metters' gravestone originally completed his task, omitting Norton's name in his description of the murder and referring only to 'her servant' as the man responsible. As the inscription clearly indicates, the inclusion of the name was an after-thought, added as such to save the cost of a completely fresh inscription. But at whose behest was the addition made? One might guess that John Metters, or perhaps other members of the family or indeed of the wider community, decided, at a late stage, that posterity should be left in no doubt as to the identity of the perpetrator of this heinous crime. Perhaps John, the kind-hearted employer determined to give the young miscreant every chance, wanted to exercise a final act of clemency by leaving the name out, and perhaps he was, at a final stage, persuaded otherwise.

Who knows? The net result is that the immortality planned for the victim of this violent assault extends also to the murderer. Immortality is, indeed, double-edged.

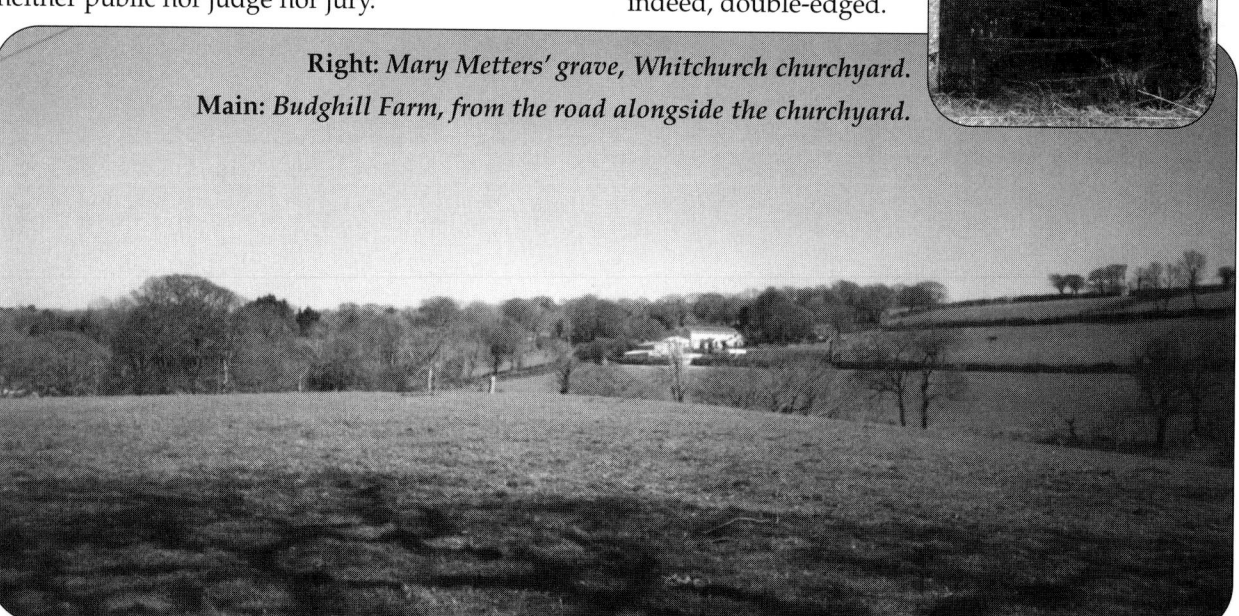

Right: *Mary Metters' grave, Whitchurch churchyard.*
Main: *Budghill Farm, from the road alongside the churchyard.*

Chapter 15

HEROES OR VILLAINS?

There follow six cameos of characters who all lived in the parish of Whitchurch for some time during the period of four centuries between 1596 and 1996.

The little procession leaves Fitzford Gatehouse, near Tavistock's Drake statue, as the clock strikes midnight. The form is the same as it has been every night for centuries. A black hound, with its one eye in the middle of its forehead, leads a carriage made of bones and drawn by headless horses. In the carriage rides the old lady. They proceed to Okehampton Park, where the hound plucks a blade of grass, and then they return to Fitzford, where the blade of grass is laid on a stone. Any residents or visitors who have missed the spectacle need have no worry. It will be re-enacted every night until Okehampton Park is denuded of grass. When that occurs the old lady will finally have paid her penance.

The punishment is certainly a terrible one. But so, it seems, was the crime. For the bones of her carriage are those of three husbands and two children, all murdered. And all murdered by the lady, who, not content with such heinous crimes, drove her fourth husband to distraction and had an affair with a servant, himself married, which resulted in at least one illegitimate child. Clearly the terrible old lady deserves everything that is coming to her, and if, after more than three centuries, the period of penance shows no sign of coming to an end, she can have no cause for complaint.

The welter of charges and accusations that were made after Lady Mary's death in 1671 came together to form a legend that was to take a prominent place in local folklore. More than 200 years later Sabine Baring-Gould included in his collection of folk-songs one called 'My Lady's Coach'. It begins:

My Lady hath a sable coach with horses two and four,
My Lady hath a black bloodhound that runneth on before,
My Lady's coach hath nodding plumes, the driver has no head,
My Lady is in ashen white, as one that is long dead.
'Now pray step in', My Lady says, 'Now pray step in and ride'.
'I thank thee, I would rather walk than gather to thy side'.

Lady Mary Howard was perhaps the most interesting, certainly the most famous, person to have been born in the parish of Whitchurch. Her father, Sir John Fitz, belonged to a family which had had a high standing in local society for generations and which, since the middle of the fifteenth century, had been settled in the great Fitzford Mansion, near the Tavy on the western edge of Tavistock. He was a drunkard, a bully and a victim of uncontrollable bouts of anger and violence. Mary was his only child. She was born on 1 August 1596 at Walreddon, which was then a dower-house to the mansion a mile away, and was baptised in St Andrew's, Whitchurch, on the same day. When she was nine years old her father's stormy life ended at an inn at Twickenham, when he put a sword first through his host and then through himself.

A print by Hollar from a portrait of Lady Mary Howard, painted by Van Dyke in about 1625. The print survives, but the portrait is lost.

The child was desirable property. Wardships were at that time the subjects of sale and Mary's wardship, having reverted to the Crown on her father's death, was quickly sold to the Earl of Northumberland. Three years later, when she was 12, her guardian married her off to his brother, Sir Allen Percy. For Sir Allen, a younger son, a marriage to an heiress was financially very convenient. Fate intervened. Sir Allen died suddenly and unexpectedly in his sleep, after appearing to have recovered fully from a chill. Mary was left a widow at the tender age of 15, but was still subject to the Northumberland guardianship.

Within a short time she had eloped from the house where she was living under the supervision of a Lady Hatton. She made off with Thomas Darcy, a young man of noble family and of about her own age. A marriage quickly followed. It may be a story of young love. On the other hand, it may be that Earl Rivers, young Darcy's father, engineered the coup in an attempt to restore the family's fortunes. No doubt a legal battle would have been waged by Northumberland had not Thomas Darcy died, of a cause – and at a date – unknown, but within a few months of his marriage.

If her second widowhood caused her more grief than her first, then she was not to be allowed a long period of mourning, for her guardian quickly arranged a third marriage, to Sir Charles Howard, son of the Earl of Suffolk. Charles and Mary lived at Audley End, where two daughters, Elizabeth and Mary, were born. Lady Mary then began an affair with George Cuttford, her husband's solicitor, which brought about, in 1619, a separation from Sir Charles, who left the country and died soon after his return, reportedly by his own hand. By then Mary had a son, born 19 months after her husband's departure for the Continent. She called him George Howard. He was almost certainly the son of George Cuttford, who had now become Mary's steward and whom she installed at Walreddon Manor.

Now 26 and a widow for the third time, she re-established herself at Fitzford, close to her lover. Marriage to Cuttford was, of course, socially unthinkable, even if either partner had fancied that path. But the 'richest match in the west', as Clarendon called her, would not be likely to remain long unmarried. Husband number four was Richard Grenville. A country gentleman, baronet and JP, he was also haughty, arrogant and quick-tempered, and he could not adjust at Fitzford to a condition of financial dependence on his rich wife. His wrath was turned, first against Mary, and then, when he discovered more of what had been going on, against Cuttford, with whom he locked horns in a legal war. After three years of the marriage, relations had deteriorated to the level at which divorce proceedings began. The court heard from one side that 'he tooke hold of her petty coate and tore it, and threw her on the ground, and made her eye blacke and Blewe', and from the other that 'she sunge unseemly songs to his face to provoke him and bid him go to such a woman and such a woman, and told him that she loved Cuttford better than him.' A divorce was granted. Grenville, financially ruined, thereupon began a five-year exile as a mercenary soldier on the Continent.

After his return to England, Grenville became embroiled in the Civil War. Given a regiment by Parliament, he marched it out of London, defected, and handed himself and it over to the Royalist side. In 1644 he was in Devon, armed with a royal warrant to take over all his ex-wife's property. Establishing himself at Fitzford, he had Cuttford thrown into gaol and the Cuttford family evicted from Walreddon. For the next two years Grenville managed to alienate or annoy everyone he came into contact with. In 1646, realising which way the war was going, he again fled to the Continent, this time permanently. Mary thereupon reoccupied a battered Fitzford and reinstalled the Cuttfords at Walreddon, though without George, who had died soon after his release from prison.

The final phase of her life was to last for 25 years. Her son, George, became MP for Tavistock but died heirless in 1671. Mary thereupon made her will, in which she left Walreddon to her cousin, Sir William Courtenay. She signed the will 'Mary Grinvil', using a name that she had not used for 40 years. She then turned her face to the wall and three days later she died. One of her last acts was to make a sizeable contribution of 10s. to a collection made in the locality 'towards the redemption of the p'sent captives nowe in Turkey.' Hers was the largest of the 730 donations.

When Lady Mary Howard died in 1671 she bequeathed her birthplace, Walreddon Manor, to her cousin, Sir William Courtenay. It was to remain in Sir William's family for almost three centuries until, in 1953, a descendent, the seventeenth Earl of Devon, sold it. During that long period it was occupied either by junior members of the family or by tenants. There is no doubt about the identity of the most illustrious of the long line of distinguished occupants. He, perhaps more than any other, exemplified the kind of resident who one might most readily associate with this remote, half-concealed mansion. In the late 1890s curious bystanders on street corners would observe on Sunday mornings the only public appearances of this semi-recluse, as he was driven to and from worship at Whitchurch Parish Church. Although by then he was in his eighties and was quite deaf, his gait remained stiff-backed, and a flowing white beard gave particular distinction to his striking visage. In November 1901, in the sixth year of his Walreddon retreat, and just three weeks after the last of his weekly outings, he died. Four years older than Queen Victoria, he had outlived her by ten months. The polished oak coffin in which he was lowered into his Whitchurch grave four days later bore a brass plate on which was inscribed: 'Edward John Eyre. Formerly Governor of Jamaica. Died November 30th 1901, aged 86.' The granite cross that was later to mark the plot added a further distinction, 'Australian Explorer', and a one-sentence eulogy: 'He did his duty in that state of life into which it pleased God to call him.'

Edward Eyre was born in Yorkshire in 1815, the son of a clergyman. At the age of 17 he emigrated to Australia. Success as a sheep farmer was followed by a period of extensive exploration, in which he led expeditions which opened up vast areas of the interior and earned him a reputation as one of

HEROES OR VILLAINS?

Edward John Eyre and his grave.

the most resourceful explorers of the century. Significantly, in the light of later events, he was considered to have a philanthropic and progressive view of the rights of the aborigines, and it was largely on the strength of this reputation that the British Government appointed him Deputy Governor of New Zealand, a post that he held until 1853. There followed governorships of St Vincent and the Leeward Islands, and then, in 1861, he went to Jamaica. The events that followed were to cast their shadow over the rest of his career, and indeed his life. Had he never set foot in Kingston he would have been remembered as one of the greatest of Australian explorers. As it was he was to go to his grave as the butcher of Surrey. Surrey was the county that saw the worst of the violence in the Jamaican rebellion of October 1865. The rising, among the black underclass of former slaves, led to attacks on whites and to atrocities that persuaded the Governor that martial law should be imposed. During the 30 days of the emergency the authorities, under Eyre's direction, carried out 439 executions and 600 floggings of both men and women. About 1,000 dwellings were burned down. The rising was suppressed and the emergency powers were then withdrawn. Such leaders of the rising as had survived became subject to the ordinary processes of the law, before being hanged.

Eyre's conduct sharply divided opinion within Jamaica and this division was mirrored in Britain, where a storm of public controversy was aroused by press reports of what had taken place. Prime Minister Russell set up a Commission of Enquiry. It published a report which, on the one hand, praised Eyre for acting promptly and thus preventing further bloodshed, and, on the other hand, charged him with reacting with unnecessary harshness to an event that was not an organised conspiracy. The Government accepted the findings and relieved Eyre of his duties. He arrived back in Britain, straight into a deluge of public debate, in which the great opinion-formers of mid-Victorian England lined up, for or against. Five years of legal wrangling followed, at the end of which the Government agreed to give him a pension, and Eyre accepted that his career was over.

He retired to Adderley Hall in Shropshire, listing his hobbies in *Who's Who* as shooting and fishing. From there he moved, finally, to Walreddon in 1896, at the age of 80. It was the action of a man seeking total seclusion for the final chapter of his life. He played no part in the social affairs of the local community during these last years, although the *Western Morning News* did suggest, in its obituary, that he had shown himself 'ever ready to respond liberally to appeals on behalf of the poor or any other good object.'

Among the domestic staff who attended to the old man's needs at Walreddon was a girl who was later to become Mrs Clampit. More than 60 years later she spoke of her old employer. She had no great secrets about him to reveal. But she knew what to call him. 'I was', she began her recollections, 'the house parlourmaid at Walreddon to Hangman Eyre.'

By the time of Eyre's death the passions that had been evoked a generation earlier had largely subsided, and he died an almost forgotten figure, having, as one obituarist put it, 'outlived his generation'. His family, in order to compensate, as it almost seemed, for his delayed departure, brought forward the day of the funeral from the date that was originally announced. This was probably done to avoid the attendance of reporters and others who might have used the occasion to re-ignite the old embers. If the family had in mind a wish to avoid any possible demonstrations at the funeral, then the plan worked. In the event, only a small number of friends, neighbours and servants followed his four sons, all of them in the Forces or the Colonial service, and his daughter, to the Whitchurch graveside on that December afternoon. The 'he did his duty' tribute that was to appear on the stone was to be a final, defiant gesture from a loyal family. It may be fair to offer, a century after his death, the thought that Edward Eyre is not the only man to have suffered the fate of having a positive reputation, based upon strong qualities and formidable achievements, buried under the weight of one blunder, crime, or indiscretion. Shakespeare, as always, got it right: 'The evil that men do lives after them, The good is oft interred in their bones.'

Mark Patrick (moustached, standing in the back row) entertains constituents on the House of Commons terrace.

Not all of the Members of Parliament who have represented the local area over the past seven centuries have felt it important to live here. Indeed, in earlier periods even visits were considered unnecessary. Mark Patrick took a different view. When, in 1931, he was elected as Member for the Tavistock Constituency, he decided that he would need a home in the heart of the constituency, without sacrificing his two other residences in Hampshire and in London or his two other addresses at London clubs. And what could be closer to the heart of his constituency than Whitchurch Down? The result was the construction of a house at the crossroads where the road west–east from Tavistock to Sampford Spiney crosses the old north–south route from Peter Tavy to Horrabridge. This is Warren's Cross. The house was built with stone quarried nearby at Pennycomequick, the largest of the quarries on the Down.

Colin Mark Patrick was adopted as the Prospective Conservative candidate for the Tavistock seat in 1930, when the sitting member, General Wallace Wright, announced that he would stand down at the forthcoming election. Born in 1893, Patrick had been educated at Eton and Oxford, and had been commissioned in 1914. He had served with the 16th Lancers and been severely wounded at Ypres. After the war he had entered the diplomatic service and had served in Berne, The Hague and Cairo, as well as on a special mission to Abyssinia. His last posting before his adoption was in Moscow. He was, as he freely admitted, neither an orator nor a political philosopher. His selection by the caucus of the local Conservative Association occasioned no surprise. His two predecessors (and his successor) were men of similar background and stamp.

He claimed that he was driven by neither ideology nor ambition, but responded to a strong sense of public duty. In 1914, he had felt that his country called him to fight in the First World War. In 1919 the call on his duty was to defend the interests of his nation diplomatically. In the 1930s, he felt that there was a need to defend the country, as he saw it, from the threat of socialism. He harboured no doubts about what constituted the national need, and his country's need was his command. Some saw him as an uncomplicated, if honourable, man. He was, however, an intellectual heavyweight, who was seen by those who knew him as having the qualities to rise to the very top in the world of politics. Among his close political associates and personal friends were his contemporaries Lord Salisbury and R.A. Butler. His qualities were noted and respected across the political spectrum. Such a man was Colin Mark Patrick, the Honourable Member for Tavistock and the owner of Warren's Cross, Whitchurch parish.

Patrick held the seat through the rest of the decade. Having won it in 1931, he only had to defend it once, in 1935. This latter campaign revealed some of his limitations. When, at a public meeting, the raising of some issues threw him on to the back foot, he took refuge in a claim that some of his opponents had shown their colours by not doffing their hats for the National Anthem. On the floor of the Commons he could generally be relied upon to support the leadership of his party. When challenged on this, he responded by saying: 'I have no intention of trying to gain cheap notoriety by asking silly questions.' And there was only one occasion when he defied the party whip. But those who had pencilled him into the 'poodles' column soon had to think again.

Patrick's diplomatic experience was of considerable value to the Government and he served as a Parliamentary Private Secretary at both the India Office and the Foreign Office. His work as a member of the Parliamentary Commission that made recommendations about the future government of India was much admired. He wrote a book titled *Hammer and Sickle*, which was based on his Moscow experiences, and his knowledge of Europe gave him insights into the political realities of the situation, particularly in Germany and Italy, that many ministers, notably Prime Minister Chamberlain, so obviously lacked. By 1938 the Member for Tavistock was making speeches, both in Parliament and in the constituency, challenging the policy of appeasement and warning of its dangers. After the Munich Agreement in August 1938 he helped to form the 'Eden Group', which included the former Foreign Minister, Anthony Eden, and another future Prime Minister, Harold Macmillan. Harold Nicolson records, in his diary, a meeting of the group at Patrick's London house on the day in March 1939 when Hitler occupied Prague. The man who emerged as the chief mouthpiece for this anti-appeasement opinion was, of course, Winston Churchill, but one of its most persistent, and consistent, exponents was Mark Patrick.

When war came in September 1939 Patrick behaved characteristically by rejoining his old regiment. He served in uniform for two years, before returning to politics in December 1941. One month later, on the evening of 7 January 1942, when he was at home putting the finishing touches to a speech he planned to make in the Commons on the following day, he suffered a heart attack and died. He was 49 years old.

When looking at the stand on appeasement that men like Churchill, Eden, Macmillan and Patrick took in the 1930s, it is important to remember how unpopular they were at the time over this issue. The majority of people either chose not to listen to them, or dismissed them as scaremongers. When Mark Patrick told his constituents that re-armament was necessary most of them preferred not to believe such an unwelcome message. The judgement of the man from Warren's Cross was to be amply justified by events. It was a pity he did not live to see the victory that was to follow.

Warren's Cross was to provide a home for a Mark Patrick after the war. The son, and namesake, of the MP returned from childhood evacuation in Canada to live in the house for some time.

The Beavers arrived in Whitchurch in 1938. Noel Herbrand Beaver was a retired naval commander with First World War experience. He came with his wife, originally Marjorie Eleanor Worsley Smith, and his son Martin and stepson David. They bought, from the Church Commissioners, Whitchurch House, which had been the vicarage for more than 100 years but which had been empty since the death of Revd Beebe. Almost immediately the Second World War broke out and the Commander was recalled to the service. Mrs Beaver, with her sons still young and her husband absent, occupied a central position in a household that became a village institution. Commander Beaver returned after the war, but died in 1949, leaving his middle-aged widow to resume her pivotal role.

Marjorie Beaver had been brought up in a vicarage, the daughter of an Anglican parson. His last years were spent at Whitchurch House and he lies buried in the churchyard beside his daughter. Marjorie continued to live at the house until her death in 1987 at the age of 91. She had by then assumed a position of an almost matriarchal nature in the local community. Her occupancy of Whitchurch House finally extended to 48 years. The house became the centre for a whole range of activities. Societies met there. Clubs had their parties there. Good causes benefited from events held in the house or the grounds. In a number of ways it became an alternative community centre. Hospitality also always seemed to be on offer. Many people over the years who found themselves in the area and needed accommodation, either in the short or the longer term, found it under the Beaver roof. There also appeared to be an endless supply of visitors, coming, it seemed, from all parts of the world – friends and acquaintances, contacts from earlier occasions here or elsewhere, people who just wanted to renew a friendship or to express gratitude for a service once performed. At the centre of what sometimes appeared an endless whirl of activity, was the lady of the house, versatile, unflappable, and ready and willing to do herself any of the jobs in or around the house that needed to be done.

Both the pattern for these kinds of activities, and the style with which they were carried out, were set in the first few years of 'the Beaver era', and were the result of the war emergency. The first evacuees to be provided with a home in Whitchurch House were the members of the Bell family from London, consisting of mother and six children. They were followed by a number of soldiers who had escaped from Dunkirk and were billeted in the house for several months.

Marjorie Beaver, surrounded by members of the Wayfarers Cricket Club, of which she was president. Left to right, back row: ?, Bob McCall, Rex Murrain, Bill Crocker, ?, Mike Gill, Brian Perry, ?, Den Crocker, Frank Sprague; front row: Bill Parkin, Ted Gent, Les Tucker, Tony Glanville, Den Towl, Derek Glanville.

Later, a second family of evacuees appeared, Mrs Meager arrived from Kent with five children and a sixth on the way. The two families remained for the duration of the war, after which the Meagers returned to Kent and the Bells decided to settle in the area. Other wartime visitors, who stayed for varying lengths of time, were two elderly ladies who were bombed out of their homes by the Plymouth blitz, and several refugees from Austria. Some of the latter were Jewish exiles fleeing from Nazi rule, who had made the journey to freedom with the help of Angela Smith, Marjorie's sister, who lived in Austria for some time between the wars. There were also two Czech brothers called Horitz. John, a practising lawyer, flew with Bomber Command and, having survived numerous missions, ended the war as one of his country's most decorated veterans. Karl was a professional musician who was later to play a great deal with Sir Thomas Beecham. Another musician who was a visitor at Whitchurch House, as well as at the home of his relations, the Shaws at Edgemoor, in Middlemoor, was Lionel Tertis, a viola player of world renown. In addition there were many friends, or friends of friends, who arrived and departed in an ad hoc manner. Two Land Girls lived in a caravan by the house. In the period before D-Day, when troops from a Yorkshire Regiment were camped on Whitchurch Down, the wives of two of the soldiers stayed for a while and established close friendships.

In a rapidly changing situation in which the only constant was a policy of open-door hospitality, there were occasional organisational problems. Although Whitchurch House was by most standards a substantial residence, with eight bedrooms, it took some organisation to ensure that everyone who needed accommodation was helped. There was no gas, but there was electricity and a rather erratic water-supply provided by a temperamental ram which slowly pumped water into tanks in the roof, powered by hydraulic pressure from springs above the house. There was a single large stove, an Esse, with which Mrs Beaver became so closely identified that one of her friends enquired at her funeral whether it was going to be buried with her. She taught the other two mothers who stayed with her how to cook. The diet was supplemented from the farm and the garden which supplied chickens, eggs, ducks, geese, guinea fowl, cows, milk, cream, goats, pigs, fruit and vegetables. As the farm had been allocated a small petrol ration it was possible to make occasional forays into Tavistock to stock up with other essential supplies.

Mrs Beaver's extraordinary capacity for making people feel welcome, whether they were ordinary parishioners or national celebrities, outlived these remarkable war years, and outlived also the early death of her husband and the departure from the nest of her two sons. Her reputation for liberal hospitality and for encouraging and supporting local organisations remained with her for the rest of her long life. She died on 9 April 1987 and her ashes were buried in the churchyard, close to the house which she had adorned for 48 years.

HEROES OR VILLAINS?

Tom Balment.

Tom Balment was born on 20 March 1977. On both sides his parents bore names that were well-known in the local community. His mother Sue is a member of the Kerswill family, who at one time operated the premier building firm in the area. His father David is an estate agent, whose commercial enterprise extends to the sponsorship of such deserving causes as the Whitchurch Cricket Club. Tom was an elder child. His brother Jamie arrived 19 months later. The boys grew up in the family home, Strawberry Hill, on Whitchurch Road.

A very able and intelligent pupil, Tom did well academically at each of the four local schools that he attended – St Rumon's, St Peter's, Kelly College and Tavistock College. He was also a natural all-round sportsman who enjoyed, and excelled at, a range of activities. He represented his schools at all age-levels at football, rugby, cricket, tennis and swimming, but also became highly proficient at surfing and skiing. He spent time in France and loved it, but it would be fair to say that he was happiest in the area he knew best, in his native South West. Here, on the coasts and moors of Devon and Cornwall, he swam, surfed and walked. Sometimes it was sheer recreation. Sometimes, as with the Tavistock College Ten Tors Team, it was also competition. He was a good team member. One can imagine gang leaders in the playground at St Peter's vying for his membership. One of the keys to this popularity, a condition that stayed with him throughout his life, was a deep sense of loyalty to the group and of commitment to the welfare of its other members. This characteristic was to show itself in a most dramatic way in the final acts of his life.

There are many examples of people who show an aggressive quality in relation to physical endeavour, but who in other ways display a marked gentleness of nature. Tom was one such. His natural style was reserved and self-effacing. He had a nice, laconic sense of humour, and one of the many attractive features of his personality was a capacity, some might say rare in the young, to smile at himself. An example of this concerned his absent-mindedness. Here was no affectation, but a genuine doubt on occasions as to where he was and where he should be. It gave rise to much good-natured banter with colleagues and with teachers. His head of sixth form at Tavistock College recalls such situations, and remembers that they always ended with grins on all sides. 'Not to like Tom', he says, 'was simply not possible.'

The 27 September 1996 was the last day of the long summer university break. Tom had enjoyed a holiday after completing his first year as a student at Sussex University, where he was studying French and International Relations. Just enough time to slot in one final surf before his return on the following day to Brighton to begin his second year. And where else to go but Polzeath, a beach second only to Newquay as a surfing mecca, and one that Tom had known since early childhood? He arranged a visit with his brother Jamie, then in the middle of his sixth-form career, and Jamie's friend Nick Woods. They left Tavistock in late afternoon in fine weather. What happened next is told in the words of Sue Balment, Tom's mother:

Wet-suited, they went to assess the surf. The sea was rough because of a spring tide and a full moon, but conditions were great for the habitual surfer, which they all three were. Several surfers were already in the water. At this point Nick either slipped or was washed into the water by a freak wave and was pushed by the high tide into a gully which narrowed and deepened towards the cliff. Initially, Tom and Jamie went together to get help, but Tom turned back as Nick was already in some distress and was calling out. Tom almost succeeded in pulling Nick out of the water several times, but was hindered by the fact that Nick still had on his fins. At some point Tom was also washed or inadvertently pulled into the sea. For the next 45 minutes Tom hung on with one hand to Nick and with the other to the rope that was thrown to him. On several occasions Nick was swept from his grasp but Tom managed to get him back.

Finally Tom lost Nick, and it was at this point that the coastguards, helped by some others including Jamie, decided to pull Tom out with the rope. The rope frayed on the rocks. Tom fell back. He hit his head and drowned.

At the inquest, held four months after the tragedy, it was testified that Tom, 6'4" tall and a strong and confident swimmer, was still strong, and was in fact walking up the rock-face, when the rope broke. We later learned that the coastguard equipment at Polzeath, and at other beaches around the coast, had been cut back in 1985 by the government of the day when huge changes in the coastguard service had been made. The rope that had been thrown to Tom had been intended only for horizontal rescues from sea to shore and was unsuitable for vertical cliff rescues. At that time the Polzeath Coastguards did not have a dedicated vehicle – let alone a 4WD – or any cliff rescue equipment. On the evening in question they turned up in their own vehicles, with only torches, radios, and dayglo jackets, and with no ropes.

We, Tom's family and friends, looked for ways in which we might be able to turn our grief to a positive end. With the support of the media, local and national, over an intense period of six months of campaigning, improvements, including the provision of a fully-equipped 4WD at Polzeath, were made. We cannot forget that, had this equipment been in place at the time, our son would almost certainly have survived. Tom was posthumously awarded the Royal Humane Society's 'In Memoriam' award for bravery. This, the highest award in the Society's gift, was received by his brother Jamie on behalf of family and friends at a ceremony held on the first anniversary of the tragedy. Tom now lies in the peace of Whitchurch churchyard.

Angela Rippon was born in Plymouth in 1944. She cut her teeth in the media world as a junior reporter with the *Sunday Independent*, a regional weekly paper based in her home city. There followed periods with the BBC and ITV, as reporter, editor and producer of regional television. Her appearance nationally as a BBC newsreader projected her to media stardom and iconic status, and she became well known, nationally and internationally. Among the high-profile roles that she assumed was the chairmanship of the English National Ballet. She has always, however, claimed to retain a special affection for the area that she has called 'My West Country', at the centre of which lies Dartmoor.

In 1969 Angela and her husband Chris bought Gem Cottage, above the River Walkham and just off the main road from Tavistock to Horrabridge. They thus became parishioners of Whitchurch. The house derives its name from the time when it served as the Count House for the nearby Gem Mine. It was here that the ore from the mine was weighed and here that the supervising bailiff exacted his dues of one shilling for every ton of ore that he weighed. For a time in the 1870s this was the only mine in the parish that was actually in production.

Angela has described the discovery of the house:

At first we had no idea that the river was so close to the bottom of our garden. The thickly-wooded banks running steeply down from the fence effectively concealed both the sight and the sound of water. What we saw first, after the jungle of garden and simple charm of the old stone house, was a cloud of bluebells swamping the wood with colour. It was only after we'd wandered through the trees and around the edge of the blue and green carpet, that we caught sight of the water sparkling and chasing through the trees. We'd already fallen for the house and the garden, but the sight of the river and the cool green of the wood convinced us that this was where we wanted to put down roots. There's nothing lazy about the progress that the Walkham makes seaward, forever rushing and tumbling over itself as if it cannot reach its destination fast enough, hurtling along at breakneck speed and living up to its reputation of being one of the fastest-flowing waterways in Devon. Before reaching us, the river has washed over the salmon-spawning beds above Ward Bridge, gurgled cheekily past the attractive riverside hamlet at Huckworthy, skidded over the weir and under the ancient bridge at Horrabridge, and tickled the toes of visitors at the beauty spot at Magpie Bridge. It comes to us as a seasoned traveller, anxious to rush on to its next milestone at Grenofen Bridge, too busy to stop and admire the valley.

Most of Angela Rippon's Whitchurch days included a ride from her Walkhampton stable, and one of her favourite routes, enjoyed, she believes, also by her horse, involved the climb to Pew Tor. She writes:

HEROES OR VILLAINS?

Angela Rippon is the patron of the locally-based Stannary Band. She is seen here in 2002 with two of its members, Stephen Grey (left) and John Benzie (right).

At the foot of the tor there is a formal pattern of fields in which our friends Mike and Wendy Doidge (of Wilsetton) rear their fine flock of Devon Closewool and Whiteface Dartmoor sheep. A few yards beyond is the unmistakeable roof style of a Devon longhouse where John Hearn, his father, and his father before him, have tamed the rough moorland turf into fine grazing. If you visit John (at Oakley) you have to watch out for his geriatric geese. There are three of them, all bought eight years previously to fatten for Christmas. John and his wife got so fond of them that they didn't have the heart to slaughter them, so they continued to wander around like family pets, along with the 21-year-old Dartmoor pony and the 18-year-old donkey. From the back of the Hearns's house, Pew Tor looms large and solid, and, looking up at it from the farmyard, it's easy to see how it has earned the family nickname of 'The Old Grey Battleship', for that's just what it looks like. Most weekend visitors and dog-walkers are happy to storm the bulk of the 'battleship' and go no deeper into the moor.

The ground behind the tor is covered in clitter, and you have to pick your way carefully between the sharp edges and overlapping stones and usually follow one of the narrow sheep tracks that run like fine pencil-lines all across the moor. From the side of Pew Tor you can look out towards Princetown and see a different face of Dartmoor. There are no lush green fields or convenient network of roads here. Only the open barren common land, its bracken and coarse grass punctured by a smattering of small tors, old quarries, and its landscape littered with the remains of hut circles which were the homes of the moor's earliest inhabitants.

In every community the lists of heroes and villains are, in both cases, short. This tribute to Whitchurch and its people ends with an appreciative nod in the direction of the others, the anonymous 99 per centage, who belong, or once belonged, to Whitchurch – a parish, a village, a community, to applaud, to savour and to enjoy.

Subscribers

Clifford and Margaret Alford, Tavistock
Mr Jeremy Allison
Malcolm and Jenny Ashfold
John and Mary Baker, Yelverton, Devon
Angela Ball (née Jeffery)
Martin Beaver, formerly of Whitchurch House
Ewart and Margaret Blowey, Tavistock, Devon
Geoffrey P. Bradford, Tavistock, Devon
Sandra C. Bray, Whitchurch, Devon
Muriel I.B. Brown
K.J. Burrow, Bucks Cross, Devon
Mr and Mrs Kenneth H. Cook, Tavistock, Devon
John Cooke, Waterways Garage, Tavistock
Miss R. Cundy, Lamerton, Devon
PC Simon Dell M.B.E., Tavistock
Mr Ian W. Doidge, Whitchurch, Devon
Miss J.C. Doidge
Ian and Gillian Douglas, Whitchurch
David and Christine Eggins, Middlemore, Whitchurch
Kathleen E. Evans (née Giles), Woodbury Salterton
John and Dorothy Findell, Whitchurch, Devon
Nicholas Findell, Dunstable, Bedfordshire
John Foxhall, Wembury, Devon
Brian A. Fyfield-Shayler, Tavistock, Devon

SUBSCRIBERS

Tom and Jacqueline Gale, Whitchurch, Devon
Peter E. Giles, West Buckland
G.M. (Mort) Glanville Q.C., Michelle and Gillian Glanville, London, Canada
Paul and Kate Glanville, Tavistock
R. Grace Glen-Leary
Christopher Goodwyn, Plymouth
Hugo and Ana Gorziglia, Chile
Mr and Mrs G.B. Harland, Whitchurch, Devon
Ray and Pamela Heale, Whitchurch, Devon
Peter and Liz Heaton, Whitchurch
Mr B.P. and Mrs P.E. Hill
Wing Commander and Mrs G. Hingston-Jones and Amanda (Tavyside School, 1965–69)
E.A. Ingram, Whitchurch
N.J. Ingram, Whitchurch
Mr Bernard T. James, Whitchurch
Mr Colin James, Bristol
Gloria Janku, Whitchurch, Devon
Joan Jeeves
Mrs Lesley Johnson, North Beer, Launceston
Brian and Sheila Jones, Whitchurch, Devon
Ann Keelan and Richard Cosgrave, Whitchurch, Tavistock, Devon
Graham and Brenda Kirkpatrick, Tavistock
Rev Mike Lapage, Tavistock
Phil and Yvonne Maker, Kingskerswell
Joan Marshall, Whitchurch, Devon
Ida McCabe, Whitchurch, Devon
Linda and Chris Mooney, Tavistock, Devon
Jane E. Moses
Shirley Nicholl (Toye), Whitchurch, Devon
Michael and Mary Parriss, married Whitchurch, December 1956
Keith and Pene Pendrill, Whitchurch, Devon
Mr Harold Penhall, Whitchurch
Mr and Mrs R.M. Perry, Plymouth, Devon
Mike and Sue Pesterfield, Tavistock, Devon
Sheila and Peter Plumb, Tavistock, Devon
Miss A.J. Prizeman, Plymouth
Mr and Mrs Puttick, Eastbourne, East Sussex
Mr and Mrs P. Radgick, Tavistock
Jennifer A. Robson (Woodford), Whitchurch, Devon
Ann and Eric Rowland, Whitchurch, Devon

Mrs Jenny Sanders, Tavistock, Devon
Jenny Sanders, Whitchurch, Devon
Peter Saunders, Ringwood
Steve and Janis Shipman
Dr J.C. Speller, Tavistock, Devon
Tavistock Subscription Library
Doreen Toye, Whitchurch
Frank Toye and Family, Whitchurch, Devon
Ralph Toye, Whitchurch
John and Sarah Treays, Tavistock, Devon
Mr G. Waldron, Plymouth, Devon
John F.W. Walling, Newton Abbot, Devon
June E. Warren, Whitchurch, Devon
Louise C. Watson, Whitchurch, Devon
Whitchurch Community Primary School
P.D. Whitcomb, Salisbury, Wiltshire
Peter R. Williams, Whitchurch, Devon
Mark and Cameron Woodcock, Philadelphia, USA
Norma Woodcock, Tavistock
Mrs J. Woodland, Tavistock, Devon
John and Ann Wright, Whitchurch
John F. Wyatt and Family

❦ FURTHER TITLES ❦

Community Histories

The Book of Addiscombe • Canning and Clyde Road Residents Association and Friends
The Book of Addiscombe, Vol. II • Canning and Clyde Road Residents Association and Friends
The Book of Ashburton • Stuart Hands and Pete Webb
The Book of Axminster with Kilmington • Les Berry and Gerald Gosling
The Book of Bampton • Caroline Seward
The Book of Barnstaple • Avril Stone
The Book of Barnstaple, Vol. II • Avril Stone
The Book of The Bedwyns • Bedwyn History Society
The Book of Bickington • Stuart Hands
Blandford Forum: A Millennium Portrait • Blandford Forum Town Council
The Book of Boscastle • Rod and Anne Knight
The Book of Bramford • Bramford Local History Group
The Book of Breage & Germoe • Stephen Polglase
The Book of Bridestowe • D. Richard Cann
The Book of Bridport • Rodney Legg
The Book of Brixham • Frank Pearce
The Book of Buckfastleigh • Sandra Coleman
The Book of Buckland Monachorum & Yelverton • Pauline Hamilton-Leggett
The Book of Carharrack • Carharrack Old Cornwall Society
The Book of Carshalton • Stella Wilks and Gordon Rookledge
The Parish Book of Cerne Abbas • Vivian and Patricia Vale
The Book of Chagford • Iain Rice
The Book of Chapel-en-le-Frith • Mike Smith
The Book of Chittlehamholt with Warkleigh & Satterleigh • Richard Lethbridge
The Book of Chittlehampton • Various
The Book of Colney Heath • Bryan Lilley
The Book of Constantine • Moore and Trethowan
The Book of Cornwood and Lutton • Compiled by the People of the Parish
The Book of Crediton • John Heal
The Book of Creech St Michael • June Small
The Book of Cullompton • Compiled by the People of the Parish
The Book of Dawlish • Frank Pearce
The Book of Dulverton, Brushford, Bury & Exebridge • Dulverton and District Civic Society
The Book of Dunster • Hilary Binding
The Book of Easton • Easton Village History Project
The Book of Edale • Gordon Miller
The Ellacombe Book • Sydney R. Langmead
The Book of Exmouth • W.H. Pascoe
The Book of Grampound with Creed • Bane and Oliver
The Book of Gosport • Lesley Burton and Brian Musselwhite
The Book of Hayling Island & Langstone • Peter Rogers
The Book of Helston • Jenkin with Carter
The Book of Hemyock • Clist and Dracott
The Book of Herne Hill • Patricia Jenkyns
The Book of Hethersett • Hethersett Society Research Group
The Book of High Bickington • Avril Stone
The Book of Ilsington • Dick Wills
The Book of Kingskerswell • Carsewella Local History Group
The Book of Lamerton • Ann Cole and Friends
Lanner, A Cornish Mining Parish • Sharron Schwartz and Roger Parker
The Book of Leigh & Bransford • Malcolm Scott
The Book of Litcham with Lexham & Mileham • Litcham Historical and Amenity Society
The Book of Loddiswell • Loddiswell Parish History Group
The New Book of Lostwithiel • Barbara Fraser
The Book of Lulworth • Rodney Legg
The Book of Lustleigh • Joe Crowdy
The Book of Lydford • Compiled by Barbara Weeks
The Book of Lyme Regis • Rodney Legg
The Book of Manaton • Compiled by the People of the Parish
The Book of Markyate • Markyate Local History Society
The Book of Mawnan • Mawnan Local History Group
The Book of Meavy • Pauline Hemery
The Book of Mere • Dr David Longbourne
The Book of Minehead with Alcombe • Hilary Binding and Douglas Stevens
The Book of Monks Orchard and Eden Park • Ian Muir and Pat Manning
The Book of Morchard Bishop • Jeff Kingaby
The Book of Mylor • Mylor Local History Group
The Book of Narborough • Narborough Local History Society
The Book of Newdigate • John Callcut
The Book of Newtown • Keir Foss
The Book of Nidderdale • Nidderdale Museum Society

The Book of Northlew with Ashbury • Northlew History Group
The Book of North Newton • J.C. and K.C. Robins
The Book of North Tawton • Baker, Hoare and Shields
The Book of Nynehead • Nynehead & District History Society
The Book of Okehampton • Roy and Ursula Radford
The Book of Ottery St Mary • Gerald Gosling and Peter Harris
The Book of Paignton • Frank Pearce
The Book of Penge, Anerley & Crystal Palace • Peter Abbott
The Book of Peter Tavy with Cudlipptown • Peter Tavy Heritage Group
The Book of Pimperne • Jean Coull
The Book of Plymtree • Tony Eames
The Book of Porlock • Dennis Corner
Postbridge – The Heart of Dartmoor • Reg Bellamy
The Book of Priddy • Albert Thompson
The Book of Princetown • Dr Gardner-Thorpe
The Book of Probus • Alan Kent and Danny Merrifield
The Book of Rattery • By the People of the Parish
The Book of Roadwater, Leighland and Treborough • Clare and Glyn Court
The Book of St Day • Joseph Mills and Paul Annear
The Book of St Dennis and Goss Moor • Kenneth Rickard
The Book of St Levan and Porthcurno • St Levan Local History Group
The Book of Sampford Courtenay with Honeychurch • Stephanie Pouya
The Book of Sculthorpe • Gary Windeler
The Book of Seaton • Ted Gosling
The Book of Sherborne • Rodney Legg
The Book of Sidmouth • Ted Gosling and Sheila Luxton
The Book of Silverton • Silverton Local History Society
The Book of South Molton • Jonathan Edmunds
The Book of South Stoke with Midford • Edited by Robert Parfitt
South Tawton & South Zeal with Sticklepath • Roy and Ursula Radford
The Book of Sparkwell with Hemerdon & Lee Mill • Pam James

The Book of Staverton • Pete Lavis
The Book of Stithians • Stithians Parish History Group
The Book of Stogumber, Monksilver, Nettlecombe & Elworthy • Maurice and Joyce Chidgey
The Book of Studland • Rodney Legg
The Book of Swanage • Rodney Legg
The Book of Tavistock • Gerry Woodcock
The Book of Thorley • Sylvia McDonald and Bill Hardy
The Book of Torbay • Frank Pearce
The Book of Truro • Christine Parnell
The Book of Uplyme • Gerald Gosling and Jack Thomas
The Book of Watchet • Compiled by David Banks
The Book of West Huntspill • By the People of the Parish
The Book of Weston-super-Mare • Sharon Poole
The Book of Whitchurch • Gerry Woodcock
Widecombe-in-the-Moor • Stephen Woods
Widecombe – Uncle Tom Cobley & All • Stephen Woods
The Book of Williton • Michael Williams
The Book of Winscombe • Margaret Tucker
The Book of Witheridge • Peter and Freda Tout and John Usmar
The Book of Withycombe • Chris Boyles
Woodbury: The Twentieth Century Revisited • Roger Stokes
The Book of Woolmer Green • Compiled by the People of the Parish

For details of any of the above titles or if you are interested in writing your own history, please contact: Commissioning Editor, Community Histories, Halsgrove House, Lower Moor Way, Tiverton, Devon EX16 6SS, England; email: katyc@halsgrove.com

In order to include as many historical photographs as possible in this volume, a printed index is not included. However, the Devon titles in the Community History Series are indexed by Genuki. For further information and indexes to various volumes in the series, please visit: http://www.cs.ncl.ac.uk/genuki/DEV/indexingproject.html

St Andrew's Whitchurch

Guide to the Church

£1

St Andrew's Church Guide

Contents

700 years of worship	3
St Andrew's Story	4
Monks & Money	8
Vicars & Hounds	10
'Stiff Paper over the Holes'	11
Porch & Font	12
The Chancel	13
The Chapel & South Transept	16
North Aisle	17
Bells & Tower	18
Saints & Stained glass	19
Structure & Roof	20
Outside in the Churchyard	21
Stables & Inn	22
Index	23

With Thanks to:

Jean Wans	Research
Jacqui Humphries	Artwork
Ben Sanham	Artwork
Jane Sanham	Editing & layout

"Reaching out to people with the love of Christ in word and action"

700 Years of Worship

Continuity & Change

Christians have been worshipping God in this church of St Andrew's for at least 700 years.

Worship and prayer go on here today as they have through the centuries, giving the church its atmosphere of ageless, unchanging peace and security.

Over 700 years the building has seen many changes. The way worship is conducted has altered many times over the years. Technology has advanced, and new things have come into the church. Electricity, central heating, Bibles in English rather than Latin, and more recently a public address system.

In 1882 the old harmonium was replaced by a brand new pipe organ – this was replaced by an electronic organ in 1974. Before the harmonium, music would have been provided by a small orchestra.

Each generation has inherited the building and its traditions from the previous one and has in turn left its own impression. The building has been neglected and restored. Continually, things have been added and things have been taken away. The processes of change, maintenance and continuity have worked together throughout the years to produce the building as it is today.

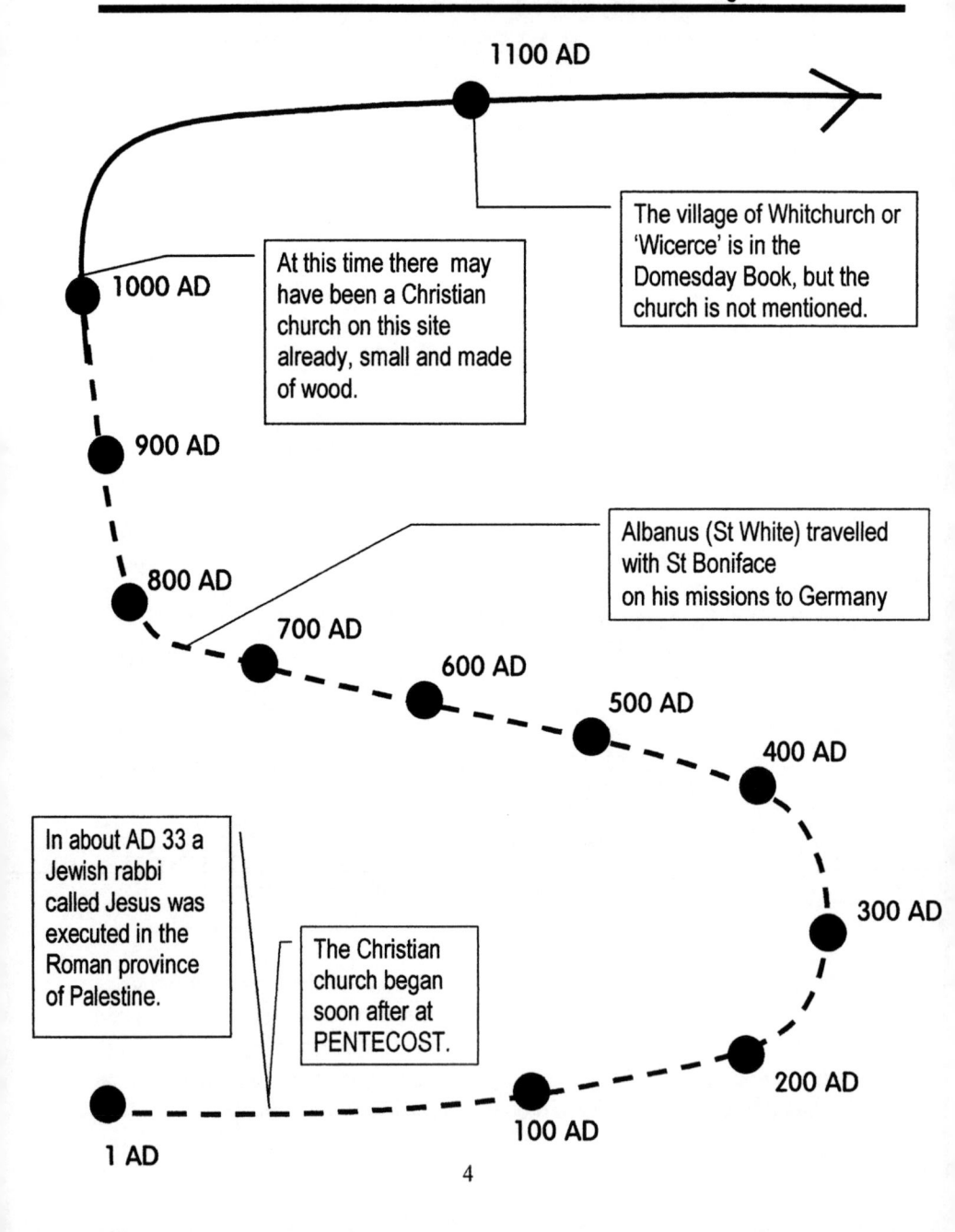

St Andrew's Story

1100 AD — The village of Whitchurch or 'Wicerce' is in the Domesday Book, but the church is not mentioned.

1000 AD — At this time there may have been a Christian church on this site already, small and made of wood.

900 AD

800 AD — Albanus (St White) travelled with St Boniface on his missions to Germany

700 AD

600 AD

500 AD

400 AD

300 AD

200 AD

100 AD — The Christian church began soon after at PENTECOST.

1 AD — In about AD 33 a Jewish rabbi called Jesus was executed in the Roman province of Palestine.

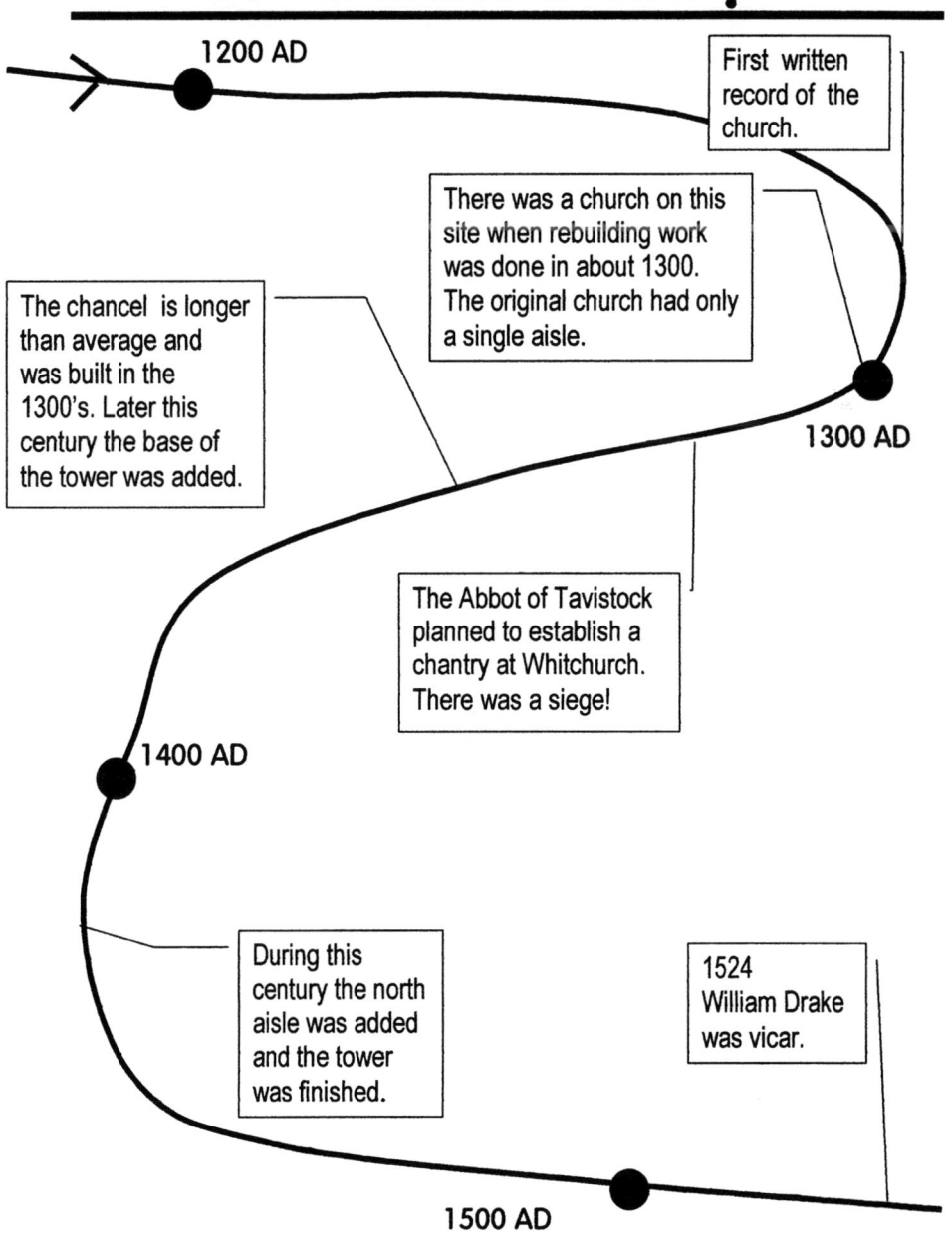

St Andrew's Story

1200 AD

First written record of the church.

There was a church on this site when rebuilding work was done in about 1300. The original church had only a single aisle.

The chancel is longer than average and was built in the 1300's. Later this century the base of the tower was added.

1300 AD

The Abbot of Tavistock planned to establish a chantry at Whitchurch. There was a siege!

1400 AD

During this century the north aisle was added and the tower was finished.

1524 William Drake was vicar.

1500 AD

St Andrew's Story

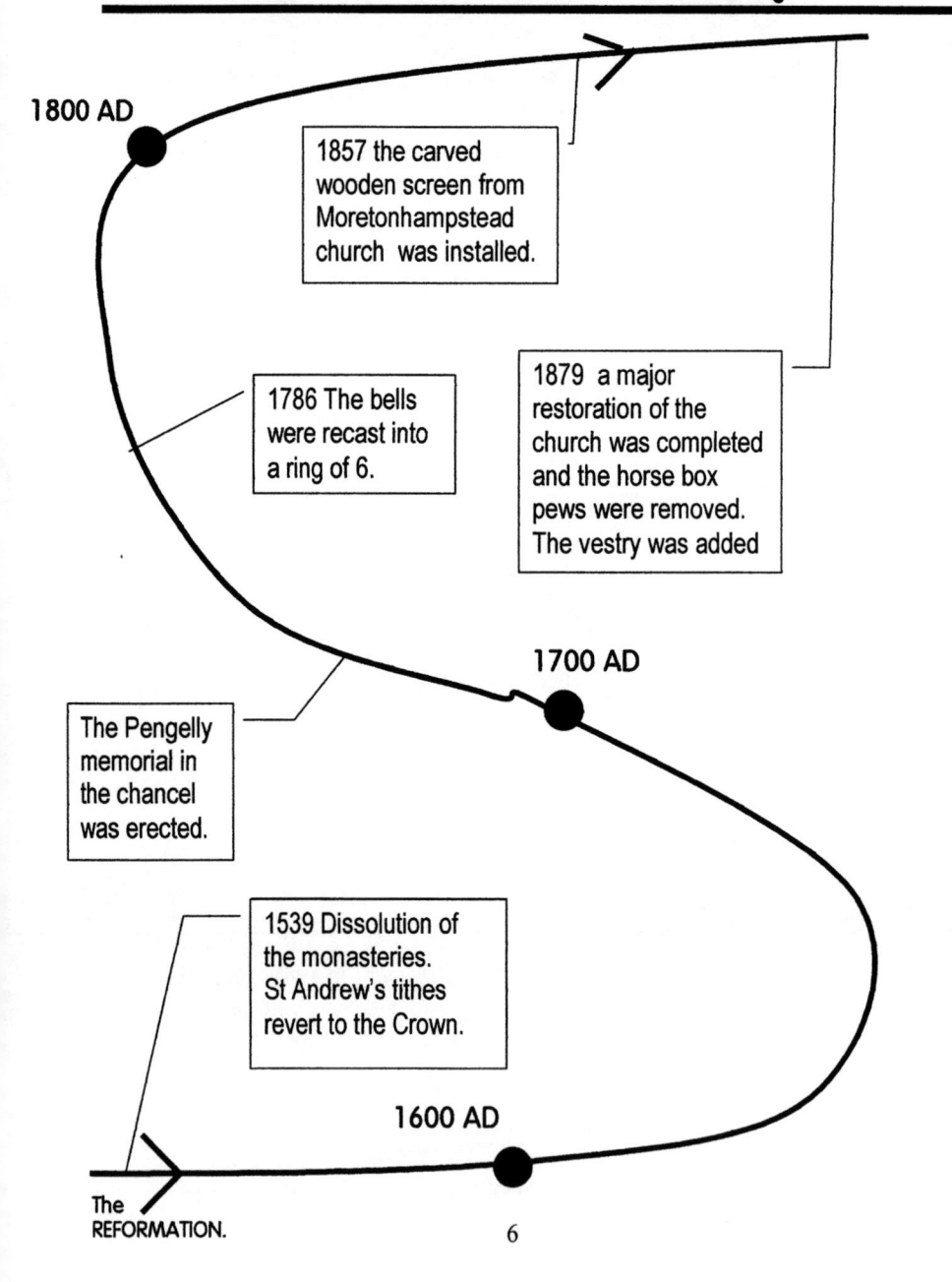

1800 AD

1857 the carved wooden screen from Moretonhampstead church was installed.

1786 The bells were recast into a ring of 6.

1879 a major restoration of the church was completed and the horse box pews were removed. The vestry was added

1700 AD

The Pengelly memorial in the chancel was erected.

1539 Dissolution of the monasteries. St Andrew's tithes revert to the Crown.

1600 AD

The REFORMATION.

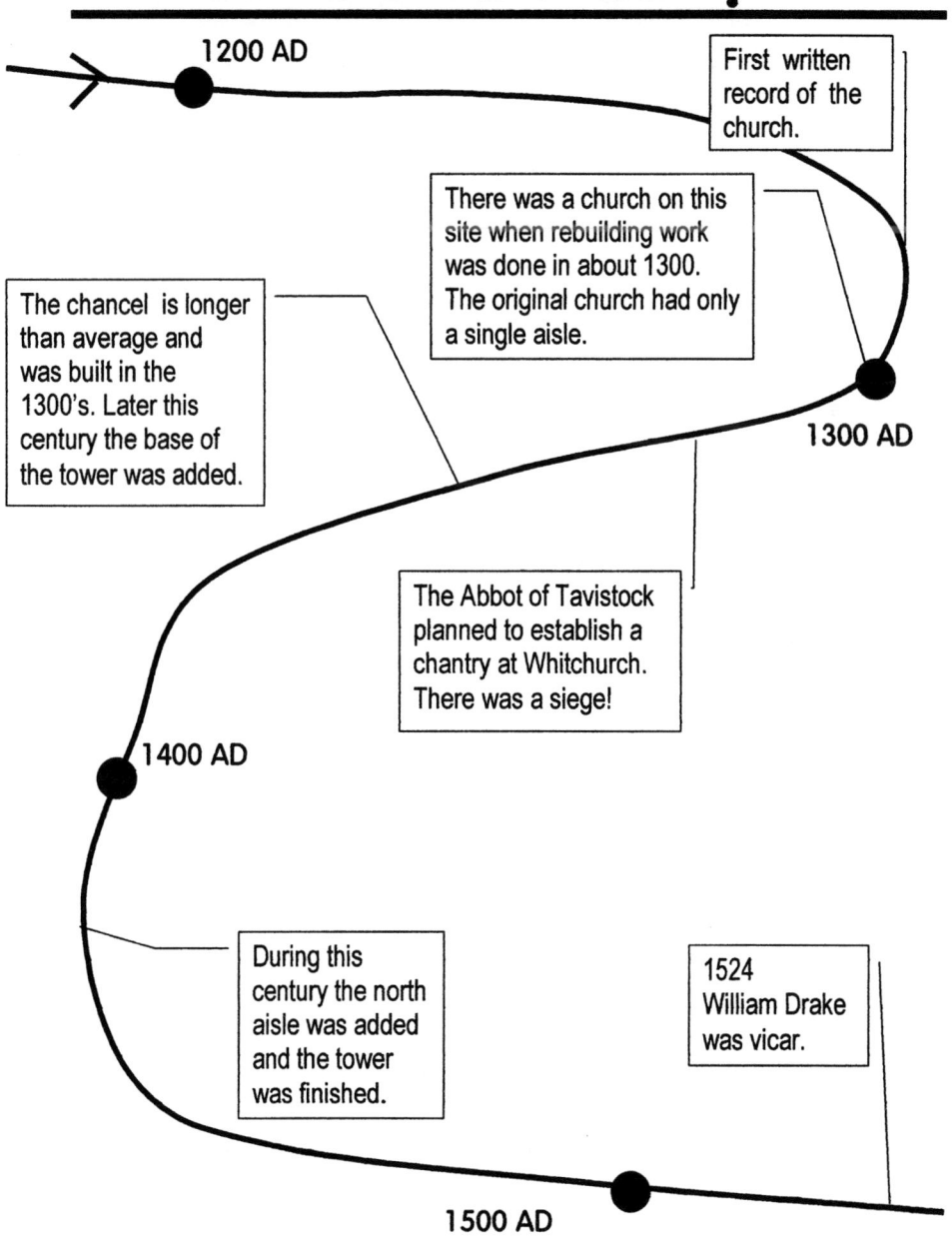

St Andrew's Story

1200 AD

First written record of the church.

There was a church on this site when rebuilding work was done in about 1300. The original church had only a single aisle.

The chancel is longer than average and was built in the 1300's. Later this century the base of the tower was added.

1300 AD

The Abbot of Tavistock planned to establish a chantry at Whitchurch. There was a siege!

1400 AD

During this century the north aisle was added and the tower was finished.

1524 William Drake was vicar.

1500 AD

St Andrew's Story

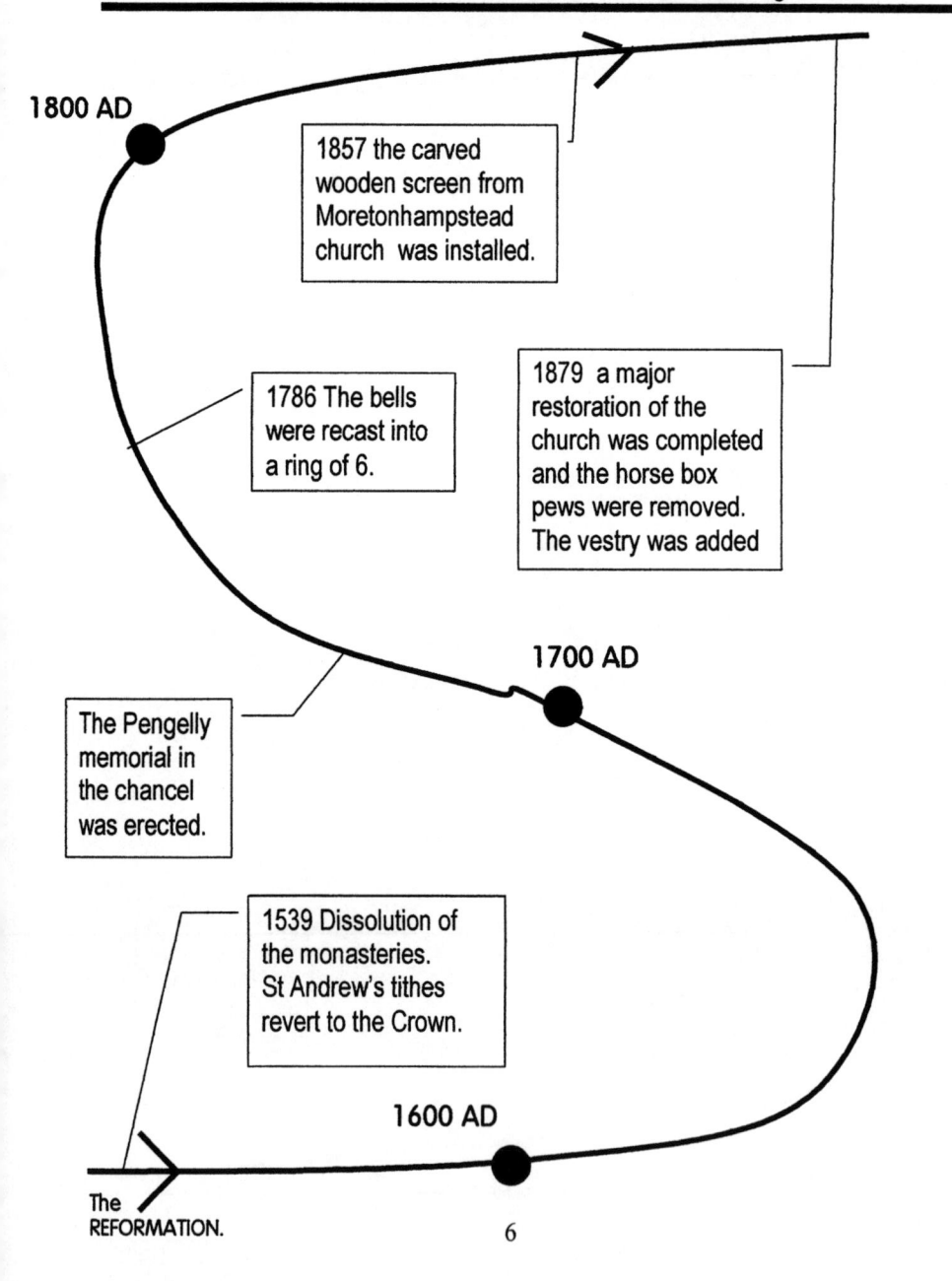

1800 AD

1857 the carved wooden screen from Moretonhampstead church was installed.

1786 The bells were recast into a ring of 6.

1879 a major restoration of the church was completed and the horse box pews were removed. The vestry was added

1700 AD

The Pengelly memorial in the chancel was erected.

1539 Dissolution of the monasteries. St Andrew's tithes revert to the Crown.

1600 AD

The REFORMATION.

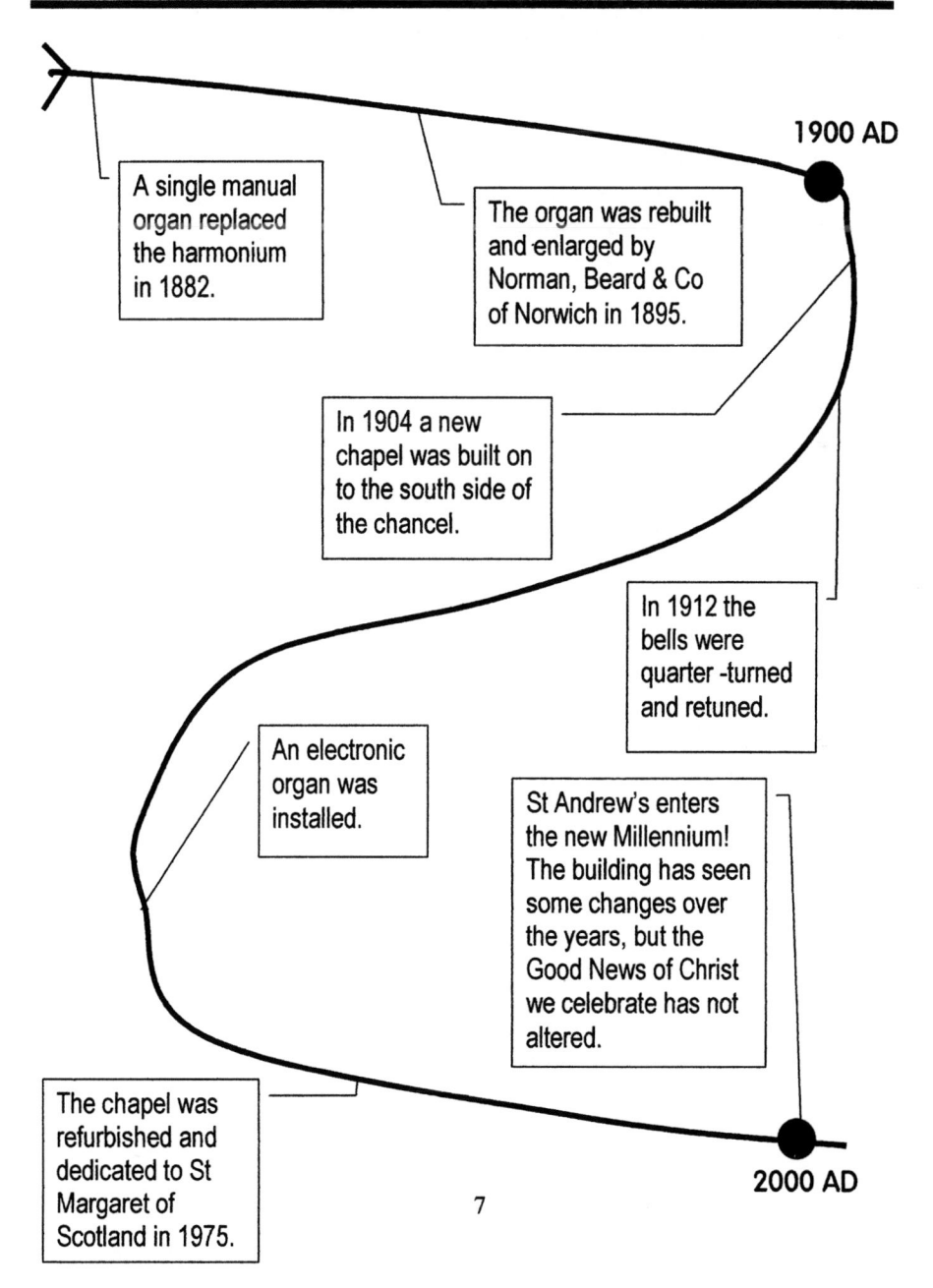

St Andrew's Story

1900 AD

A single manual organ replaced the harmonium in 1882.

The organ was rebuilt and enlarged by Norman, Beard & Co of Norwich in 1895.

In 1904 a new chapel was built on to the south side of the chancel.

In 1912 the bells were quarter-turned and retuned.

An electronic organ was installed.

St Andrew's enters the new Millennium! The building has seen some changes over the years, but the Good News of Christ we celebrate has not altered.

The chapel was refurbished and dedicated to St Margaret of Scotland in 1975.

2000 AD

Monks & Money

The First Record
The earliest written record of the church comes from 1288, when this church was assessed as having a considerable income. Soon afterwards, the church and its tithes came into the possession of the large and powerful neighbouring Tavistock Abbey.

A Chantry?
In 1321, the Abbot of Tavistock, Abbot Campbell, decided to establish a chantry at Whitchurch. The chantry would have an arch-priest, three assistant priests and appropriate servers to assist him in maintaining services in the church. Their main job would be to say regular masses for the souls of a specific list of people. This would allow the Abbot to take possession of the bulk of the parish income from tithes, leaving just enough to pay the expenses of the chantry.

At the time, the Vicar of Whitchurch was Sir James Fraunceis. The Abbot's scheme could only have come into effect after he ceased to be Vicar. But in fact the Abbot died before Sir James did (1331/2), so the chantry plan was abandoned.

Monks & Money

The Siege

The next drama in the life of St Andrew's happened soon afterwards when the Vicar Sir James also died. The gift of the living was shared by the Lord of the Manor of Whitchurch, Lubbe, and alternately the Abbots of Tavistock and Buckland. On this occasion, it was Buckland's turn to choose the next vicar after Sir James, and a David Aliam was nominated.

Tavistock Abbey

But the new Abbot of Tavistock, Bonus, would not accept this nomination.

The next thing was that the Abbot of Buckland Abbey, as instructed by the Bishop of Exeter, came to Whitchurch to conduct a service to induct Aliam as Vicar. He was surprised to be met by a posse of soldiers commanded by four monks from Tavistock Abbey! They were blocking the entrance to the church, and defending a mound and ditch. The Abbot beat a retreat!

This caused a lengthy wrangle and Abbot Bonus was dismissed. David Aliam eventually became Vicar, but Tavistock Abbey retained the great tithes of the parish right up until the Dissolution of the monasteries in 1539, when they reverted to the Crown.

Vicars & Hounds

After the Reformation, the tithes and patronage were sold into the hands of a succession of local families. Two of these families, the Pengellys of Sortridge, who had a fine Elizabethan mansion, and the Sleemans provided vicars for the parish.

Francis Pengelly had set up the Pengelly Charity to pay for a school and a teacher but Henry Pengelly who was vicar 1785 – 1832 delayed implementation of the Charity and it eventually lapsed under the Statute of Mortmain in 1865.

Two vicars also came from the Sleeman family. Peter Sleeman, Vicar from 1848 – 1870, trained as a curate under the Reverend John Russell who was renowned for being the breeder of the Jack Russell Terrier.

Peter Sleeman was himself famous for having fifteen children, hunting regularly and keeping his pack of hounds at the vicarage! When the Bishop of Exeter forbade him to keep hounds for hunting, he gave them to his wife, and continued to hunt as before.

'Stiff Paper over the Holes'

A Major Restoration

By 1877 the church building was in a very dilapidated condition and it was time for major renovations. The old horse-box pews were rickety and awkwardly positioned, the walls were damp and discoloured, and the gallery at the back of the nave was unsafe.

Part of the chancel roof had also collapsed, with *'stiff paper put over the holes'* to protect the clergy on wet days!

The church decided to take action and money was raised for a major restoration of the building, which began in 1877 and was completed in 1879.

The work consisted of:
- Repairing the fabric of the building
- Re-roofing the chancel..
- Installing a new east window using the original tracery
- Cleaning and colour-washing the walls
- Re-flooring and tiling the chancel.
- Moving the railings from around the Pengelly memorial in the chancel to the back of the church to make a screen at the entrance of the tower.
- Building a new vestry to open into the chancel through the ancient priest's doorway.
- Installing new pews, choirstalls, pulpit and clergy desks.

Total Cost = £1,500

All this work cost the enormous sum of £1500, but the fundraising was so successful that there was even some money left over. That was used to replace the existing harmonium with a single manual organ built by Hele & Co of Plymouth in 1882. This organ was itself later rebuilt and enlarged by Norman, Beard & Co of Norwich in 1895. In 1974 an electronic organ was installed.

Porch & Font

The South Porch

Usually people come into the church through the south porch. There is an ancient sundial over the doorway, and looking up you can see an unusual feature, the quatre-foil carvings in the angles on the outside of the lintel which are also repeated on the inside.

The outer doorway, the stone benches and the holy water stoup in the porch are among the oldest parts of the church. Notice the empty niche over the inner doorway into the church, which would have held a statue.

The Font

The font is from the late fourteenth century, and is octagonal in the perpendicular style. There are alternate carved shields bearing St Andrew's and St George's crosses.

It was originally in Fitzford House in Tavistock, and Mary Fitz, Lady Howard, took it to Walreddon when she retired there. Later she gave the font to St Andrew's Church.

The Chancel

There is a stained glass window of the Good Shepherd on the north wall. Its frame and that of the doorway leading to the clergy vestry are from the 13th century, and so is some of the stonework around the east window.

Piscina

There is an unusual square-shaped 14th century piscina in the wall of the chancel near the altar. It has a shallow bowl with a drain hole which was originally used to allow holy water to drain straight into the ground.

The pulpit, clergy desks and choir stalls were installed in the 1879 renovations. Underneath the chancel are the vaults of the Courtenay family which were sealed and tiled in the 1880's to prevent subsidence of the floor.

East Window

The east window is a low arch with stained glass in shades of gold, yellow and green which gives an almost sunlit appearance to the chancel even on dull days.

The tracery is very old and was re-used when the window was remade in the 1879 restoration.

The coloured glass was designed by Fouracres & Watson of Plymouth.

St Andrew fills the central light, flanked by the four Evangelists, Saints Matthew and Mark to the left and Saints Luke and John on the right. Above each evangelist is a winged symbol, a man (Matthew), a lion (Mark), a bull (Luke), and an eagle (John).

The Chancel

Pengelly Monument

This imposing memorial commemorates Francis Pengelly who founded the Pengelly Charity to provide a school and pay a teacher.

The memorial was made by John Weston of Exeter, who was a highly regarded sculptor of the time, and it was erected in 1723.

It consists of two female figures holding an oval plaque, showing the gulf fixed at the Last Judgement.

There are souls being conducted by angels into the presence of God, some still struggling upwards attended by angels and demons, and others, rather ominously, trapped under an overhanging ledge.

The Pengelly family lived at Sortridge for many years and held the advowson, or patronage of the church. There were two Pengelly vicars, and Henry Pengelly (vicar 1785 – 1832) allowed the Pengelly charity to lapse.

Above the tomb is a shield with the Pengelly arms. Originally the memorial was protected by the railings which now close off the tower room.

There are three Pengelly memorials on the chancel walls and two more in the south transept.

The Chancel

Moringe Memorial

On the north wall is a box-tomb with an arch. The archway of Hurdwick stone was built first, in the 14th century, and the recess in the arch was originally used as an Easter Sepulchre.

In about 1630, the slate panels were fitted into the back of the recess of the arch, perhaps they were moved from somewhere else. They are early 17th century and commemorate the Moringe family of Moortown. The tomb may originally have had recumbent figures.

The carved row of kneeling figures under the inscription represents the family, and some of the children are shown holding a skull. These skulls are thought to represent other children who died as infants.

The five arches on the front of the tomb have carvings of a fleur-de lys, a six-petalled flower, a five-petalled flower, a fleur-de-lys and crossed bones, shovel and pick. Above the arch are the Moringe arms, six birds either side of a central shield showing a crowned death's head with cornflail and arrow on one side, an hour-glass on the other, crossed bones, pick and shovel below and 'Nobis mores lucrum' inscribed above.

The Chapel & South Transept

Chapel

St Margaret's Chapel, on the south of the chancel, was built and dedicated in 1904. It was originally called the Michell chapel, after the donor.

The outside wall of the church was taken down and replaced with archways for access and communication between the chancel and the chapel, and the window frames were re-used in the outside wall. It was refurbished and dedicated to St Margaret of Scotland in 1975. The chapel roof is barrel-vaulted. The altar is polished Merrivale granite, and the candlesticks and cross on the wall behind it were made by the chief blacksmith at Dartmoor Prison.

Below the St Michael and St George window, there is a plaster cast of a fossilised fish, often used as a Christian symbol, found when work was done on the floor in the tower room. Near the fish there is an account of the life of St Margaret of Scotland, and above the doorway is a copy of the prayer preserved in her chapel in Edinburgh Castle.

South Transept

This is one of the oldest parts of the church. The archway (or squint) and the massive wall beside it are from the fourteenth century. The transept was used as a vestry for many years until a new vestry was built on to the north of the chancel. Some of the roof bosses have carved shields with St Andrew's and St George's crosses. The window features the Annunciation, with the angel and Mary. Below it is a double sill which may have been used as an altar.

North Aisle

St Peter
The medallion of St Peter's head in the window is the oldest of the coloured glass in the church. Its exact age is unknown, but it was made before 1876.

The Screen
A carved wooden screen was installed in about 1857, cutting off the end of the north aisle which was originally part of the main body of the church. The area it encloses is now used as an outer vestry. This screen was from Moretonhampstead Church. When it was removed, the Earl of Devon gave part of it to St Andrew's and the other part went to Powderham Castle.

The carvings are medieval and show great skill. The top border of intertwined vines and tendrils has long-beaked birds, stealing grapes. Look for oak leaves, acorns and acanthus leaves.

Rood Loft
In the enclosed area of the outer vestry behind the screen is a cupboard in which is a stairway which used to lead up to the rood loft. There are memorials to the Courtenay family on the walls and this area is known as the Courtenay aisle.

Mary Fitz, Lady Howard, was related to the Courtenays and Walreddon House passed from her to a branch of the Courtenay family when she died in 1671. This area was used to house the organ installed in 1882.

Bells & Tower

The Tower Room

At the back of the church is a wrought iron screen with gates, originally part of the Pengelly memorial in the chancel, and now moved here in 1879 when the church was being refurbished.

Through the gates is the tower room, and in the floor an ancient gravestone commemorates William Drake, vicar of Whitchurch 1524-47. He was a great uncle of the famous Sir Francis Drake, who was born locally at Crowndale. There are also the gravestones of Thomas Drake and his wife Margaret (d1655) and John Drake who died in 1640.

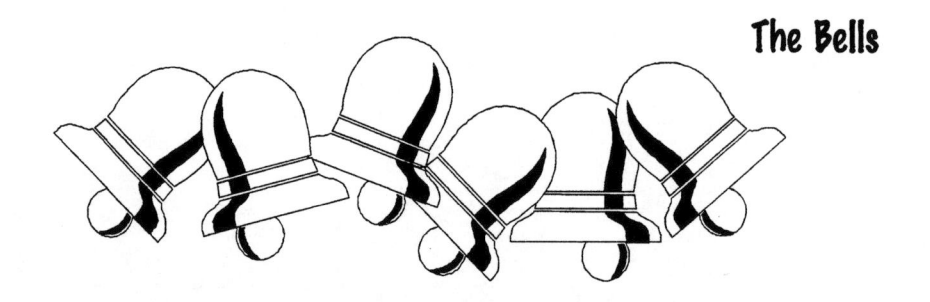

The Bells

At present there are six bells in the tower, but at the time of the Reformation there were three or four huge bells, so large that they had to hollow out the tower walls to fit them in. These big bells were later recast into five bells.

In 1786 the Penningtons, two Cornish brothers who were itinerant bell-founders, recast the bells yet again, into a ring of six. For this they charged £70, plus £31.16s for extra metal at 1/- per lb. Four of the bells are inscribed with the initials of the Penningtons, I.P. and C.P. and the date, 1786, while the fifth is inscribed:
> *' John Moor Knighton and John Berriball C.W. 1786'*

The sixth bell is inscribed
> *'Henry Pengelly Vicar 1786'.*

In 1912 the bells were quarter-turned and retuned, and the walls of the bell-chamber were reinforced. There is an enthusiastic group of bell ringers here today.

Saints & Stained Glass

Saints
At first the church was dedicated to St White. There are two saints with this name, this was likely to have been Albanus, later known as St White. He was a Devon man and went with Boniface of Crediton on his missionary journeys to Germany, where he was martyred in 754.

The church was rededicated to St Andrew in the fourteenth century. St Andrew was a fisherman, and the brother of St Peter. He was the one who introduced Peter to Jesus. He is also the patron saint of Scotland.

Stained Glass
The oldest of the coloured glass is the medallion of St Peter's head in a window in the north aisle; its exact age is unknown, but it is before 1876. The glass of the east window was installed in 1879 and is the oldest of the rest of the stained glass in the church. A document from 1644 mentions coloured windows of coats of arms (England, France, and Tavistock Abbey), and one of a saint with nails piercing his head, but what happened to these windows is not known.

In the Margaret Chapel the window of St Michael and St George is the most recent coloured glass in the church (1946). The memorial window to Lavinia Lampen was made by C. E. Kempe. If you look closely you can see his mark, a golden wheatsheaf, at the bottom of the left border. The black castle superimposed on it shows that this window was made after 1909 when his nephew Towers became his partner.

Structure & Roof

Stone

The church is built mainly of elvan, granite and Hurdwick stone from local quarries. The oldest stonework in the church is probably early Norman or Saxon. The base of the east window in the chancel, the north chancel wall, parts of the south transept and the south porch are the oldest parts of the building.

Roofs

The church has barrel roofs, whose timbers are original apart from repair work, except for the chancel whose roof was renewed in 1879, and St Margaret's Chapel which was only built in 1904.

The roof bosses appear similar; but, look closely and you will see carvings of angels on the bosses at the back of the church and a face on one above the pulpit. '1656' is carved on a boss in the south transept. Some of the bosses of the south transept have shields with St Andrew's and St George's crosses carved on them.

Tower

The church tower is rectangular in ground plan with the longer sides parallel with the west wall of the church. Notice the enormous stones which form the jambs of the tower door and the tower buttresses. The first stage has a double buttress at each corner except the NE, and the upper stages have a single oblique buttress at the three corners.

At the top are battlements with pinnacles at the corners; the NE is shorter and marks the top of the tower stairway as it climbs up inside a built-out shaft.

Stairs

As you walk along outside the north wall of the church, look out for the bulge of the shaft holding the stairway which once led to the rood loft.

Saints & Stained Glass

Saints

At first the church was dedicated to St White. There are two saints with this name, this was likely to have been Albanus, later known as St White. He was a Devon man and went with Boniface of Crediton on his missionary journeys to Germany, where he was martyred in 754.

The church was rededicated to St Andrew in the fourteenth century. St Andrew was a fisherman, and the brother of St Peter. He was the one who introduced Peter to Jesus. He is also the patron saint of Scotland.

Stained Glass

The oldest of the coloured glass is the medallion of St Peter's head in a window in the north aisle; its exact age is unknown, but it is before 1876. The glass of the east window was installed in 1879 and is the oldest of the rest of the stained glass in the church. A document from 1644 mentions coloured windows of coats of arms (England, France, and Tavistock Abbey), and one of a saint with nails piercing his head, but what happened to these windows is not known.

In the Margaret Chapel the window of St Michael and St George is the most recent coloured glass in the church (1946). The memorial window to Lavinia Lampen was made by C. E. Kempe. If you look closely you can see his mark, a golden wheatsheaf, at the bottom of the left border. The black castle superimposed on it shows that this window was made after 1909 when his nephew Towers became his partner.

Structure & Roof

Stone
The church is built mainly of elvan, granite and Hurdwick stone from local quarries. The oldest stonework in the church is probably early Norman or Saxon. The base of the east window in the chancel, the north chancel wall, parts of the south transept and the south porch are the oldest parts of the building.

Roofs
The church has barrel roofs, whose timbers are original apart from repair work, except for the chancel whose roof was renewed in 1879, and St Margaret's Chapel which was only built in 1904.

The roof bosses appear similar; but, look closely and you will see carvings of angels on the bosses at the back of the church and a face on one above the pulpit. '1656' is carved on a boss in the south transept. Some of the bosses of the south transept have shields with St Andrew's and St George's crosses carved on them.

Tower
The church tower is rectangular in ground plan with the longer sides parallel with the west wall of the church. Notice the enormous stones which form the jambs of the tower door and the tower buttresses. The first stage has a double buttress at each corner except the NE, and the upper stages have a single oblique buttress at the three corners.

At the top are battlements with pinnacles at the corners; the NE is shorter and marks the top of the tower stairway as it climbs up inside a built-out shaft.

Stairs
As you walk along outside the north wall of the church, look out for the bulge of the shaft holding the stairway which once led to the rood loft.

Outside in the Churchyard

The Stocks
The Parish stocks of 1809 are in the graveyard behind the Inn. They were discovered in a farm building in the 1970's.

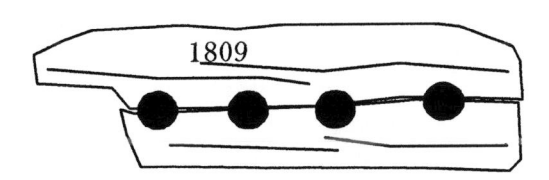

Edward Eyre
A few yards from the NW end of the church is a tall memorial of bluish stone which marks the grave of Edward Eyre.

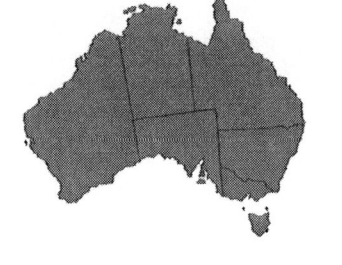

Edward Eyre was a famous 19th century explorer, cattle drover and administrator in Australia and New Zealand and also later Governor of Jamaica. He retired and came to live at Walreddon, where he died in 1901.

Lake Eyre, a huge dry lake in the desert of Western Australia, was named after him.

Mary Metters
Close to the church on the north side is her grave with this inscription.

> In Remembrance of Mary Metters
> barbarously murdered by Sam'l Norton her servant,
> with a billhook at Budghill in this Parish
> the 16th February 1815 aged 45 years
> leaving a disconsolate husband and
> five children to mourn her untimely end
> For which horrid deed he was
> Tried and Executed at Exeter
> the Lent Assizes following

Stables & Inn

The Stables

Opposite the church gate is 'The Stables', which was used to shelter horses belonging to parishioners (for a fee) when they attended services in bad weather.

Now it is used for meetings, coffee mornings etc.
The cottage next to it also belongs to the church and is used for youth and children's work.

The Whitchurch Inn

The ancient Whitchurch Inn next door to the church started life as a Church House belonging to the parish, and was originally used to accommodate visiting Tavistock monks and travellers.

In Elizabethan days it was used for parish meetings and Saint's Day feasts. At times it was also used as a temporary store-house or brew-house and to accommodate parishioners from outside the village cut off by bad weather.

In 1702 its name was changed to the Whitchurch Inn, and even today the Vicar and Churchwardens are still the Trustees of the property.

The stonework at the back of the Inn dates from the 12th century. A medieval dome-shaped oven was found in a six-foot thick wall at the back.

Index

Albanus, St White	4,19	Pengelly memorial	6,11,14
Andrew, St	19	Pengellys of Sortridge	10,14
Abbot of Tavistock	5,8,9	Penningtons	18
Aliam, David	9	Pews, Horse box	6,11
Bells	6,7,18	Piscina	13
Bonus, Abbot of Tavistock	9	Porch	12
Bosses, roof	16	Restoration of church	11
Campbell, Abbot of Tavistock	8	Roofs	20
Chancel	13	Screen, wooden	6,17
Chapel	7,16	Sleeman, Peter	10
Churchyard	21	South transept	16
Courtenay family	13,17	Stables	22
Drake, William	5,18	Stained glass	19
East window	13	Stairs (rood loft)	20
Eyre, Edward	21	Stocks	21
Fish	16	Stone	20
Fitz, Mary	12,17	Tithes	8,9,10
Font	12	Tower	18, 20
Fraunceis, Sir James	8	Tower room	18
Harmonium	7	Vestry	6,17
Holy water stoup	12	Weston, John	14
Kempe, C. E.	19	Whitchurch Inn	22
Lubbe, Lord of Manor	9	Window, Good Shepherd	13
Margaret of Scotland (St)	16	Annunciation	16
Metters, Mary	21	St Peter	17,19
Moringe memorial	15	St Michael & St George	19
North Aisle	17		
Organ	7,11		

Groundplan of the church
(not to scale)

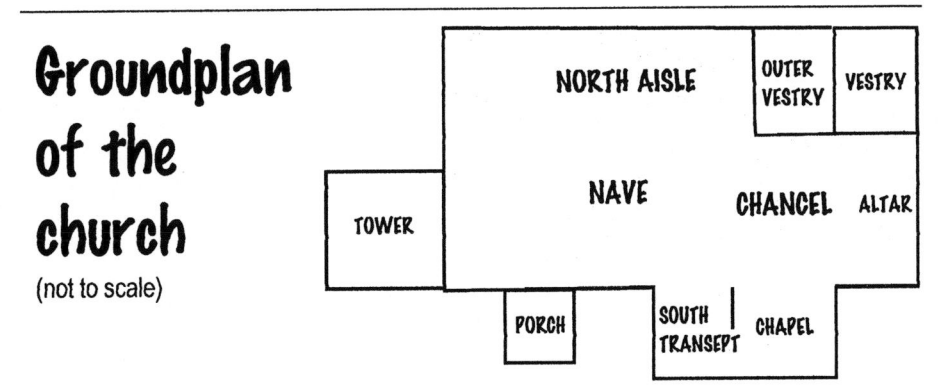

23